TH

The Biblical Seminar
30

THE ANCIENT LIBRARY OF QUMRAN

THE ANCIENT LIBRARY OF QUMRAN

3rd Edition

Frank Moore Cross

Sheffield Academic Press

1st edition published 1958
2nd edition published 1961

3rd revised and extended edition
Copyright © 1995 Sheffield Academic Press

Published by
Sheffield Academic Press Ltd
Mansion House
19 Kingfield Road
Sheffield, S11 9AS
England

Typeset by Sheffield Academic Press
and
Printed on acid-free paper in Great Britain
by The Cromwell Press
Melksham, Wiltshire

British Library Cataloguing in Publication Data

A catalogue record for this book is available
from the British Library

ISBN 1-85075-511-6

CONTENTS

PREFACE TO THE FIRST EDITION

The study of the scrolls and fragments of scrolls from the wilderness of the Dead Sea has barely begun. Only a small part of the fund of discoveries is published. Although much of the unpublished material will duplicate or confirm what already is known or suspected, there is much which is of revolutionary import. Positions which must be won now by complicated combinations of bits and tatters of evidence will automatically establish themselves once the vast corpus is laid out for all to see. Certain new documents will sweep away much of the nonsense now swelling the secondary literature on the scrolls, delivering sober scholars from the burden of continuing controversy, or rather freeing them to enter into new debates.

The time has not yet come, obviously, when it is possible or desirable to attempt total, much less final syntheses in the several major areas of Qumrân research. Nevertheless, Qumrân studies are ready to enter into a new phase. It is not too early to discern some of the coherent patterns emerging from the mass of fact accumulated by a decade of discoveries in the wilderness of Judah. And it is time to lay many of the early discussions to rest. The combination of newly found and partially published documentary material and the results of recent archaeological research has established new positions from which the entire field of inquiry can be viewed in a fresh perspective.

Decisive gains have been made by the paleographer and archaeologist. The study of early Jewish scripts has reached a stage of precision, thanks to the wealth of typological data furnished by recent finds and excavations, which now permits the specialist to date the Qumrân manuscripts within the interval of a half century. Five seasons of excavation at the community center of the scroll sect have been completed. The evidence dredged up by these researches has fixed the chronological framework of the sect's life in the desert within narrow and immovable limits.

Although the new documents from recent discoveries have had only preliminary examination, the importance of the data which have been extracted from them can scarcely be overestimated. In the first find, a narrow sample of the literature composed by the sect was recovered. Now we know the full scope of their religious writings. Historical allusions in the documents of the first discovery were scarce and never quite explicit. In the new manuscripts allusions are rare, to be sure, but Greek kings, Hasmonaean rulers, and a Roman official, all well known to the historian, are named by name. Alongside the few biblical manuscripts from the first cave, all of them of more or less traditional character, we can place now more than a hundred texts, many of nontraditional types. For the reconstruction of the religious and community life of the people of Qumrân, for the tracing of the early development of the Old Testament text, for the determination of the historical relationships of the Qumrân sect, these data are crucial. They enable us to proceed with some boldness to fresh attempts at historical synthesis.

This volume contains the text of the Haskell Lectures for 1956–57, delivered to the Graduate School of Theology, Oberlin College, March 12–21, 1957. The form of the book is shaped by its origin in a series of lectures. Each of the lectures after the first deals with a single, but major area of scroll research. No serious effort is made to give a comprehensive treatment of the field of scroll study as a whole. Each lecture records, however, an attempt to achieve in a given area a synthesis or at least a systematic interpretation of the facts now available. Old and new, published and unpublished data are drawn upon.

The text of the lectures was written with public presentation in view, and at the same time expanded by extensive footnoting, not merely for the usual purposes of documentation, but to enable the writer to elaborate on the restricted material suitable to his text. The longer notes are written at two levels; most contain technical discussions, especially at points where unpublished material or unpublished views are alluded to in the text; at the same time a number of explanatory notes are directed to the reader with less background in the field under discussion than the academic audience to whom the lectures were originally addressed.

There are many acknowledgments to be made. First of all I wish to thank Professor David Noel Freedman. He has been a constant source of encouragement, criticism, and aid. To the Haskell Lectureship Committee, especially to Professor Herbert G. May and Dean Leonard Stidley, I owe a debt of gratitude for hospitality shown me during my pleasant days in Oberlin on the occasion of the delivery of the lectures.

To Professor W.F. Albright, my former teacher and perennial mentor, Professor Krister Stendahl, and Mr. John Strugnell who have read my manuscript and offered many helpful suggestions; to R.P. Roland de Vaux, Mr. G. Lankester Harding, and the members of the scroll staff in Jerusalem whose influence is evident throughout the pages of this book; and to my patient wife, who wishes, I am sure, that the scrolls had been fed to the goat responsible for their discovery; to all these I wish to acknowledge my indebtedness and express my thanks.

July 13, 1957   F.M.C., Jr.

PREFACE TO THE SECOND [REVISED] EDITION

The revised edition of these lectures was destined for publication in a German edition in the fall of 1959, and, owing to a series of vicissitudes, including the destruction in fire of my files on Qumrân studies and the draft of the revision, has been delayed until now.

My loss of materials has precluded the systematic revision which I had planned. Chapters 1 through 3 have been revised fairly extensively, especially where new or primary evidence has appeared; major discussions are noted. Chapters 4 and 5 have virtually escaped revision. No major advances in our knowledge of the history of the Old Testament text (Chapter 4) can be expected until the one hundred or so biblical manuscripts from Cave Four, Qumrân are published in full. On the other hand, the topics dealing with the Scrolls and the New Testament (Chapter 5) are now represented by a burgeoning literature. Had I chosen to deal adequately with publications since 1957 (when the lecture was originally prepared), publication would have been delayed indefinitely.

In addition to those mentioned in my earlier preface, I wish to thank heartily Professor Arthur Derby Nock (†) and Professor Helmet Koester for helpful suggestions, and Mr Clement Alexander for his patient and efficient help in guiding this volume through press.

June 30, 1960   F.M.C., Jr.

PREFACE TO THE THIRD EDITION

The edition of 1961 has not been extensively rewritten. Errors in fact have been removed, and some supplemental material added, chiefly in the footnotes. A Supplement to Chapter 1, based in part on the German edition (1967), has been added to bring up to date recent discoveries and to point to sources for further study. A full set of script charts has been included, taken from my monograph, *The Development of the Jewish Scripts* (DJS). Also a new chapter, Chapter 6, has been added at the end detailing some of the author's views of and reactions to recent discussion and publications, not found in the earlier editions. However, the original lectures, which formed the basis for the book, have been left essentially intact, recording a stage in the history of my scroll research.

I am grateful to Professor Douglas Knight, to Professor David J.A. Clines, and to Dr Marshall Johnson for initiating the project of republishing *The Ancient Library of Qumran*, to Rene Kuhn Bryant for editorial assistance, and to Andrew Kirk for guiding it through press.

Thanksgiving Day, 1994   F.M.C., Jr.

LIST OF ILLUSTRATIONS
following page 128

Figure 1. Cave IV, Qumrân viewed from the floor of the Wâdī Qumrân. The ruin of the community center is situated above on the marl terrace through which the wâdī cuts. Photograph: F.M. Cross.

Figure 2. Cave IV as it appeared undisturbed in the 1920s before secondary openings were made by Bedouin. The cave may be seen high in the column of marl immediately to the left of the side torrent bed. Photograph: Harvard Semitic Museum.

Figure 3. Khirbet Qumrân and vicinity.

Figure 4. The sites of the caves which produced manuscripts. Cave IV–X are located in the marl terrace adjacent to the community center; Caves I, III, and XI are high in the limestone cliffs.

Figure 5. The entrance to Cave XI (after clearance by Ta'âmireh shepherds). Photograph: F.M. Cross.

Figure 6. Excavations at the northwest tower of community buildings at Qumrân. Photograph: Jean Starcky.

Figure 7. R.P. Roland de Vaux in his excavation togs. He is standing in the commons of the community. Photograph: F.M. Cross.

Figure 8. Five of the seven original members of the international committee preparing and piecing together Cave IV manuscripts. Shown are (from left to right) John Strugnell, John Allegro, Monsignor Patrick Skehan, Claus-Hunno Hunzinger, and J.T. Milik. Missing are Abbé Jean Starcky and Frank Moore Cross. Photo: Jean Starcky.

Figure 9. The author, stranded in the wilderness above Qumrân (ca. 1955).

Figure 10. Qumrân Cave IV manuscript fragments in a lot purchased with a grant of $15,000 from McGill University.

Figure 11. The Psalms Scroll from Qumrân, Cave XI (4QPs^a). The scroll is shown in the condition it was found, before unrolling. Photograph: Israel Antiquities Authority.

Figure 12. Fragments of a Jeremiah manuscript from Cave IV (4QJer^b). It contains an edition of the text of Jeremiah shorter than that preserved in the Masoretic Text. This shorter text is found also (in translation) in the Old Greek version of Jeremiah. Photograph: Israel Antiquities Authority.

Figure 13. A manuscript of Qohelet (4QQoh^a) dating to *ca.* 175–150 BC. Photograph: Israel Antiquities Authority.

LIST OF ABBREVIATIONS AND SIGLA

AASOR	Annual of the American Schools of Oriental Research
ADSS	R. de Vaux, *Archaeology and the Dead Sea Scrolls* (Oxford, 1973)
Antiq.	Flavius Josephus, *Jewish Antiquities*
ASOR	American Schools of Oriental Research
ATR	*Anglican Theological Review*
BA	*Biblical Archaeologist*
BAR	*Biblical Archaeology Review*
BASOR	*Bulletin of the American Schools of Oriental Research*
CBQ	*Catholic Biblical Quarterly*
CMHE	F.M. Cross, *Canaanite Myth and Hebrew Epic* (Cambridge, 1973)
Découvertes	J.T. Milik, *Dix ans de découvertes dans le Desert de Juda* (Paris, 1957)
DJD I	D. Barthélemy, O.P., J.T. Milik, *et al.*, *Qumrân Cave I. Discoveries in the Judaean Desert I* (Oxford, 1955)
DJS	F.M. Cross, 'The Development of the Jewish Scripts', in *The Bible and the Ancient Near East* (ed. G.E. Wright; Garden City, N.Y.: Doubleday, 1961), pp. 133-202
DSS I	M. Burrows, John C. Trever, and W.H. Brownlee, eds., The Dead Sea Scrolls of St. Mark's Monastery, Vol. I (New Haven, 1950)
DSS II	M. Burrows, John C. Trever, and W.H. Brownlee, eds., *The Dead Sea Scrolls of St. Mark's Monastery*, Vol. II: 2 (New Haven, 1951)
ET	*Evangelische Theologie*
Gen. Apoc.	N. Avigad and Y. Yadin, *A Genesis Apocryphon. A Scroll from the Wilderness of Judaea* (Jerusalem, 1956)
Geschichte[3]	E. Schürer, *Geschichte des jüdischen Volkes im Zeitalter Jesu Christi*, 3. Aufl. (Leipzig, 1901)
HSM	Harvard Semitic Monographs
HTR	*Harvard Theological Review*
HUCA	*Hebrew Union College Annual*
IEJ	*Israel Exploration Journal*
JAOS	*Journal of the American Oriental Society*
JBL	*Journal of Biblical Literature*
JBR	*Journal of Bible and Religion*
JJS	*Journal of Jewish Studies*
JNES	*Journal of Near Eastern Studies*
JQR	*Jewish Quarterly Review*

JSS	*Journal of Semitic Studies*
LXX	Septuagint
MT	Masoretic Text
MQC	Julio Trebolle Barrera and Luis Vegas Montaner, eds., *The Madrid Qumran Congress*: Proceedings of the International Congress on the Dead Sea Scrolls, Madrid 18-21 March, 1991, 2 vols. (Leiden and Madrid: Brill and Editorial Complutense, 1992)
NTS	*New Testament Studies*
OG	*Old Greek*
OMG	E.L. Sukenik and N. Avigad, *'ôṣar ham-mĕgillôt hag-gĕnûzôt* (Jerusalem, 1954)
PAAJR	*Proceedings of the American Academy of Jewish Research*
PEQ	*Palestine Exploration Quarterly*
QHBT	F.M. Cross and S. Talmon (eds.), *Qumran and the History of the Biblical Text* (Cambridge: Harvard University Press, 1975)
Rapport I	R. de Vaux, 'Fouilles au Khirbet Qumrân', *RB* 60 (1953), pp. 83-106
Rapport II	R. de Vaux, 'Fouilles au Khirbet Qumrân. Rapport préliminaire sur la deuxième campagne', *RB* 61 (1954), pp. 206-36
Rapport III	R. de Vaux, 'Fouilles de Khirbet Qumrân. Rapport préliminaire sur les 3ᵉ, 4ᵉ, et 5ᵉ campagnes', *RB* 63 (1956), pp. 533-77
RB	*Revue biblique*
RHPR	*Revue d'histoire et de philosophie religieuses*
RHR	*Revue de l'histoire des religions*
RevQ	*Revue de Qumrân*
SQI	F.M. Cross, *et al.* (eds.), *Scrolls from the Qumrân Cave I: The Great Isaiah Scroll, the Order of the Community, the Pesher to Habakkuk* (Cambridge and Jerusalem: Albright Institute of Archaeological Research and the Shrine of the Book, 1972)
ST	*Studia Theologica*
SzHk	K. Elliger, *Studien zum Habakuk–Kommentar vom Toten Meer* (Tübingen, 1953)
TLZ	*Theologische Literaturzeitung*
ThR	*Theologische Rundschau*
TSK	*Theologische Studien und Kritiken*
TWzNT	*Theologisches Wörterbuch zum Neuen Testament*, ed., G. Kittel (Stuttgart)
ThZ	*Theologische Zeitschrift*
VT	*Vetus Testamentum*
VTSup	*Vetus Testamentum*, Supplements
War	Flavius Josephus, *The Jewish War*
ZAW	*Zeitschrift für die alttestamentliche Wissenschaft*
ZDPV	*Zeitschrift des Deutschen Palästina-Vereins*
ZNW	*Zeitschrift für die neutestamentliche Wissenschaft*
ZTK	*Zeitschrift für Theologie und Kirche*

The sigla used in designating the manuscripts of Qumrân follow the standard system adopted in the series, *Discoveries in the Judaean Desert*. A full listing is given in *DJD I*, pp. 46-48. Among the more important documents discussed in the text or notes are the following:

1QS [*sérek hay-yaḥad*]	The sectarian Rule of the Community, exemplar from Cave 1, Qumrân. Published in *SQI*.
1QSa, 1QSb	Adjuncts to the Rule of the Community (1QS). Published in *DJD I* as 1Q28a and 1Q28b.
pap4QS^e	A papyrus exemplar of the Rule of the Community, from Cave 4, Qumrân. Unpublished.
1QH [*hôdāyôt*]	The sectarian roll of Psalms of Thanksgiving from Cave 1. Published in *OMG*
1QM [*milḥāmāh*]	The sectarian War of the Children of Light Against the Children of Darkness. Published in *OMG*.
1QIsa^a	The Great Isaiah Scroll from Cave 1. Published in *SQI*.
1QIsa^b	A manuscript of Isaiah from Cave 1; published in *OMG*
1QpMic	A *pešer* (commentary) on Micah from Cave 1. Published in *DJD I*.
1QpHab [*pešer* Habakkuk]	The commentary on Habakkuk from Cave 1. Published in *SQI*.
1QM [*milḥāmāh*]	The sectarian War of the Children of Light Against the Children of Darkness. Published in *OMG*.
1Q34^{bis} (= 1Q LitPrb)	A collection of liturgical prayers. Published in *DJD I*.
1QGenApoc	The Genesis Apocryphon published in *Gen. Apoc.*
4QpaleoGen-Exod^l	Formerly Exod^a. A manuscript of Genesis and Exodus in paleo-Hebrew script. Published in *DJD IX*.
4QExod^b	A manuscript of Exodus from Cave 4. Formerly 4QExod^a. Published in *DJD XI* (in press).
4QExod-Lev^f	A manuscript of Exodus and Leviticus from Cave 4. Formerly 4QExod^f. Published in *DJD XI* (in press).
4QpaleoExod^m	An Exodus manuscript written in Paleo-Hebrew script. Published in *DJD IX*, pp. 53-130
4QNum^b	A manuscript of Numbers from Cave 4. Published in *DJD XI* (in press).
4QDeut^a	A manuscript of Deuteronomy from Cave 4. Published in *DJD XI* (in press).
4QDeut. 32 [= 4QDeut^q]	Published in *DJD XI* (in press).

4QSam^a	A manuscript of 1 and 2 Samuel from Cave 4. Partially published by F.M. Cross, *BASOR* 132 (1953), pp. 15-26.
4QSam^b	An archaic manuscript of Samuel from Cave 4. Partially published by F.M. Cross, *JBL* 74 (1955), pp. 15-26.
4QJer^a	A manuscript of Jeremiah from Cave 4. Unpublished. See provisionally, E. Tov, *RevQ* 54 (1989), pp. 189-205.
4QJer^b	A manuscript of Jeremiah from Cave 4. See provisionally, E. Tov, *RevQ* 54 (1989), pp. 189-205.
4QXII^a, 4QXII^c	Manuscripts of the Twelve Minor Prophets from Cave 4. See provisionally, R.E. Fuller, 'The Minor Prophets Manuscripts from Qumrân, Cave IV' (unpublished dissertation, Harvard University, 1988).
4QPs^a	A manuscript of Psalms from Cave 4. Unpublished.
4QpPs^a	A *pešer* (commentary) on Psalms from Cave 4. Published in *DJD V*.
4QJob^a	A manuscript of Job fom Cave 4. Unpublished.
4QQoh	A manuscript of Qohelet (Ecclesiastes) from Cave 4.
4Q Flor[ilegium]	A manuscript from Cave 4. Published in *DJD V*, pp. 53-57.
4QM	Manuscripts of the War of the Children of Light Against the Children of Darkness. Published in *DJD VII*.
4QPr[ayer of] Nab[onidus]	A document belonging to the lost Daniel literature from Cave 4. See F.M. Cross, 'Fragments of the Prayer of Nabonidus', *IEJ* 34 (1984), pp. 260-64.
4QTLevi ar^a	The Testament of Levi in Aramaic from Cave 4. Partially published by J.T. Milik, *RB* 62 (1955), pp. 398-406.
4Q Testimonia	The sheet of testimonia from Cave 4. Published in *DJD V*.
11QPs^a	A collection of canonical and non-canonical psalms from Cave 11, Qumrân. Published in *DJD IV*.
CD	The Cairo Damascus Document
6QD	A copy of the Damascus Document from Cave VI, Qumrân. Published in *DJD III*.

Chapter 1

DISCOVERY OF AN ANCIENT LIBRARY

In 1947 seven antique rolls of leather were found by shepherds in the Judaean wilderness near the northwestern shore of the Dead Sea. This discovery set off a series of manuscript finds which are without precedent in the history of modern archaeology. Since the first cave and its manuscripts were found, the lonely precincts of the desert have been invaded successfully again and again by seekers of leather and papyrus treasure. A competition has developed between clandestine Bedouin diggers and accredited archaeologists, with laurels going frequently to the scientists, more often to the ignorant but patient shepherds.

The most important as well as the best known finds have come from caves in the vicinity of Wâdī Qumrân, a gorge cut by winter torrents through the cliffs which border the Dead Sea, some seven or eight miles south of modern Jericho. But other districts in the Judaean wasteland have yielded precious antiquities as by-products of the intense search. Groups of documents, scarcely less interesting than those of Qumrân, have been dug out of the gargantuan caves of the Wâdī Murabba'ât, which lies about twelve miles southwest of Qumrân; others have come from an unknown place—known precisely only to Bedouin—further south along the Dead Sea [see further in the supplement to this chapter]; yet another group has been found in the ruins of Khirbet Mird (ancient Hyrcania) situated on a peak inland from Qumrân in the western flank of the Judaean Buqê'.

Eleven caves clustered about ruins on the Wâdī Qumrân have now produced manuscripts or manuscript fragments. These include the cave of the initial discovery in 1947 (Qumrân I), and the most recent find, a cave discovered in January 1956 (Qumrân XI). Of the Qumrân caves, only Caves I and XI have produced relatively intact manuscripts. The largest single cache, however, and probably the most important, was dug from the ancient floor levels of Cave IV found in 1952: tens of thousands of fragments belonging to a corpus of more than five hundred and seventy manuscripts at latest count. From the caves of Qumrân alone there are now in the museums of Palestine a total of more than eight hundred manuscripts, a few well preserved, most extremely fragmentary, all invaluable. And there is no reason to suppose that the discoveries in this lonely land are at an end.

When the majority of these documents from the wilderness of the Dead Sea are published the main labors of research will not be done. Scholars will be occupied for decades in the tedious studies required to assimilate adequately the knowledge available in these new sources, and to relate this new learning to biblical and ancillary disciplines.

1. *The First Cave*

The story of the first cave has been obscured by time and legend. This circumstance, it must be confessed, is due less to the faulty memories of the native discoverers than to the fervid imagination of Western writers. Even so, while a full history of the find may never be reconstructed, certain essential facts are well established, partly by cross-examination of tribesmen and their middlemen, partly by subsequent events.[1]

In the spring of the year 1947 two shepherd lads were grazing their mixed flocks of sheep and goats along the foot of the crumbling cliffs that line the Dead Sea in the vicinity of Qumrân. There was nothing unusual about their being in this terrain. The few clans of their tribe, the Ta'âmireh, that still live in 'houses of hair' following flocks, customarily use the bubbling springs of Feshkhah immediately south of Qumrân as a watering place, and often in the spring, when the desert turns green for a brief few weeks, may be found in these wild pastures.[2]

---

1.   The most authoritative account—as well as one of the briefest—is that given by G. Lankester Harding in *Qumrân Cave I, Discoveries in the Judaean Desert I* [*DJD I*], by D. Barthélemy, O.P., J.T. Milik, *et al.* (Oxford, 1955), pp. 1-7; cf. 'The Dead Sea Scrolls', *PEQ* 81 (1949), pp. 112-16.

2.   The writer, engaged in explorations in the Judaean wilderness to the west of Khirbet Qumrân, has come by chance upon an encampment of the Ta'âmireh clan involved in the discoveries. Actually the traditional range of the Ta'âmireh lies mostly south of the Wâdī–Nâr. The region of 'En Feshkhah and Qumrân is disputed with the 'Arab ibn 'Ubêd. However, one of the old burying grounds of the 'Arab et-Ta'âmireh is immediately north of the cave area near Hajar el-'Asba'. (Cf. Cross and Milik, 'Explorations in the Judaean Buqê'ah', *BASOR* 142 [April 1956], pp. 5-17; especially p. 5, n. 1). For a tribal history of the Ta'âmireh, see B. Couroyer, 'Histoire

According to their account, one of their animals strayed. In searching for it, one of the shepherds, Muhammed ed-Dîb by name, casually threw a stone into a small circular opening in the cliff face. Instead of the expected smack of rock against rock, he heard a shattering sound. He was frightened and fled. Later, presumably when the fear of *jinn* or hyenas finally gave way to the lure of buried gold, he and his companion Ahmed Muhammed returned and crept into the cave and found decaying rolls of leather in one of a number of strange elongated jars embedded in the floor of the cave. These were the original 'Dead Sea Scrolls'.

In the year between the Bedouin discovery and the first press releases announcing the discovery to the world, there was confusion, blundering, and intrigue, as is associated often, unfortunately, with spectacular, chance finds. At least one, and probably several clandestine excavations ravaged the cave site; additional materials came to light; there is evidence that a considerable amount of precious material was destroyed in the process. The details of this phase of the vicissitudes of the scrolls of Cave I are most difficult to establish. In any case, after some of the scrolls (three, according to Ta'âmireh claims) had been passed about in the tents of clansmen, they were brought to Bethlehem for sale and fell into the hands of antiquities dealers. At some point they were joined with a portion of the manuscript materials from clandestine excavations. Ultimately one lot came into the possession of the Syrian Orthodox Metropolitan of Jerusalem, a Syrian cobbler of Bethlehem acting as broker;[1] another was

d'une tribu semi-nomade de Palestine', *RB* 58 (1951), pp. 75-91.

It is to be noted that the Ta'âmireh were not without experience in archaeological matters before the manuscript discoveries. M. R. Neuville, the late French prehistorian, used these tribesmen in his excavation of caves in Ta'âmireh country; and tribal traditions reflect pride in these caves and their antiquities.

1. One Khalil Iskander Shahin, better known as Kando. It is rather evident that Kando, a henchman named George Isaiah, and probably representatives of the Syrian monastery in Jerusalem were responsible for at least one of the clandestine forays on the cave. However this may be, Kando since has won the trust, not only of the Ta'âmireh, but also of antiquities officials handling purchase of newer Bedouin finds, and so has become the regular middleman for virtually all transactions in scroll materials. Such a person was necessary to both sides. Theoretically the manuscripts acquired by clandestine excavations could be confiscated by the Department of Antiquities. In fact it was necessary to establish a standard but indirect procedure for purchasing the precious leather. Otherwise the materials would have been smuggled and scattered, broken up and held for higher and higher prices, or, worst of all,

purchased by the late E.L. Sukenik for the Hebrew University.[1]

The metropolitan, Athanasius Yeshue Samuel, upon acquiring his lot of manuscripts, was anxious to have them authenticated, or to be more precise, perhaps, evaluated. A series of persons, including reputable scholars, was consulted and given opportunity to examine them. No one, however, who was competent in Hebrew paleography saw the scrolls. The episodes which mark this interlude are quite amusing in retrospect but are best forgotten, perhaps, in kindness to the scholars who failed.

The Syrian scrolls finally were brought to the American School of Oriental Research in February 1948, nearly a year after their discovery. Their antiquity and value were then recognized by a young scholar of the school, John C. Trever, who, together with William Brownlee, began first studies of the lot and systematically photographed it. Some prints of sections of one scroll, the great Isaiah scroll, were immediately dispatched to the distinguished orientalist, W.F. Albright, a leading authority in matters of Jewish paleography. He quickly replied, confirming Trever's judgments of the scrolls, congratulating him on 'the greatest discovery of modern times'. In the meantime, the Director of the American School, Professor Millar Burrows, had returned after an absence in Iraq to find his staff absorbed with the old leather rolls. He also convinced himself of

destroyed in the face of threatened seizure. Fixed prices by centimeter of inscribed surface were agreed upon early with the Bedouin, and a fixed commission for Kando. All sides have kept faith, with the result that the manuscripts have flowed into the Palestine Museum with a minimum of loss to the scientific world, and at a minimum cost.

1.   Accounts of the early history of the scrolls as told by principals may be found in the following: M. Burrows, *The Dead Sea Scrolls* (New York, 1955), pp. 3-28; E.L. Sukenik, *'wṣr hmgylwt hgnwzwt* (Jerusalem, 1954) (*OMG*), pp. 13-20; A.Y. Samuel, 'The Purchase of the Dead Sea Scrolls', *BA* 12 (1949), pp. 26-31; John C. Trever, 'The Discovery of the Scrolls', *BA* 11 (1948), pp. 46-68. The enormous secondary literature on the early discoveries is recorded by H.H. Rowley, *The Zadokite Fragments and the Dead Sea Scrolls* (Oxford, 1952), pp. 3-6. Newer developments have wholly antiquated the early discussion, though it retains some human interest. To these may be added the account of J.M. Allegro, *The Dead Sea Scrolls* (Penguin Books), 1956, pp. 15-34. It may be noted that while Allegro's account draws on interviews with the principals, his account, like others, is at best a reconstruction. Many discrepancies remain. For example, we still are not sure which scrolls came from the shepherd find, which from Syrian (illegal) excavations. And the precise fashion in which Sukenik's lot arrived in his possession is thoroughly obscure. We know only that they were purchased from a Muslim dealer of Bethlehem (not directly, at least, from Kando), through a well-known Jerusalem dealer in antiquities.

the extreme age and importance of the new finds, and on April 11, 1948, made the first announcement of the discovery of the manuscripts to the press of the world.[1] Two weeks later (on April 26), Professor Sukenik announced the existence of the Hebrew University collection.

In point of fact, Sukenik had recognized the scrolls for what they were before the metropolitan approached the American School with his collection. In late November, Sukenik was shown fragments in a Jerusalem antiquities shop. His familiarity with Hebrew inscriptions of the period had prepared him as few were prepared for the discovery. He relates, however, that he could scarcely believe what his knowledge and senses told him was true![2] His delay in announcing the discoveries was occasioned, no doubt, by his reluctance to alert Bedouin and their middlemen to the value of their finds before as much material as possible had been acquired by scientists. The Hebrew University lot was acquired in purchases in November and December 1947. In December, Sukenik also learned of the Syrian collection, and during the following month attempted to arrange its purchase through one Anton Kiraz, a member of the Syrian Orthodox community. Actually, the St. Mark's scrolls came into Sukenik's hands for some days, but negotiations were broken off, presumably after the Syrian monks had approached the scholars of the American School.[3]

Ultimately the four scrolls belonging to the Syrian monastery were smuggled to America by the metropolitan, and after the publication of three of them by the American Schools of Oriental Research in 1950 and 1951, were purchased through indirect channels for the Hebrew University in the summer of 1954. Professor Sukenik's negotiations were thus completed more than six years later; and scrolls which would have sold for a few hundred dollars in 1948 brought a reported $250,000 in 1954.[4]

Arab–Israeli fighting began so to disturb Palestine in the spring of

1.   Cf. G. Ernest Wright, 'A Phenomenal Discovery', *BA* 11 (1948), pp. 21-23; W.F. Albright, 'Notes from the President's Desk', *BASOR* 110 (April 1948), pp. 2-3.

2.   Cf. the excerpts from Sukenik's diary, *OMG*, p. 20.

3.   The account related by the metropolitan differs at this point from that of Sukenik. Samuel maintains that the scrolls were shown to Sukenik by Kiraz after they had been taken to the American school and photographed. However, the precise dates given by Sukenik, presumably drawn from his diary, are evidently to be followed in reconstructing the sequence of events.

4.   Actually the purchase—worked out by Yigael Yadin, Sukenik's son—was not announced until February of 1955.

1948 that attempts to locate and excavate the site of the extraordinary find were frustrated. With the war that followed the end of the British mandate in May 1948 communications were cut between the scholars who knew of the finds and the antiquities officials resident in Palestine (now Arab Jordan). Indeed, Mr. G. Lankester Harding, the Director of the Department of Antiquities of Jordan, learned of the discoveries only upon reading the April 1948 issue of the *Bulletin of the American Schools of Oriental Research*, which reached him in Ammân in November 1948! As soon as arrangements could be made, Arab legion-naires were dispatched to comb the cliffs of the Dead Sea in search of the cave. After only two or three days' search, in late January 1949, whitish debris which had cascaded down a ravine in the cliffside revealed the position of the cave to Captain (later Colonel) Akkash el-Zebn. It lay about .6 mile (1 kilometer) north of Wâdī Qumrân, low in the six- or seven-hundred-foot cordon of cliffs, at a point just over a mile distant from the shore of the Dead Sea.[1]

Scientific excavations were carried out successfully (February 15–March 5, 1949), and fragments belonging to about seventy documents, including fragments of two of the original seven manuscripts, were found.[2] However, the fragments recovered by the archaeologists were taken from Bedouin debris, and from more or less disturbed levels in the cave, so that none was impressive in size. Nevertheless, the provenience of the purchased lots was established, and sufficient archaeological data were recovered to date the context of the scrolls roughly, confirming earlier paleographical results.[3]

2. *New Treasures from the Wilderness*

The fantastic episode seemed closed. For nearly two years the desert was left undisturbed. It was generally assumed that by a stroke of

1.   The cave is located at map co-ordinate 193.3:128.9. Owing to a *lapsus calami*, the position is wrongly given in *DJD I*. Cf. Cross, 'Qumrân Cave I', *JBL* 75 (1956), p. 121, and the references in n. 2.

2.   Bits of 1QM and 1QH were discovered in controlled excavations. In addition lots from clandestine digs were later purchased from Kando and included extensive portions of the Rule of the Community (1QS), smaller bits of the Hebrew University Isaiah (1QIsa[b]), and of the Genesis Apocryphon (1Q20).

3.   *DJD I*, pp. 6-38. Cf. Harding, 'The Dead Sea Scrolls'; R. de Vaux, 'La grotte des manuscrits hébreux', *RB* 56 (1949), pp. 586-609; O.R. Sellers, 'Excavation of the 'Manuscript Cave', *BASOR* 114 (April 1949), pp. 5-9.

fortune an isolated cache had been found. Apparently it occurred to few scholars that Cave I was other than a chance hiding place, or storage place, chosen by some odd but happy quirk of an ancient mind. The discovery was unique; to the sophisticated, the odds against parallel discoveries seemed staggering. The Ta'âmireh clansmen, however, having made a successful debut in the archaeological field, were inclined to make a vocation of it. They ranged the sterile wastes of the Judaean desert, peering into caves, scratching in their floors, oblivious to passing months, patient and undiscouraged by persistent failure. Their range lands were rich only in caves and they proposed to exploit them.

In the fall of 1951 the Bedouin made new discoveries in caves far to the southwest of the first cave, somewhere in the heart of the Judaean badlands. Scholars were alerted to the find when documents of a new order—unrelated to the Qumrân finds—were offered for sale in Jerusalem. Investigation was made; in fact the caves of the Wâdī Murabba'ât which produced the finds were actually visited; but the search was inconclusive, and only later was the site of the new discoveries surely confirmed. Meanwhile it was supposed that a small find had been made and exhausted.[1]

In November and December of 1951, G. Lankester Harding, Director of Antiquities, and R.P. Roland de Vaux, Director of the École Biblique et Archéologique Française in Jerusalem, proposed to make soundings at the ancient ruins to the south of Cave I on the Wâdī Qumrân. The ruin was by no means unknown. De Saulcy in the nineteenth century had identified it as biblical Gomorrah; and soberer scientists in the modern period of archaeology had noted evidence of its Roman date.[2] The excavations at Cave I had brought the curious ruin to immediate attention, and speculation as to its possible connection with the people who deposited the scrolls made its systematic excavation desirable.[3]

1.　See R. de Vaux, 'Les grottes de Murabba'ât et leur documents', *RB* 60 (1953), pp. 245-75; especially p. 245.

2.　De Vaux lists the older published materials relating to Khirbet Qumrân in his article, 'Fouille au Khirbet Qumrân', *RB* 60 (1953), p. 89, notes 1-8; unpublished material is available in the files of the Palestine Archaeological Museum.

3.　De Vaux and Harding made surface explorations and dug two tombs at Khirbet Qumrân in 1949. However, they were disinclined to see any connection between the cave and the ruin. See De Vaux, *op. cit.*, p. 89, and 'La grotte des manuscrits hébreux', *RB* 56 (1949), p. 586, n. 1. These scholars were not satisfied, however, with the superficial character of their examination of the site; moreover, other scholars were clamoring for further study of the site (see P. Kahle, *Die hebräischen*

Excavations in 1951 initiated a series of five campaigns, the most recent in the spring of 1956.[1] The first soundings at Khirbet Qumrân yielded enough evidence to permit the tentative suggestion that the site was an ancient community-center of the Essenes,[2] one of the major religious parties in Judaism, who, together with the Pharisees and Sadducees, competed for the loyalty of Jews in late pre-Christian and early Christian times. Already the internal evidence of certain of the sectarian manuscripts had led scholars to assign them an Essene authorship.[3] Slowly a new pattern began to emerge: the scrolls belonged to an ancient people who occupied the caves north and south of Khirbet Qumrân, and the ruin was precisely the Essene desert retreat remarked by the Roman historian Pliny.[4] However, in late 1951 this construction of the origin of the scrolls and the character of the site on the Wâdī Qumrân was yet to be established securely.

Concurrently, at the end of November 1951 a new large lot of documents was presented for sale at the École Biblique. It became clear, now, that the Ta'âmireh had continued their enterprise in the caves of the wilderness, and that their finds were of major importance. Père de Vaux entered directly into conversations with representatives of the Ta'âmireh, both to negotiate purchase and to seek information about the locality of the new series of caves. If unusual wit was needed to bargain successfully with the Bedouin for their precious manuscripts, one can only speculate on the adroitness required to educe the secret of the

Handschriften aus der Höhle, [Stuttgart, 1951], pp. 59-60).

1.   See De Vaux, 'Fouille au Khirbet Qumrân', *RB* 60 (1953), pp. 83-106; Harding, 'Khirbet Qumrân and Wady Muraba'at', *PEQ* 84 (1952), pp. 104-9; De Vaux, 'Fouille au Khirbet Qumrân. Rapport préliminaire sur la deuxième campagne', *RB* 61 (1954), pp. 206-36; 'Chronique archéologique: Khirbet Qumrân', *RB* 61 (1954), pp. 567f.; *RB* 63 (1956), pp. 73f.; and especially, 'Fouilles de Khirbet Qumrân. Rapport préliminaire sur les 3ᵉ, 4ᵉ et 5ᵉ campagnes', *RB* 63 (1956), pp. 533-77. Cf. E. Vogt, 'Effossiones in Hirbet Qumrân', *Biblica* 36 (1955), pp. 562-64 (with diagram of the ruins); J.A. Kelso, 'The Archaeology of Qumran', *JBL* 74 (1955), pp. 141-46; A. Parrot, 'Les manuscrits de la Mer Morte: le point de vue archéologique', *RHPR* 35 (1955), pp. 61-67. [See now the superb synthesis of R. de Vaux, *Archaeology and the Dead Sea Scrolls* (The Schweich Lectures, 1959; London: Oxford University Press for the British Academy, rev. edn, 1973)].

2.   See De Vaux, 'Fouille au Khirbet Qumrân', p. 105.

3.   See especially A. Dupont-Sommer, *Aperçus préliminaires sur les Manuscrits de la Mer Morte* (Paris, 1950), pp. 105-17.

4.   Pliny, *Naturalis historia*, V, xv, 73. Cf. *Dio apud Synesium* 39 (ed. Migne).

source of their treasure. Père de Vaux was equal to the task. At a visit of the tribesmen, when a rather high price was suggested for a fragment, De Vaux was openly, if not ostentatiously, horrified. The Bedouin then spoke eloquently of their 'operations', the gargantuan caverns in which they worked, forty or fifty strong, for days and weeks, to recover the pieces presented for sale. When De Vaux appeared dubious about the details of their tale they energetically defended the account of their hardships, and argued (rhetorically) that if he would come and see, he would find them vindicated. Père de Vaux was not one to turn down even an oblique invitation. He would go! But, he hastened to remark, was there not danger from the police? Less energetically, no doubt, they allayed any fears of the police De Vaux might have entertained. They had sentinels posted in the hills. If police appeared in the neighborhood, signals flashed through the wilderness and the workmen vanished into 'the caverns of the rock and the clefts of the crags.' De Vaux was reassured, and had a helpful suggestion to make as well. Perhaps he could get permission from the Department of Antiquities for the journey, so that neither he nor his guides need go to prison if caught. The Bedouin agreed that this was a capital idea. So he added another suggestion. Perhaps he could prevail on the Director of Antiquities himself to accompany them. The Bedouins indicated that they would be highly honored.

The expedition could not be launched until after the season of excavations at Khirbet Qumrân; but in late January a party set out including Harding and De Vaux, an Arab foreman, a police escort(!), and the Bedouin guides. A trip by truck into the edge of the wilderness, and a three-hour march farther brought them into the Wâdī Murabba'ât, a portion of the Wâdī Darâjeh. They came upon the site of the caves at a point about twelve miles southwest of the Qumrân caves, about twelve miles southeast of Bethlehem, in a landscape comparable to that ascribed to the moon. They were in a gorge whose vertical sides cut more than six hundred feet into the desolate mountains, about three miles short of its mouth in the Dead Sea. The caves were in the north face, about two hundred feet above the floor of the *wâdī* bed.

The first glimpse of the caves assured the party that they had come to the right place. A stream of Bedouin were fleeing the caves; De Vaux counted no less than thirty-four clandestine diggers slipping out! Four caves were found. Two of them contained inscribed material and evidence of ancient occupation. Each of the latter two attains a length of more than one hundred fifty feet, one of them (Cave II) dividing into two long galleries which plunge deep into the cliff. The Bedouin proved Père de Vaux's skepticism ill-founded—to his delight—and while their description of the magnificence of the caves had been mildly exaggerated, their account of the hardships of working at the site had been understated. The excavations which followed were perhaps the most testing and arduous ever undertaken in Palestine.[1]

Scientific excavations were carried out in the caves of Wâdī Murabba'ât from January 21 to March 3, 1952. Occupation levels and documentary materials of several periods were discovered. The caves had been the hiding places for guerillas, refugees, and brigand bands through the long troubled history of Palestine. There were evidences of men who had huddled in the caves three millennia before David hid from Saul's jealous wrath in the caves of this same hinterland. In the days of the Hyksos and the kings of Judah, in the era of the Jewish revolts against Rome and the Arab conquest, desperate men found shelter in the caverns of Murabba'ât and left behind bits of pottery and tools, and in the later periods scraps of their 'papers' and books.[2]

Although the documents of the library of Qumrân are to be discussed following the narrative of the series of discoveries, perhaps it is best to describe the literary remains of unrelated discoveries in the context of our story.

Of considerable interest among written materials from Murabba'ât[3] is the earliest papyrus in Hebrew ever found in Palestine. Unfortunately, it is not a literary text; rather it is a list of names and numbers written in

1.   The description of De Vaux's negotiations is told in his article, 'Les grottes de Murabba'at et leur documents', *RB* 60 (1953), pp. 245-48. For the full color of the events leading to the discovery of the caves, however, one needs to hear the story from his own lips. Both Harding ('Khirbet Qumran and Wady Muraba'at', *PEQ* 84 [1952], pp. 104-9) and De Vaux (*op. cit.*, pp. 249-75) give vivid, detailed descriptions of the work in the caves. [See now *DJD II (Les grottes de Murabba'ât)*].

2.   That is, Chalcolithic, Middle Bronze II, Iron II, Roman, and Arab levels appeared superimposed in excavation.

3.   Several texts have been given preliminary publication: De Vaux , 'Quelques textes hébreux de Murabba'at', *RB* 60 (1953), pp. 268-75; Milik, 'Une lettre de Siméon Bar Kokheba', *ibid.*, pp. 276-94. For recent literature on the last-mentioned text, see Cross, 'La lettre de Siméon Bar Kosba', *RB* 63 (1956), pp. 45-48; to which is to be added S. Yeivin, *'Atiqot* I (1955), pp. 95-108. The reports of the excavation in the Wâdī Murabba'ât, together with the publication of the texts have now appeared in *DJD II*.

the script of the seventh century BC.[1] Moreover, the piece is a palimp-sest. The underwriting is dim, but appears to be a letter of roughly the same date. More important, no doubt, are a series of texts of the late first and early second centuries AD from a cache belonging, apparently, to remnants of the army of Simon bar Kokheba, the 'pseudo-Messiah' who led the second Jewish revolt against Rome (AD 132–35). They include Greek, Aramaic, and Hebrew documents, among them dated letters and contracts, as well as a few biblical fragments.

Actually, the most important of the Murabba'ât finds, a magnificent scroll of the Minor Prophets from the second century AD, came to light early in 1955. The preserved portion of the manuscript extends from the middle of Joel to the beginning of Zechariah, including (in traditional order) Amos, Obadiah, Jonah, Micah, Nahum, Habakkuk, Zephaniah, and Haggai. Four columns are almost perfectly preserved.[2]

While the archaeologists busied themselves in the Wâdī Murabba'ât in the early part of 1952, the Ta'âmireh, forced away from their new set of caves, took advantage of the absence of scientists from Qumrân to begin searches and soundings in the original area of discovery. In February 1952 the tribesmen found the fragmentary remains of manuscripts in a new cave hard by Cave I, no more than a few hundred yards to the south of it. Cave II, Qumrân, was not an impressive find.[3] However, the find was enough to bring the archaeologists—too late—out of the Wâdī Murabba'ât in a frantic effort to keep up with the chain of discoveries.

With evidence now that more than one cave in the area of Qumrân held pre-Christian manuscripts, and the growing realization that the manuscripts actually derived from a community with its center at Khirbet Qumrân, the various archaeological schools in Jerusalem were galvanized. They mounted an expedition to explore all the caves of the high rocky cliffs north and south of Khirbet Qumrân on a line some five

1.   Abbé Milik, who is to publish the text, prefers an eighth-century date (oral communication). The script is an unusual cursive; perhaps we should await publica-tion and detailed paleographical analysis before committing ourselves too closely to a dating. One thing is clear, however, the script is archaic, not archaizing, and therefore is not to be compared with the Paleo-Hebrew series of Qumrân.

2.   The MS, found by *bedu*, purportedly comes from a fifth Murabba'ât cave a kilometer or so west of the four investigated in 1952. As we shall see, the text of the Murabba'ât manuscript of the Twelve Prophets, like that of the more fragmentary biblical material, is virtually identical with the Masoretic consonantal tradition. See further in Chap. 4; and *DJD II*.

3.   See *DJD VII*.

miles long. The exploration was carried out during the month of March 1952.[1] Teams of archaeologists, with foremen and the obliging Ta'âmireh in their pay, clambered over the dizzying heights, systematically combing the cliffs. The excitement of the search turned aging scientists into a new breed of archaeological mountain goats. Soundings were made in more than two hundred caves. In twenty-five the pottery recovered proved to come from the same potteries[2] which had served the building complex at Khirbet Qumrân and Cave I. Moreover, evidence was detected of tents and lean-tos adjacent to clefts or caves containing domestic pottery of the period, giving indication of an extensive occupation radiating out from the communal buildings at Qumrân. However, only one new cave produced inscribed materials. This was Cave III, found on March 14, 1952. Its most spectacular treasure was dug out nearly a week later (the doorway of the cave had collapsed in antiquity), the so-called 'Copper Scrolls'.

The 'Copper Scrolls' are actually a single work, preserved in two oxidized rolls of beaten copper. After a delay in which experiments were made to discover a way in which the rolls could be opened and deciphered, they were cut into small strips at the Manchester College of Technology. The first announcement of their contents was made on June 1, 1956.[3]

The unique find had caused considerable speculation in the interim between its discovery and decipherment. Hints of the contents of the document had been gained by examination of its exterior where reverse impressions of letters showed through, thanks to the force of the

1.   See De Vaux, 'Exploration de la région de Qumrân', *RB* 60 (1953), pp. 540-56; W.L. Reed, 'The Qumrân Caves Expedition of March, 1952', *BASOR* 135 (October, 1954), pp. 8-13.

2.   That is, the pottery was not merely that common to the late Hellenistic and early Roman period (first century BC–first century AD); its paste, form, and decoration were sufficiently homogeneous to suggest a common place of manufacture. As we shall see, this common pottery is almost certainly the elaborate installation found in the excavations of the community center.

3.   The scrolls are scheduled to be published in the third volume of *Discoveries in the Judaean Desert* along with other materials from the 'minor caves'. Meanwhile, a provisional report on their opening and contents may be found in J.T. Milik's article, 'The Copper Document from Cave III, Qumran', *BA* 19 (1956), pp. 60-64. [The Copper Document together with the other materials of the 'Minor Caves' is published in *DJD III*.]

engraver's hammer. It was inscribed in Hebrew, more or less in the format of a leather or papyrus scroll. Evidently it had to do with treasures and their hiding places.

Lost scrolls of high antiquity containing secrets of hidden hoards of gold and silver: here was a subject to stir the imagination! One can excuse the soberest scientist being bitten by the Gold Bug. But, as is virtually inevitable in the case of legends of treasure, on full examination the Copper Document proved disappointing.

The twelve columns of writing on the strips of copper list some sixty treasures. The gold and silver, not to mention other precious stuffs, come to more than two hundred tons of precious metal according to a minimal calculation. The specifications of the hiding places of the treasures are also given in each case. Both the fabulous amounts of the treasures, and the vague or traditional character of their hiding places are sufficient evidence of the folkloristic character of the document. In any case, none of the decipherers of the Copper Document has come into sudden wealth.

Presumably the strange text records the priestly or royal treasures which popular imagination assigned to old Israel, and supposed had survived in caches distributed over Palestine.[1] In some respects, indeed, the chief interest of the text—now that it is open—is in the proto-Mishnaic dialect in which it is written.

---

1.   On the Copper Document, K.G. Kuhn's provisional study, 'Les rouleaux de cuivre de Qumrân', *RB* 61 (1954), pp. 193-205, is still useful. It is a bold and discerning attempt to reconstruct its text from what could be read in reverse on the outside of the rolls. However, his natural supposition that the treasures were actual Essene hoards buried in the neighborhood of Qumrân has proved untenable.

Mr. John Allegro's recent statements supporting the original form of the Kuhn hypothesis (*The Dead Sea Scrolls*, pp. 181-84) are, to the writer, quite bewildering. To be sure, the document is difficult, and a number of ambiguities are as yet unsolved. The points which are clear, however, can in no fashion be fitted into the picture drawn earlier by Kuhn: the size and type of the treasure, the vague or traditional places of concealment (coupled with precise measurements!), the vulgar dialect in which it is written, and the clumsiness of the scribe.

Professor Kuhn, himself, in an article published since the opening of the document ('...Bericht über neue Qumranfunde und über die Offnung der Kupferrollen', *TLZ* 1956 cols. 541-46), proposes an alternate suggestion that the rolls may contain a record of real treasures, presumably those of the Herodian Temple destroyed in AD 70, and that this record may have been put into the hands of the Essenes for safekeeping.

The attrition of heat, malaria, and simple fatigue brought the expedition to a halt at the end of March. It had succeeded in investigating most of the natural caves of the limestone cliffs. On the other hand, it had

Though it is clear from Josephus' notices that the Temple treasures were burned or taken by the Romans, at least in considerable part, as Kuhn observes, it is not impossible that some treasures were secretly hidden.

I am in agreement that the treasures probably are meant to be national and/or temple treasures of Israel. But I am dubious that even the temple of Herod could have mustered such glittering heaps of gold and silver, much less that such amounts escaped the greedy besiegers. Moreover, in this hypothesis, the treasures would necessarily have been smuggled out and hidden in the early days of the Revolt, and the lists transmitted to Qumrân before the latter's demise early in the Revolt (AD 68). Perhaps this is possible; in any case it must be admitted that the date of the Copper Scroll—scarcely earlier than the middle of the first century AD—raises no objection.

A more serious objection comes when one recognizes that under such a hypothesis we must assume that temple officials gave a list to the counter-priesthood at Qumrân, whose open contempt for their orthodox brethren in Jerusalem can scarcely have been unilateral. This dilemma is avoided if the document was made up after Zealot forces took control of the temple, but in this case we are in chronological difficulties again.

Again, I cannot believe that the document in hand was in any sense official. Too much has been made (by the writer as well as others) of the costliness of copper. The scribe appears unskilled. Even taking into account the awkward material in which he worked, he cannot be compared with the facile scribes of Qumrân. And the notion of a priestly official having a record of treasure made up in copper and hidden against the future in a remote cave seems overly dramatic.

I should prefer to propose, tentatively to be sure, that we have to do with traditional, i.e., fabulous treasures, perhaps of the temple of Solomon. Such would 'appropriately' be hidden in the monument of Absalom, the cairn of Achan, and in Mount Gerizim (of the Samaritans!). And it is just possible to imagine a priestly hermit of Qumrân taking such folkloristic traditions seriously enough to preserve them in copper. Mr. J. Strugnell has called my attention to II Baruch 6.7-10 in this connection. Professor Stendahl has reminded me of the curious tale of 'holy vessels' hidden (by Moses according to Josephus' text) in Mount Gerizim, told in the days of Pilate (*Antiq.* XVIII, 85-87).

It may be observed in this connection that Cave III, like most of the 'minor caves', should not be thought of as a 'hiding place', much less a *genîzāh* for Essene documents. Rather the minor caves are to be designated as repositories for members of the Essene community who lived in the cliffs. Presumably the remnants from the minor caves constitute the remains of scrolls in private use, most of them no doubt copied at the Qumrân center, and 'lent out from the main library', so to speak. The Copper Document, like other texts from this and other caves, was left behind lying openly on the ancient floor, presumably at the time of the Roman attack of AD 68. Cave IV, with its massive remains of nearly 575 MSS, and possibly Cave I, with some ignored the artificial caves and clefts in the marl terrace at the foot of the cliffs.[1] Time and funds were short, and logical Western minds, noting that the caves which had yielded manuscripts all were located in the upper level, concluded that exploration of the marl caves was to no purpose. So the archaeologists retired from the desert of Qumrân. The Bedouin continued the search. Being less logical, and perhaps less energetic, they attacked the marl terrace supporting Khirbet Qumrân. In the late summer of 1952 they discovered a cave two hundred yards or less from the site of the Essene center and, some feet beneath the modern floor of the cave, came upon the matted and decayed remains of manuscripts. They had struck the main lode: Qumrân Cave IV.

The clandestine diggings of the Ta'âmireh were halted, fortunately, before the contents of the cave were exhausted.[2] In the month of September (22-29) 1952 controlled excavations replaced Bedouin efforts and met with good finds in the remaining untouched levels of the cave. To be sure, the lion's share fell to the clansmen; but Harding, De Vaux, and their co-workers succeeded in recovering fragments belonging to more than a hundred manuscripts, including pieces of most of the chief manuscripts of the cave. Obviously this circumstance has proved important in establishing beyond doubt the provenience of lots of Cave IV

seventy documents, at least three of which were in a jar, are to be treated as exceptions. Cave I may have been a hiding place, sought out when the settlement appeared doomed; Cave IV almost certainly contained the remnants of the great collection originally housed in the community center only a stone's throw distant from its opening.

1.   The marl caves (Caves IV-X) are clearly the work of human hands in ancient times. No doubt they made handy living quarters immediately adjacent to the communal buildings, which, to judge from the function of the architectural details, made little provision for the living accommodations of the large community at Qumrân. It is likely that the caves were originally cut for tombs for the Iron II (ninth–sixth century BC) settlement which underlies the Essene structures. Despite search, no Iron Age tombs have come to light. Against this it must be said that no Iron Age deposits have been found in the floor levels of the marl caves, an extraordinary circumstance even if the caves had been thoroughly cleaned and expanded in Hellenistic–Roman times.

2.   According to reports, the well-organized Ta'âmireh had teams working in shifts to hasten their exploitation of the cave. At least one new entrance was opened into the cave. More than a meter of debris appears to have been removed in the process of their diggings. But so well had they learned their new trade that few scraps remained in their dumps.

fragments bought from Bedouin over the following five years.[1]

Caves V and VI were found in conjunction with the discovery of Cave IV. Cave VI, situated near the waterfall of Wâdī Qumrân, low in the rocky face where in geological times the marl terrace was cut away by the cascade, was discovered by Ta'âmireh in the late summer. Cave V was discovered by scientists during the excavations in Cave IV; it is located immediately north of Cave IV in the marl terrace. Both V and VI contained significant but minor finds.

The summer of 1952 brought as by-products of the desert search other series of manuscript discoveries in precincts of the wilderness remote from Qumrân. The most significant of these is a cave or caves discovered by the Ta'âmireh in a locality which has never been precisely fixed, though it seems clear enough that it lies to the south of Murabba'ât in one or more of the *wâdīs* that empty into the Dead Sea. These documents of undesignated provenience made their appearance in Jerusalem in July 1952 and were bought up in several purchases in the month following. Like Murabba'ât, the bulk of them must be attributed to the era between the Jewish revolts against Rome.[2] The most important text for our purposes, no doubt, is a manuscript of the Minor Prophets in Greek, a lost recension of the Septuagint, the old Greek version of the third–second centuries BC. When combined with three 'standard' Septuagint manuscripts from Cave IV, Qumrân,[3] this newly

1.   Among the scientifically excavated materials deep in undisturbed soil were such odd items as Septuagint fragments, phylacteries, Paleo-Hebrew materials, cursive bits of Exodus, as well as the usual Qumrân run of Hebrew and Aramaic documents on papyrus and leather. The writer had the opportunity to begin his labors on the scrolls by examining and doing preliminary identification of the excavated materials before they were combined with the great mass of purchased fragments. I was struck with the fact that the relatively small quantity of fragments from the deepest levels of the cave nevertheless represented a fair cross section of the whole deposit in the cave, which suggests, among other things, that deterioration of the manuscripts must have begun even before time sealed the manuscripts in the stratified soil, and that the manuscripts may have been in great disorder when originally abandoned in the cave. The paucity of sherds in the cave certainly indicates that the scrolls of Cave IV were not left stored away in jars.

2.   Several of the texts of the find have been published together with brief notices of the find as a whole: Barthélemy, 'Redécouverte d'un chaînon manquant de l'histoire de la Septante', *RB* 60 (1953), pp. 18-29 [see now the *editio princeps*, *DJD VIII*]; J. Starcky, 'Un contrat nabatéen sur papyrus', *RB* 61 (1954), pp. 161-81; J.T. Milik, 'Un contrat juif de l'an 134 après J.-C', *RB* (1954), pp. 182-90.

3.   Qumrân IV has produced leather fragments of two MSS of the LXX—one of

found recension will place textual critics in a much improved position to reconstruct the early history of the text of the Septuagint.[1] [2]

Quiet descended upon the desert for nearly three years, save for the seasonal excavations at the site of Khirbet Qumrân. Then, in the spring of 1955 came a new cycle of finds.[3] During the fourth campaign at Qumrân four additional productive caves were located and exploited: VII-X. Like Caves IV and V, these latter were found in the marl terrace adjacent to the settlement. Unlike Cave IV, they had collapsed in ancient times as a result of erosion along the ravines which make up the complex of the Wâdī Qumrân. Only a handful of fragments was recovered from all of these caves combined, enough to prove, only, that manuscripts had once been deposited in them. Most of the treasures had washed with the winter torrents into the sea.[4]

Leviticus, the other of Numbers. A third MS, represented by papyrus fragments, is a second copy of Leviticus. These documents are probably to be dated in the first century BC paleographically; in any case, none can be later than the early first century of our era. There is no doubt that they belong to the common LXX tradition. This is noteworthy in as much as they derive from a pre-Christian Jewish community in Palestine. Otherwise only two fragmentary papyri of comparable age are known, both of Egyptian provenience. I am indebted to Patrick W. Skehan for permitting me to read in manuscript his treatment of the Qumrân LXX fragments published in *Actes du 2ᵉ Congrès international pour l'étude de l'Ancien Testament, Strasbourg*, 1956. [See now *DJD IX*.]

1.   In addition to Barthélemy's preliminary publication (see p. 34, n. 2) see also his *Les devanciers d'Aquila* (Leiden: E.J. Brill, 1963), cf. Vogt, 'Fragmenta Prophetarum minorum deserti Iuda', *Biblica* 34 (1953), pp. 423-26; J.W. Wevers, 'Septuaginta-Forschungen I', *TR* 22 (1954), pp. 136-38; K. Stendahl, *The School of St. Matthew* (Copenhagen, 1954), pp. 177-80; Cross, 'The Manuscripts of the Dead Sea Caves', *BA* 17 (1954), pp. 12f.; P. Kahle, '...Die im August 1952 entdeckte Lederrolle mit dem griechischen Text der kleinen Propheten und das Problem der Septuaginta', *TLZ* 79 (1954), pp. 82-94; P. Katz, 'Septuagintal Studies in the Mid-Century', in *The Background of the New Testament and its Eschatology*, W.D. Davies and D. Daube, eds. (Cambridge, 1956), pp. 206-8.

2.   Mention also may be made at this point in our narrative of the late Byzantine and early Arabic finds from the cisterns of Khirbet Mird (ancient Hyrcania) by Bedouin in the summer of 1952. For references to the discoveries and the subsequent expedition of the Mission Archéologique Belge de Louvain in February–April 1953, see Milik, 'Un inscription et une lettre en araméen christo–palestinien', *RB* 60 (1953), pp. 526-39, especially pp. 526f.; De Vaux, 'Fouille au Khirbet Qumrân', *ibid.*, p. 85; and Cross, 'The Manuscripts of the Dead Sea Caves', p. 12.

3.   For the discovery in the Wâdī Murabba'ât in early 1955, see p. 28, n. 1.

4.   See provisionally, De Vaux, 'Fouilles de Khirbet Qumrân...3ᵉ, 4ᵉ et 5ᵉ

Finally, or perhaps we should say most recently, the ubiquitous tribesmen detected another cave not far from Cave III, well over a mile to the north of the ruin.[1] Its entrance was collapsed, but crevices remained open through which hosts of bats fluttered at dusk and dawn. By Herculean efforts the cave was opened and excavated by the finders. Their labors were thorough; when archaeologists pitched their tents on the plain below and halted the unauthorized digging, little more than Iron Age and Chalcolithic levels remained untouched, sealed in millennial deposits of bat guano. Several virtually complete scrolls were taken by Ta'âmireh, and significant fragments of at least five other works by Ta'âmireh and archaeologists. Cave XI thus rivals Caves I and IV in importance.

3. *A Catalogue of the Library of Qumrân*

We shall be concerned here chiefly with the great collection from Cave IV. Cave I texts are now almost completely published and relatively well known. The 'minor caves' have been published, and the most important of the Cave 11 texts.[2]

From Cave I came the seven manuscripts of the original shepherd find. These are the great Isaiah scroll (1QIsa^a), a commentary (*péšer*) on Habakkuk (1QpHab), and the Rule of the Community (1QS), all three published by the American Schools of Oriental Research in 1950–51.[3]

---

campagnes', pp. 572f. Of especial interest are some papyrus bits of the Greek Epistle of Jeremiah from Cave VII. [See now *DJD III*.]

1.   Cave III lies at map co-ordinates 193.5:129.8 (cave no. 8 of the exploration map [*RB* 60, 1953), Pl. XX opposite p. 560]). No co-ordinates are published for Cave XI; however, the cave lies low in the *falaise*, well to the north of Cave I, and slightly south of Cave III.

2.   The 'Minor Caves' are published in *DJD III* (with bibliography). For a listing of manuscripts of Cave 11 and their editions, see J.A. Fitzmyer, *The Dead Sea Scrolls: Major Publications and Tools for Study* (Atlanta: Scholars Press, rev. edn, 1990), and Florentino García Martínez, 'Texts from Qumran Cave 11', in D. Dimant and U. Rappaport eds., *The Dead Sea Scrolls: Forty Years of Research* [Leiden and Jerusalem: E.J. Brill, Magnes Press, and Yad Izhak Ben-Zvi], 1992).

3.   Burrows, Trever, Brownlee, eds., *The Dead Sea Scrolls of St. Mark's Monastery*; Vol. I, *The Isaiah Manuscript and the Habakkuk Commentary* (New Haven, 1950); Vol. II: 2, *Plates and Transcription of the Manual of Discipline* (New Haven, 1951); and F.M. Cross, *et al.*, eds., *Scrolls from Qumrân Cave I: The Great Isaiah Scroll, the Order of the Community, the Pesher to Habakkuk* (Cambridge and Jerusalem: Albright Institute of Archaeological Research and the Shrine of the Book, 1972).

Another group of three, published in 1954 by Hebrew University scholars, includes a second, fragmentary copy of Isaiah (1QIsaᵇ); a sectarian collection of thanksgiving psalms (*hôdāyôt*; 1QH);[1] and an extraordinary document called the Order of the War Between the Children of Light and the Children of Darkness (1QM).[2] The seventh of these scrolls recently has had preliminary publication under the title *A Genesis Apocryphon*.[3] It is an elaboration of Genesis in Aramaic, and will prove most useful as a basis for linguistic analyses of the Aramaic of Palestine in a little-known era. To these seven are to be added nearly seventy fragmentary manuscripts, biblical, apocryphal, apocalyptic, liturgical, published in 1955 in the first volume of *Discoveries in the Judaean Desert*.[4]

Most of the scroll materials from Cave 11 are now published. Four scrolls are in a particularly good state of preservation: the great Temple Scroll, perhaps the most important manuscript from Cave 11,[5] a scroll containing a mixture of canonical and non-canonical psalms designated, perhaps incorrectly, as 11Q Psᵃ, under the presumption that it is a manuscript of the biblical Psalter in an alternate edition,[6] a Targum of Job,[7] and a copy of Leviticus in paleo-Hebrew script.[8] The Temple

1. Sukenik and Avigad, *OMG*.

2. The best and most thorough treatment of 1QM is that of Y. Yadin, *The Scroll of the Sons of Light Against the Sons of Darkness*, trans. B. and C. Rabin (Oxford, Oxford University Press, 1962).

3. Edited by N. Avigad and Y. Yadin (Jerusalem, 1956).

4. Among the several longer reviews and review articles dealing with *DJD I*, see especially F.M. Cross, 'Qumran Cave I', *JBL* 75 (1956), pp. 121-25; J. Hempel, 'Randbemerkungen zu Qumran I', *ZAW* 67 (1955), pp. 131-39; H.M. Orlinsky, *Jewish Social Studies* 18 (1956), pp. 217-20; E. Vogt, *Biblica* 37 (1956), pp. 231-35.

5. See Y. Yadin's monumental work, *The Temple Scroll*. 3 vols. (Jerusalem: Israel Exploration Society, the Hebrew University of Jerusalem, and the Shrine of the Book, 1983).

6. See J.A. Sanders, ed., *The Psalms Scroll of the Qumrân Cave 11 (DJD IV)*.

7. See J.P.M. van der Ploeg and A.S. van der Woude, *Le Targum de Job de la grotte XI de Qumrân* (Leiden: Brill, 1971).

8. This script, sometimes incorrectly called 'Phoenician', or 'Samaritan', derives from the old pre-Exilic Hebrew script. Apparently it survived as a book hand and enjoyed a renascence in the period of Maccabean nationalism and archaism. In any case, at Qumrân it appears in documents contemporary with the Jewish hand, a derivative of the official Aramaic cursive of the late Persian Empire. The Samaritan is a descendant of this Paleo-Hebrew script of the Hasmonaean period. See now D.N. Freedman and K.A. Matthews, *The Paleo-Hebrew Leviticus Scroll*

Scroll is concerned with halakhic matters, particularly laws of purity, and projects in the eschatological future a perfect temple which it describes in detail, and a pure and holy Jerusalem. It is a sectarian work, probably Essene, dating to the era of the Maccabaean priest-kings. The Targum of Job is of particular interest since it appears to be the targum condemned by the Rabbi Gamaliel II (Paul's alleged teacher, cf. Acts 22.3), and among the earliest targumim committed to writing.[1]

From Cave IV have come tens of thousands of fragments, as we have remarked, and the collection is unrivaled in its size and import. It seems clear that the great library once housed in the Essene community center was abandoned in Cave IV; in its texts we find a cross section of the literature of sectarian Judaism at the end of the pre-Christian era.

Unlike the several scrolls of Caves I and XI which are preserved in good condition, with only minor lacunae, the manuscripts of Cave IV are in an advanced state of decay. Many fragments are so brittle or friable that they can scarcely be touched with a camel's-hair brush. Most are warped, crinkled, or shrunken, crusted with soil chemicals, blackened by moisture and age. The problems of cleaning, flattening, identifying, and piecing them together are formidable.[2]

The fragments when they are purchased from tribesmen generally come in boxes; cigarette boxes, film boxes, or shoe boxes, depending on the size of the fragments. The precious leather and papyrus is delicately handled by rough Bedouin hands, for the value of the material is all too keenly appreciated. Often cotton wool or tissue paper has been used by Bedouin to separate and protect the scraps of scrolls; and on occasion they have applied bits of gummed paper to pieces which threatened to crack apart or disintegrate. Not since the clandestine digs of Cave I have owners broken up large sheets or columns to sell them piecemeal.

Since 1952 when the cave was found, its myriad of fragments have slowly been gathered into the Palestine Archaeological Museum in Jerusalem. The major share was acquired by a purchase of the government of Jordan from Ta'âmireh, and by the controlled excavations. However, these initial acquisitions by no means exhausted the cave's treasures. After the Department of Antiquities, the Palestine Museum,

---

(11 QpaleoLev) (Cambridge: American Schools of Oriental Research, 1985).

1. Talmud Babl., Shabbat 115a; Talm. Jer., Shabbat 16a; The addition at the end of the Septuagint to Job may be quoted from this Targum.

2. Cf. Père Benoit's description of the process of editing the fragments in 'Le travail d'édition...' pp. 52ff. ('Editing the Manuscript Fragments...' pp. 79ff.)

and other institutions in Jordan had expended their financial resources for the purchase of antiquities, the Council of Ministers of Jordan passed legislation permitting reputable foreign institutions to purchase additional lots of manuscripts of Cave IV remaining in Bedouin hands. Such purchases were arranged by the Director of Antiquities, on the condition that scrolls so purchased remain in the Palestine Archaeological Museum for editing, after which they are to be distributed to their owners. Such an arrangement had several advantages. First of all, it prevented loss by destruction or smuggling at the hands of Bedouin; it permitted the fragments to be bought through established official channels at standard prices (about $2.80 per square centimeter of inscribed surface); and more important, it kept the great mass of fragments in one center for editing. Had they been scattered, much of their usefulness would have been destroyed, since obviously much of the joining of fragments into large complexes can be done only with the original leather. Finally donors were to receive in this plan, not the unsorted fragments belonging to the actual lot which their money happened to purchase, but *all* fragments belonging to a group of manuscripts equivalent in size to the amount contributed for purchase.

On this basis lots were acquired by McGill, Manchester, and Heidelberg universities, the Vatican Library, and McCormick Theological Seminary (Chicago).

An international, interconfessional team of eight scholars was appointed to prepare and publish the manuscripts of Cave IV. From France are two scholars, Fathers D. Barthélemy, O.P., and J. Starcky; from Poland, Father J.T. Milik (now attached to the Centre National de la Recherche Scientifique); from England, Messrs. John Allegro of Manchester and John Strugnell, of Jesus College, Oxford; from Germany, Dr Claus–Hunno Hunzinger of Göttingen; and from America Monsignor Patrick W. Skehan of the Catholic University of America, and the writer. The workroom of the Palestine Museum is a veritable Babel of languages. Actually the staff exhibits a remarkably ecumenical spirit. There is a harmony of scientific presuppositions, shared excitement in new discoveries, and a common good humor. Only at night in the café gardens is theology argued.

On arrival at the Palestine Museum, purchased groups of fragments were in unbelievable disorder. Many large, well-preserved fragments came in each lot. But large or small, well or ill preserved, most had to be be exposed to a process of humidification, cleaned of incrustations and dirt, and repaired or reinforced before being pressed flat between glass plates. Fragments in advanced decay, especially lumps of coagulated layers of leather, require more energy and patience and special techniques, though the same general procedure is followed. Often a fragment will exhibit an area of acute decay and shrinkage in the midst of otherwise pliable leather. The bad spot may draw the entire fragment into a crinkled or scalloped ball, so that the fragment is almost impossible to flatten. The script in such a area of decay may be shrunk to half or less the size of that in good areas. Often such decomposition in sheets of leather has caused splitting and fragmentation, and the problems of fitting into one manuscript healthy, light fragments alongside of wizened and blackened scraps are, to say the least, tedious.

Once the fragments are cleaned and flattened, they must be photographed. Normally all fragments are exposed on infrared plates; it is especially useful in the case of leather materials which have blackened. The infrared does not affect the carbon ink of the documents; it pales out the browns and deep reds of the decaying leather. Often a piece wholly illegible to the naked eye can be read easily on long-exposed plates. Occasionally, especially where the ink is dim or partially gone, ultraviolet photography and special lighting techniques have salvaged texts which seemed hopelessly illegible.

The process of identification and joining goes on apace. When a scholar has worked some years with the scribes of Qumrân they become old friends, and the date of their hands typologically, the personal idiosyncrasies of their scripts, and the various manuscripts which they prepared become so well known that they are recognized at a glance. Nevertheless, fragments belonging to a given work must be specifically identified, and joins with other fragments sought out. A single fragment may require many hours of study before it receives exact identification and is placed in a slowly growing column of a manuscript. Moreover, the action of soil and moisture, not to mention generations of ancient worms, has frayed or distorted the edges of fragments in such a fashion that joins are not obvious. This is the ultimate in jigsaw puzzles.

Biblical fragments are most quickly separated and identified. Usually they have a standard format and are written in an elegant book hand; scribal treatment of non-canonical works is rarely as careful or fine. More than that, the text is well known, and small combinations of words or even letters are readily discovered in a concordance. Rarely, biblical texts are sufficiently at variance with the traditional text that they escape immediate identification; in the case of certain of the historical books a concordance to the Septuagint is more efficient in making specific identification of fragments belonging to a recognized manuscript.

Non-biblical fragments are sorted into groups and reconstructed with much greater effort. In the case of published manuscripts of other caves a complete concordance was prepared by the staff to facilitate identification. Certain other texts are known in Greek, Latin, and Ethiopic versions and can with patience be identified by passage and put together. Texts which are wholly unknown must be reconstructed simply by discovering mechanical joins until the structure and development of the work are discerned.

Beginning in 1953, long tables filled with plates of unknown fragments were placed at one end of the museum workroom; a few tables at the other end were reserved for identified fragments. In the summer of 1956 the workroom held long tables of identified material, some twenty-odd plates only remaining of unidentified material. Meanwhile each fragment and its photograph have been studied many times by each of the staff, so often that the shape, script, and verbiage of the fragment become filed away in the memory against the moment when suddenly its place appears on a manuscript being reconstructed.

All this is preliminary work. The tasks of paleographical analysis, transcription, textual study or translation, as the case may be, and interpretation then follow before the editor is ready to publish his completed manuscript groups.

A sketch of the contents of Cave IV may be helpful in the discussions to follow. At the end of many years' labor 575 manuscripts have been identified from this cave. Of the manuscripts identified thus far, 122, slightly less than one fifth of the total, are biblical. All of the books of the Hebrew canon are now extant, with the exception of the Book of Esther.[1]

The best-preserved manuscript of the biblical lot, and in some ways the most important biblical document of all the finds, is a manuscript of Samuel designated 4QSam^a.[2] The secret of its relatively good state of

---

1. See Cross, 'A Report on the Biblical Fragments of Cave Four in Wâdī Qumrân', *BASOR* 141 (February 1956), pp. 9-13; 'Le travail d'édition...' pp. 56-58.

2. Fragments of this MS recovered in the controlled excavations of Cave IV by Harding and De Vaux have been given preliminary publication in Cross, 'A New Qumran Biblical Fragment Related to the Original Hebrew Underlying the Septuagint'. *BASOR* 132 (December 1953), pp. 15-26; cf. the corrections to the reconstruction in

preservation is a backing of papyrus applied in antiquity, perhaps a half century or so after it was copied.[1] As expected, both books of Samuel were copied on a single roll. A total of forty-seven of the fifty-seven columns of the original manuscript is preserved in fragmentary form. II Samuel is the better preserved; some pieces of each of its twenty-four columns are extant, and the disposition of its columns can be reconstructed rather closely. The best-preserved columns are the first, especially 2-5 (II Sam. 2–5). On the other hand, Chapters 15–21 are represented only by a few small fragments. Of thirty-three columns originally belonging to I Samuel, columns 12, 16, 18-24, and 28 are missing. After column 12 the calculation of the columns is by no means certain, save in isolated cases. Columns 2, 3, and 6 are the best preserved of I Samuel. However, in no part of Samuel, at least for the present, do we have a complete or nearly complete column.[2]

The importance of this exemplar of Samuel lies less in its bulk than in the unusual text it records. As we shall see, it belongs to a textual family known to us hitherto only in the Septuagint.[3] Even more extraordinary, in passages where Samuel and Chronicles overlap, this manuscript often preserves a text much closer to the text of Samuel used by the author of Chronicles than to the traditional text of Samuel surviving from the Middle Ages.

At the other extreme is the single copy of the Book of Chronicles from Qumrân. It is found on a three-inch strip of leather. Parts of six lines, two columns, are preserved; but worms have gorged themselves on Holy Writ. The result is leather lace with only four complete words legible.

A fairly extensive group of fragments belong to a late (Herodian) manuscript of Numbers (4QNum[b]); its text is of great interest, taking a

---

Cross, 'The Oldest Manuscripts from Qumran', *JBL* 74 (1955), p. 165, n. 40.

1.   This is deduced from two factors: (1) The scroll was reinforced in places with leather even before the papyrus backing was applied, suggesting the scroll was considerably worn; and (2) the papyrus is inscribed (unfortunately on the side which was gummed to the leather), and while no extensive parts can be read, the script appears somewhat later than that of the leather roll.

2.   There are some sixteen plates of large quarto size filled with fragments of this manuscript.

3.   The affinities of 4QSam[a] with the tradition of the Septuagint are somewhat closer than even the published fragments might lead one to expect, to judge from the very ample cross section of its text now in process of being edited.

middle position between the Old Samaritan and the Old Greek.[1] The roll is unique in being decorated by its scribe with red ink. Headings of sections are inscribed in red; the ink is still bright enough to read easily with the naked eye; the infrared film of the photographer, however, is blind to the rubrication, and certain technical problems are thereby raised. If infrared plates are used, the black ink is visible, the red invisible. If color film is used, the reverse is true. Presumably the problem will be solved in publication by use of filters and double printing.

Three very old documents have been found in Cave IV. Presumably they are master scrolls, imported into Qumrân at the founding of the community. They include an old copy of Samuel, preserved in only a handful of fragments;[2] a patched and worn section of Jeremiah, red and translucent with age (4QJer[a]); and a copy of Exodus–Leviticus (4QExod-Lev[f]) of which only a column and a few tatters are extant. The last-mentioned was studied for the first time in the summer of 1956. Its condition is such that decipherment was successful only with the aid of both infrared and ultraviolet photographs, and by *étude par transparence*, reading by a strong light projected *through* the leather.[3]

The archaic Samuel scroll can date no later than 200 BC. A date in the mid-third century is preferable.[4] The Jeremiah is probably slightly later. The archaic Exodus is more difficult to date; its script belongs to a proto-cursive type less well known than the formal or book hand. Nevertheless it appears to be no later than the old Samuel fragments.

One copy of Daniel is inscribed in the script of the late second century BC; in some ways its antiquity is more striking than that of the oldest manuscripts from Qumrân, since it is no more than about a half century younger than the autograph of Daniel. It is thus closer to the original edition of a biblical work than any biblical manuscript in existence,

---

1.   See Nathan Jastram, 'The Text of 4QNum[b]', *The Madrid Qumran Congress*, eds. Julio Trebolle Barrera and Luis Vegas Montaner (Leiden and Madrid: Brill and Editorial Complutense, 1992), Vol. I, pp. 177-198.

2.   Published by the writer, 'The Oldest Manuscripts from Qumran'. A sample of the script of the Jeremiah scroll (see below) is given in Fig. 2 of this article. Since publication of the archaic Samuel (4QSam[b]), a number of small fragments have been added.

3.   The technique proved quite useful also in deciphering blackened portions of 1QSa (see Barthélemy, *DJD I, ad loc.*). The text will be published in *DJD XI* (in press).

4.   Cf. the extended paleographical discussion in 'The Oldest Manuscripts from Qumran', pp. 147-65. More generally on the paleography of the scrolls, see *DJS*.

unless it be the Rylands Fragment of John from the first half of the second century AD.

A special category among the biblical documents is a group written in paleo-Hebrew script.[1] These include five Pentateuchal manuscripts and some fragments of Job. Especially interesting is a superb specimen of Exodus which presents a text type related to the Samaritan recension of Exodus.

The biblical scrolls from Qumrân span in date about three centuries. A few archaic specimens carry us back to the mid-third century, as we have seen. The heavy majority, however, date in the first century BC and in the first Christian century, the series terminating with the death of the community center in AD 68.[2]

The most popular books among the sectarians, to judge from the number of copies preserved in Cave IV, are Deuteronomy, 19 MSS; Isaiah, 17 MSS; and Psalms, 20 MSS. There are also eight copies of the Book of the Twelve Prophets. None is complete. We cannot always be sure that all twelve of the Minor Prophets were copied on a given roll. There can be no doubt, however, that this was the standard practice at Qumrân, as in the case of the great Minor Prophets scroll of the second century AD from Murabba'ât.

Another large portion of Cave IV documents belongs to the category of Apocryphal and Pseudepigraphical works in both Hebrew and Aramaic: Tobit, Jubilees,[3] The Psalms of Joshua, pseudo-Jeremianic works, Testaments of Levi and Naphtali, sources of the later Testaments of the Twelve Patriarchs, Enoch, and an apocryphal Daniel literature are examples.

There is another lot of specifically sectarian works, though this category overlaps with the former. In this group fall the recensions of the Rule of the Community, best known from Cave I; the Damascus Document known otherwise from the old Karaite synagogue of Cairo;[4]

1.   See p. 37, n. 8.
2.   Specifically sectarian scrolls (as distinguished from non-biblical in general) are much more restricted in date, the earliest dating to the late second century BC; cf. the writer's remarks, 'The Oldest MSS from Qumran', p. 164, n. 35; see also *DJS*.
3.   See the lists of these documents with bibliography in Fitzmyer, *The Dead Sea Scrolls: Major Publications and Tools for Study*, pp. 48-61 (labeled Apocryphal and Sectarian Works).
4.   The best editions are those of Rabin, *The Zadokite Documents* (Oxford, 1954); and L. Rost, *Die Damaskusschrift* (Berlin, 1933). Photographs of the

and various books too numerous to list in detail, containing laws, liturgies, prayers, beatitudes, blessings, hymns, and wisdom of the Essenes.[1]

These are the biblical 'commentaries', including works on Psalms, Hosea, Isaiah, and Nahum[2] (cf. Micah, Zephaniah, Psalms, and Habakkuk from Cave I[3]). The commentary on Nahum is remarkable because of its direct allusions to known historical figures, the first such allusions among the many published documents from Qumrân.

Among the curiosities of Cave IV are several documents in a cryptic script. When they were discovered we felt certain we had in hand at last the famous secrets of the Essenes. One of the fragments provided a clue to the script. The three of us in Jerusalem at the time set up a competition in decipherment. We worked unsuccessfully until lunch time and strolled home busily discussing decipherment techniques, about which we knew little. After lunch two of us arrived back promptly at the museum. Abbé Milik was late. Allegro and I discussed the ethics of starting before he arrived, and, of course, proceeded without him. Some minutes later Milik arrived, drew from his pocket a photograph of the fragments, and announced that he had deciphered the script during lunch.

Secrets are usually more exciting before they are found out. The contents of the cryptic documents, in any case, are not startling, but belong to well-known categories of literature at Qumrân.[4] One document contains astronomical observations related to the astronomical section of Enoch (Part III); another is named the 'Exposition [*midraš*] of the Book of Moses'.

Finally, there is a series of calendrical works found in Cave IV, relating to the zodiac, to the calculation of the feast days, and the courses of the

document are published by S. Zeitlin, *The Zadokite Fragments* [*JQR* Monograph Series 1] (Philadelphia, 1952).

1.　See p. 44, n. 3.

2.　Cf. J.M. Allegro, 'A Newly Discovered Fragment of a Commentary on Psalm XXXVII from Qumrân', *PEQ* 1954, pp. 69-75; 'Further Messianic References in Qumran Literature', *JBL* 75 (1956), pp. 174-87; and 'Further Light on the History of the Qumran Sect', *ibid.*, pp. 89-95; and *DJD V*, pp. 11-52.

3.　Cf. *DJD I*, pp. 77-82.

4.　This script is labeled 'A' by Milik; another related (cursive) cryptic script, as yet undeciphered, also appears in Cave IV. Allegro has edited a further curiosity, a document in which the cryptic, Jewish, Paleo-Hebrew, and Greek scripts are intermingled. If for no other reason, the document is important as an aid to the paleographer. See *DJD V*, pp. 88-91 priests (*mišmārôt*). Already the calendar materials found in published works have enabled scholars to solve a number of long-standing problems related to the solar calendar used in Jubilees and Enoch;[1] now it appears that this calendar was at home among the Essenes at Qumrân, and that it is reflected in certain of the primitive Christian traditions in the Gospels.[2]

1.   With the publication of the *mišmārôt* (Book of the Priestly Courses) by Shemaryahu Talmon, the details of the Qumrân calendar will be clarified. See provisionally his long paper, 'The Calendar of the Covenanters of the Judean Desert', in *The World of Qumran from Within* (Jerusalem and Leiden: Magnes and Brill, 1989), pp. 147-185.

2.   For the discussion of the calendar of Qumrân, its relations to the calendrical data of Jubilees, Enoch, and the passover of the Gospels, see D. Barthélemy, 'Notes en Marge de publications récentes sur les manuscrits de Qumran', *RB* 59 (1952), pp. 187-218, especially pp. 200ff.; A. Jaubert, 'Le calendrier des Jubilés et de la secte de Qumrân. Ses origines bibliques', *VT* 3 (1953), pp. 250-64; J. Morgenstern, 'The Calendar of the Book of Jubilees; Its Origin and Its Character', *VT* 5 (1955), pp. 34-76; Jaubert, 'La date de la dernière Cène', *RHR* 146 (1954), pp. 140-73; cf. Vogt, 'Antiquum kalendarium sacerdotale', *Biblica* 36 (1955), pp. 403-8; 'Dies ultimae coenae Domini', *ibid.*, pp. 408-13; J.T. Milik, *Dix ans de découvertes dans le Désert de Juda* [Les Editions du Cerf] (Paris, 1957), pp. 70-74.

SUPPLEMENT TO CHAPTER 1: DISCOVERY OF AN ANCIENT LIBRARY
AND RELATED DISCOVERIES (1960–1993)

Discoveries in the Judaean Desert have not ceased. While a number of the finds made since 1960 remain unpublished, the tale of their discovery may be told, and a brief description given of the contents of those published in whole or part.

In the first chapter above, we have described a series of discoveries made in the caves of the southern desert, in the Wâdī Murabba'ât in 1952,[1] and in wâdī beds described as 'farther south,' that is, in Israel. As early as 1953, Yoḥanan Aharoni and a team of Israeli archaeologists began searches in the great canyon systems south of 'Ên Gedî.[2] However, it was not until large-scale expeditions were mounted in 1960 and in 1961 that important finds of written materials came to light.

From March 23 until April 5, 1960, Israeli teams led by N. Avigad, Y. Aharoni, P.Bar-Adon, and Y. Yadin explored the Naḥal Ṣě'ēlîm (Wâdī Ṣeiyâl) and the Naḥal Ḥever (Wâdī Ḥabrâ) as well as other major canyons between 'Ên Gedî and Maṣada.[3] In the so-called 'Cave of the Scrolls' in the Naḥal Ṣě'ēlîm, clear evidence of the Bar Kokhba era was found, including a few scraps of inscribed leather and papyrus, evidently left behind by clandestine Bedouin diggers. In the cave dubbed the 'Cave of Letters' in the Naḥal Ḥever, a fragment of the Book of Psalms and fifteen papyri containing letters of Bar Kokhba himself were uncovered.[4]

In the spring of 1961 (March 14-28), the expedition returned to the caves.[5] The 'Cave of Horror' in the Naḥal Ḥever produced bits of a

---

1. The Murabba'ât finds are now published: P. Benoit, J.T. Milik, R. De Vaux, et al., Les grottes de Murabba'ât (DJD II) (Oxford at the Clarendon Press, 1961).

2. Y. Aharoni, 'The Caves of the Naḥal Ḥever', 'Atiqot III (1961), pp. 148-162.

3. Avigad, Aharoni, Bar-Adon, and Yadin, The Expedition to the Judean Desert, 1960 (reprinted from IEJ 11, pp. 1-2 [1961]).

4. See Y. Yadin in the work cited in n. 3 above, pp. 40-52.

5. Avigad, Aharoni, Bar-Adon, and Y. Yadin, The Expedition to the Judean Desert, 1961 (reprinted from IEJ 12, pp. 3-4 [1962]).

Greek recension of the Minor Prophets amidst skeletons of Second Revolt refugees. The newly-found fragments proved to belong to the manuscript of the Greek Minor Prophets purchased from tribesmen in 1952, thereby establishing the provenience of this important text.[1] The 'Cave of Letters' in the same wâdī underwent a second season of excavation with sensational results. A large corpus of Nabataean, Aramaic, and Greek documents of the Bar Kokhba era were found, together with additional letters of Bar Kokhba.[2]

In the early spring of 1962, Ta'âmireh shepherds found a new cave yielding unique documents.[3] The cave, which proved to be the Mugâret 'Abū Šinjeh lay in the Wâdī ed-Dâliyeh, about 14 km. north of ancient Jericho, 12 km. west of the Jordan River (thus outside of the limits of the Judaean Desert proper). A large number of papyri, many with their sealings intact, were found mingled with heaps of grisly skulls and bones, perhaps numbering as many as two hundred skeletons before being disturbed by the clandestine diggers.

The main lot of documents were purchased by the writer in behalf of the American Schools of Oriental Research on November 19, 1962. Excavations at the cave site were directed by Paul Lapp in January, 1963, and again in February, 1964. Some few fragments of papyri, certainly belonging to the lot acquired by purchase, and bullae, as well as other associated artifacts dug from the cave, confirmed the Bedouin account of the discovery.[4]

---

1. See the provisional study of D. Barthélemy, *Les Devanciers d'Aquila: Première publication intégrale du texte des fragments du Dodécapropheton* (Leiden: Brill, 1963). The *editio princeps* has recently been published by E. Tov, *The Greek Minor Prophets Scroll from Naḥal Ḥever (8ḤevXIIgr)*. DJD VIII (Oxford: Clarendon, 1990).

2. See N. Lewis (ed.), *The Documents from the Bar Kokhba Period in the Cave of Letters: Greek Papyri*; Y. Yadin and Jonas C. Greenfield (eds), *Aramaic and Nabataean Signatures and Subscriptions* (Jerusalem: Israel Exploration Society, The Hebrew University of Jerusalem, and the Shrine of the Book, 1989), and bibliography.

3. See F.M. Cross, 'The Discovery of the Samaria Papyri,' *BA* 26 (1963), pp. 110-121; and especially Paul and Nancy Lapp, 'An Account of the Discovery', 'The Cave Clearances', and F.M. Cross, 'The Papyri and Their Historical Implications', in *Discoveries in the Wâdī ed–Dâliyeh*, eds., P.W. and Nancy L. Lapp [AASOR 41] (Cambridge, MA: American Schools of Oriental Research, 1974), pp. 1-32.

4. Remains from the cave, acquired by scientific excavation are published in the volume *Discoveries in the Wâdī ed–Dâliyeh* cited in n. 3 above.

Our study of the papyri,[1] which are in a very poor state of preservation—no papyrus is as much as fifty percent preserved—and some 128 sealings associated with the papyri, has established that the documents were executed in Samaria, many before the governor of the Persian province of Samaria, during the fourth century BC. Apparently the papyri were brought into the cave by patricians of Samaria in the days of Alexander the Great. Indeed it seems likely that the Samaritans in question were those who revolted against Alexander in 331 BC, burning his prefect Andromachus alive. We should associate the wholesale massacre of the Samaritans hiding in the cave with these events. Presumably the Macedonian troops, flying to put down this first revolt in Alexander's new Syrian territory, discovered the hiding place of the rebels and dispatched them.

The earliest of the papyri was written about 375 BC, the latest dated was written on March 18, 335 ('On 20 Adar, year 2 [of Arces, the same being] the accession year of Darius the king, in Samaria...').[2] The Documents are written in Aramaic—with the exception of two bullae inscribed in Palaeo–Hebrew—and are without exception legal in character. Slave and property conveyances constitute the majority of the papyri.

These papyri from Samaria are of especial importance to the historian and to the epigraphist and paleographer. They are the earliest extensive group of papyri ever found in Palestine; they give a series of precisely dated hands which greatly aid the paleographer in assigning dates to the earliest of the Qumrân scrolls; also they come from a dark century, a period heretofore represented by virtually no contemporary written sources, and will provide historical and especially legal data of inestimable importance.[3]

The most recent extensive discoveries come from the ancient fortress built by Herod the Great at Maṣada. Major excavations at Maṣada were

1. See especially F.M. Cross, 'Aspects of Samaritan and Jewish History in Late Persian and Hellenistic Times', *HTR* 59 (1966), pp. 201-211; 'A Reconstruction of the Judean Restoration', *JBL* 94, pp. 4-18; and 'A Report on the Samaria Papyri', *Jerusalem Congress Volume: Supplements to Vetus Testamentum* 40 (1988), pp. 17-26.

2. See F.M. Cross, 'Samaria Papyrus 1: An Aramaic Slave Conveyance of 335 BCE found in the Wâdī ed–Dâliyeh', *Eretz Israel* 18 (1985), pp. 7*-17* and Pl.II.

3. Recently a new papyrus of the early third century, to judge by its script, has been found in a cave near Jericho. See Hanan Eshel and Hagai Misgav, 'A Fourth Century BCE from Ketef Yeriḥo', *IEJ* 38 (1988), pp. 158-176 and Pls. 25-26.

carried out under the direction of Yigael Yadin in 1963–65.[1] The literary and epigraphic finds come from the era of the First Jewish Revolt when the magnificent site was seized and held by the Zealots in their last stand against Rome. The fortress fell to the Romans in AD 73 when, according to the contemporary report of Josephus, the Jewish contingent, nearly a thousand persons, committed mass suicide. Most important of the documents from the Zealot phase of the Masada is a text of Ben Sira (called Ecclesiasticus in the Latin Bible) in Hebrew, containing chapters 39.27–43.30.[2] The manuscript is much the oldest of the Masada texts published thus far, dating from ca. 75 BC, about a century after the composition of the work.[3] Biblical Fragments, Psalms, Leviticus, and Genesis have been found; they contain a text which, like that of Murabba'ât, bear the stamp, in material readings and in orthography, of the Rabbinic Recension, and push back the date of the stabilized *textus receptus* to a time no later than the First Jewish Revolt.[4]

In some ways the most interesting of the finds at Masada is a copy of the 'Scroll of the Songs of the Sabbath Sacrifice', known from Cave IV, Qumrân.[5] Since this document, to judge from its calendar especially,

1. See provisionally the popular volume of Y. Yadin, Masada: *Herod's Fortress and the Zealot's Last Stand* (New York: Random House, 1966). The final reports of the excavations have recently begun to appear: Y. Yadin and J. Naveh, *Masada I:* The Yigael Yadin Excavations 1963–1965. *The Aramaic and Hebrew Ostraca and Jar Inscriptions* ; Y. Meshorer, *The Coins of Masada* (Jerusalem: Israel Exploration Society, 1989).

2. See Y. Yadin, *The Ben Sira Scroll from Masada* (Jerusalem: Israel Exploration Society and the Shrine of the Book, 1965). Two fragments of Hebrew Ben Sira were found in Cave II, Qumrân. See M. Baillet, J.T. Milik, and R. De Vaux, *Les 'petites grottes' de Qumrân* [*DJD III*] (Oxford: Clarendon Press, 1962), No. 18, pp. 75ff. and Plate XV, p. 18.

3. The text of Masada (and Qumrân) has importance not least in providing a final answer to the character of the Geniza manuscripts of Ben Sira. There can no longer be doubt, we believe, that the Geniza material, though late and corrupt, draws on the original Hebrew tradition, and not on secondary versions.

4. See F.M. Cross, 'The Contribution of the Discoveries at Qumrân to the Study of the Biblical Text', in F.M. Cross and S. Talmon (eds), *Qumran and the History of the Biblical Texts* (Cambridge, MA: Harvard University Press, 1975), pp. 278-292; and F.M. Cross, 'The Text Behind the Text of the Hebrew Bible', in Hershel Shanks (ed.), *Understanding the Dead Sea Scrolls*, (New York: Random House, 1992), pp. 139-155.

5. See most recently, C. Newsom, *Songs of the Sabbath Sacrifice: A Critical Edition* [HSS 27] (Atlanta: Scholars Press, 1985), and the literature cited.

stems specifically from sectarian, we should say Essene circles, the presence of the work at Maṣada suggests that Essenes may also have been among the folk defending Maṣada. This should occasion no surprise. We know that the Essenes looked forward to the great Holy War of the end time, and that Josephus mentions an Essene general, as well as the heavy casualties among members of the sect, in the Roman War. A number of scholars have, in fact, suggested strong Zealot influence on the sect (and *vice versa*) in its last days.[1]

Since completion of the second English edition of this work, a number of important texts have been published, as well as a burgeoning secondary literature. We can list here only certain salient volumes of the texts, bibliographical tools, and a few important monographs and collections of papers of recent vintage. The series of principal editions of Qumrân texts, *Discoveries in the Judaean Desert (DJD)* has reached volume X, and volume XI is in press. Volume X, *Qumran Cave 4 •V* contains the interesting document *miqṣat ma'aśe ha-torah*, the so-called Halakhic Epistle, edited by Elisha Qimron and John Strugnell (Oxford at the Clarendon Press, 1994). Three major manuscripts from cave 11 have been published in principal editions outside the *DJD* series: *Le Targum de Job de la Grotte XI de Qumrân*, edited by J.M.P. Van der Ploeg and A.D. Van der Woude (Leiden: Brill for the Koninklijke Nederlandse Akademie van Wetenschappen, 1971); *The Temple Scroll*, edited by Yigael Yadin, 3 volumes (Jerusalem: The Israel Exploration Society, The Institute of the Hebrew University of Jerusalem, and the Shrine of the Book, 1983); *The Paleo-Hebrew Leviticus Scroll (11Q paleoLev)* [edited] by D.N. Freedman and K.A. Mathews (Winona Lake, Indiana: Eisenbrauns for the American Schools of Oriental Research, 1985). A new series, *Judean Desert Studies*, has been inaugurated with the publication of *The Documents from the Bar Kokhba Period in the Cave of Letters*: Greek Papyri, edited by Naphtali Lewis, Aramaic and Nabataean Signatures and Subscriptions edited by Yigael Yadin and Jonas C. Greenfield (Jerusalem: Israel Exploration Society, The Hebrew University of Jerusalem and the Shrine of the Book, 1989).

Two important journals dedicated exclusively to Qumrân studies are being published, *Revue de Qumrân* (1958–) and *Dead Sea Discoveries* (1994–). The *Revue de Qumrân* publishes an exhaustive, running

---

1. See J.T Milik, *Ten Years of Discovery in the Wilderness of Judaea* [SBT 26], (trans. J. Strugnell, Napierville and London: Allenson, 1959), pp. 94-98; and the writer, below, Chapter 2, p. 60, n. 3.

bibliography. Indispensable to scholars now and in the future is the comprehensive facsimile edition of published and unpublished texts from the Judaean Desert: *The Dead Sea Scrolls on Microfiche*, edited by Emanuel Tov with the collaboration of Stephen J. Pfann (Leiden: E.J. Brill, 1993). A useful publication of the texts in transcription and English translation is in process of publication; the first volume has appeared: *The Dead Sea Scrolls: Hebrew, Aramaic, and Greek Texts with English Translations*, Volume 1 Rule of the Community and Related Documents, edited by James H. Charlesworth with F.M. Cross, J. Milgrom, E. Qimron, L.H. Schiffman, L.T. Stuckenbruck and R.E. Whitaker (Tübingen: J.C.B. Mohr and Louisville: Westminster John Knox Press, 1994). Full lists of the documents with bibliography can be found in J.A. Fitzmyer, *The Dead Sea Scrolls: Major Publications and Tools for Study* (Atlanta: Scholars Press, rev. edn, 1990). Excellent translations in English in single volume format may be found most recently in Florentino García Martínez, *The Dead Sea Scrolls Translated: The Qumran Texts in English*, trans. Wilfred G.E. Waterson (Leiden: E.J. Brill, 1994); and Geza Vermes, *The Dead Sea Scrolls in English* (Sheffield: Sheffield Academic Press, 4th edn, 1995).

Works which place the Dead Sea Scrolls and the community which produced them into their broader Second Temple or Hellenistic Jewish context include *Jewish Writings of the Second Temple Period: Apocrypha, Pseudepigrapha, Qumran Sectarian Writings, Philo, Josephus*, edited by Michael E. Stone (Assen: Van Gorcum and Philadelphia: Fortress Press, 1984); and Emil Schürer, *The History of the Jewish People in the Age of Jesus Christ*, revised and edited by Geza Vermes, Fergus Millar, and Matthew Black, 3 vols. (Edinburgh: T. & T. Clark, 1973-1987), especially volumes 2 and 3. Noteworthy recent collections of scholarly essays include *The Dead Sea Scrolls: Forty Years of Research*, eds. D. Dimant and U. Rappaport (Leiden: Brill and Jerusalem: Magnes, 1992); and *The Madrid Qumran Congress: Proceedings of the International Congress on the Dead Sea Scrolls, Madrid, 18-21 March, 1991*, 2 volumes, edited by Julio Trebolle Barrera and Luis Vegas Montaner (Leiden, Brill and Editorial Complutense: Madrid, 1992); *The Community of the Renewed Covenant: The Notre Dame Symposium on the Dead Sea Scrolls*, edited by Eugene Ulrich and James VanderKam (Notre Dame, Indiana: The University of Notre Dame Press, 1994); and *Time to Prepare the Way in the Wilderness: Papers on the Dead Sea Scrolls*, edited by D. Dimant and

L.H. Schiffman (Leiden: E.J. Brill, 1995). A useful collection of popular essays is *Understanding the Dead Sea Scrolls*, ed. Hershel Shanks (New York, Random House, 1991).

Four excellent volumes addressed to the general reader which deal *inter alia* with recent controversies over the scrolls, including some of the more sensational theories which seem to proliferate in this field, are Joseph A. Fitzmyer, *Responses to 101 Questions on the Dead Sea Scrolls* (New York: Paulist Press, 1992); Hartmut Stegemann, *Die Essener, Qumran, Johannes der Täufer and Jesus: Ein Sachbuch* (Freiburg, Basel and Wein: Herder, 1993); and James C. VanderKam, *The Dead Sea Scrolls Today* (Grand Rapids: Eerdmans and London: SPCK, 1994); L.H. Schiffman, *Reclaiming the Dead Sea Scrolls* (Philadelphia and Jerusalem: The Jewish Publication Society, 1994).

Chapter 2

THE ESSENES, THE PEOPLE OF THE SCROLLS

There is now sufficient evidence, to be supplemented as publication of
the scrolls and reports of excavations in the vicinity of Qumrân continue,
to identify the people of the scrolls definitively with the Essenes.[1] The
community at Qumrân was an Essene settlement.[2] In the discussion to

1.   The common derivation from *ḥasên, ḥasayyâ*, the standard East Aramaic
equivalent of Hebrew *qĕdōšîm*, 'holy ones', is thoroughly suitable. This etymology
has indirect support from Philo, who in two passages connects the name with Greek
ὁσιότης 'piety', 'holiness' (*Quod omnis probus liber sit*, XII, 75 [cf. XIII, 91];
Hypothetica, apud Eusebius, Praep. evang. VIII, 11., cf. Josephus, *War* II, 119). See
below chapter 6 for confirmation of this etymology.

Attempts to provide an alternative etymology have failed, including that of
A. Dupont-Sommer, *The Jewish Sect of Qumran and the Essenes* [=*Nouveaux
aperçus sur les Manuscrits de la Mer Morte, Paris*, 1953] (London, 1954), p. 63.
The latter attempts to connect Hebrew *'ēṣâ*, 'deliberative council', 'party', with
Ἐσσαῖοι Ἐσσηνοί. He ignores the problem of middle steps in the derivation, how
'ēṣâ (root *y'ṣ*) would be turned into an adjective in Hebrew, yielding an equivalent of
the Greek gentilic, or, if he attempts to go directly from *'ēṣâ* to the Greek, how it is
that the noun is taken and made into a plural gentilic which had no Hebrew equivalent.
Even if the linguistic development were transparent, one would still ask how *'ēṣâ*,
rather than *yáḥad*, the sect's own characteristic name for its 'communion', came to be
used as an appellation.

The attempt to derive from a putative *'āsayyâ*, 'healers', and to connect this with
the Egyptian θεραπευταί breaks down in several directions: (1) the transcription
ess- suggests *ḥas-*, not *'ās-*; cf. *ḥošen* in Jos., *Antiq.* III, 163, transcribed in Greek,
ἐσσὴν. (2) 'healers' is scarcely suitable as an appellation; and (3) as observed by
Schürer among others (*Geschichte des jüdischen Volkes im Zeitalter Jesu Christi*, 3.
Aufl., II, pp. 559-60), the Alexandrian sect is always termed θεραπευταὶ θεοῦ
'servants, or worshipers of God', not 'physicians'.

2.   Among the older discussions of the identification, see R. Marcus, 'The
Qumran Scrolls and Early Judaism', *Biblical Research* 1 (1956), pp. 9-47;
B.J. Roberts, 'Qumrân Scrolls and the Essenes' *NTS* 3 (1956), pp. 58-65;
F.M. Cross, 'The Dead Sea Scrolls', in *Interpreter's Bible XII* (New York-Nashville,

follow we wish to trace the process of historical synthesis, the combination of data dug up by the spade, culled from classical writers, and sifted out of the scrolls themselves, by which the ancient Essenes have been resurrected. The reconstruction of the history and life of the Essenes is a tedious task; but the product of these historical labors is well worth the effort. These little-known Essenes have proved to be exceedingly important for our understanding of early Judaism and Christianity, supplying a lost chapter in the development and transmission of the Judaeo-Christian heritage.

1. *An Essene Community in the Wilderness*

The ruins of the Essene community center lie on a marl terrace between limestone cliffs and the maritime plain at the point where the torrent bed of the Wâdî Qumrân cuts its deep gorge through to the Dead Sea. The site is called a *khirbeh*, 'ruin', by the Arabs; and, presumably, from its location on the Wâdî Qumrân it receives the full designation *Khirbet Qumrân.*[1] Its older, biblical name has not been known until recently; but

1957), pp. 657f., especially n. 69 and the literature there cited; and J.T. Milik in his volume, *Dix ans de découvertes dans le Désert de Juda* (hereafter *Découvertes*), Chap. III. For the latest controversies, see Chapter 6.

1. The etymology of the name Qumrân remains obscure. The attempt to derive it from κάλαμος (from the Byzantine name of this district) involves too many linguistic shifts to be convincing (see J.T. Milik, *RB* 60 [1953], p. 538, n. 8). Probably it must be derived from an Arabic root *qmr*. In the simple stem, the active (*qamara*) means 'to gamble', the stative (*qamira*) 'to be white', 'to be moonlit' (or 'to be in the moonlight'). H. Michaud ('A propos du nom de Qumrân', *RHPR* 35 [1955], pp. 68-74) derives from the stative root a putative **qâmir*, pl. *qumrân*, and translates 'veilleurs (au clair de lune)'; but normally in Arabic the *qâtil* form of a stem *qatila* is *stative* in meaning, viz. 'being white, moonlit'. Moreover, the form *qutlân* may be the plural of a variety of singulars including *'aqtal*, used of colors; hence *'aqmar*, pl. *qumrân* is a more plausible combination if *qumrân* is to be explained as a plural. But in fact, we can get no certainty from a morphological analysis of the name. In Syrian Arabic *qumrân* may reflect older Arabic *qamrân* or *qimrân* (as well as *qumrân*), by the regular assimilation of the vowel to the bilabial. The form may be a common adjectival pattern (frequent in proper names), or an infinitive (cf. Brockelmann, *Grundriss d. vergl. Gramm. d. sem. Sprachen* I, §§ 210-17; Wright-de Goeje, *A Grammar of the Arabic Language* I, § 304, XIX, 6).

There is little likelihood that any memory of the Essene community was transmitted into Arab times; to be sure, the local tribesmen are quite aware that these ruins belong to the days of the *jâhiliyyah*; but this knowledge (as they explain) rests thanks to new data, including remains of Israelite constructions of the ninth to the sixth century, we may confidently identify it as the biblical *'îr ham-mélaḥ*, 'City of (the Sea of) Salt', one of a series of fortress towns in the desert province of the Judaean kings, listed in Joshua 15.[1]

The site had been designated a Roman fort by Dalman and Avi-Yonah, who had done surface explorations in the area, previous to the scroll finds.[2] Harding and De Vaux in 1949 re-examined the site, dug two tombs in the cemetery of some twelve hundred[3] tombs adjacent to the ruin, but found insufficient evidence to connect the site with the cave a kilometer north. However, they were not wholly satisfied with the then current description of the site. It was certainly of the Hellenistic–Roman period, at least on the surface; but if it were a military outpost, what could be made of the extensive, adjacent cemetery? The tombs themselves were of a type unknown at the time, but certainly not Muslim.

In 1951 there were new reasons to re-examine the ruin. Debate over the date of the scrolls raised anew the possible connection of the ruin with the scrolls, and there were demands that it be dug. Again, study of the sectarian literature of Cave I had created a plausible hypothesis that the scrolls derived from Essene circles, and it was well known that Pliny placed their settlement somewhere below Jericho, above 'Ain Geddi, near the shore of the Dead Sea; this description admirably fitted the location of Khirbet Qumrân.[4]

The first campaign was launched on November 24, 1951, and continued until December 12. It was a small series of soundings; nevertheless, the excavators found sufficient evidence to date the ruin roughly to the beginning of the Christian era, to suggest that it was neither

on the non-Muslim orientation of the tombs in the vicinity.

1.   See most recently, F.M. Cross and G.E. Wright, 'The Boundary and Province Lists of the Kingdom of Judah', *JBL* 75 (1956), pp. 202-26, especially p. 223f.; and Cross and J.T. Milik, 'Explorations in the Judaean Buqê'ah', *BASOR* 142 (April 1956), pp. 5-17, especially p. 16, n. 27. Cf. R. de Vaux, 'Fouilles de Khirbet Qumrân. Rapport préliminaire sur les 3ᵉ, 4ᵉ, et 5ᵉ campagnes', *RB* 63 (1956), pp. 535f. (hereafter, *Rapport III*), and Milik and Cross, *RB* 63 (1956), pp. 74ff. The identification of Khirbet Qumrân with biblical *'Ir ham-mélah* goes back to M. Noth, *Das Buch Josua* (Tübingen, 1938), p. 72.

2.   See above p. 25, n. 2.

3.   The figure includes the tombs of the two small cemeteries north and south of the main cemetery of some one thousand tombs. See *Rapport III*, pp. 569-72.

4.   See above, p. 25, n. 1, and p. 26, nn. 3 and 4.

military nor private, but communal in character, a conclusion reinforced by the contemporary cemetery; the pottery of the site proved to be identical with that of Cave I and suggested, at least, a direct link between the people who once inhabited the settlement, and the cave deposit. Père de Vaux suggested, on the basis of his spadework, that it was most reasonable to conclude that the people of the scrolls were indeed Essenes and, further, that Khirbet Qumrân was the Essene retreat in the wilderness alluded to in the classical sources.[1]

In the winter of 1951, however, this construction of the facts, while thoroughly plausible, was by no means securely established. Obviously, major excavations at Khirbet Qumrân were called for. Now five campaigns at the site are completed, the second in the spring of 1953, and the remaining three in successive spring seasons, the latest in the spring of 1956.[2] A sixth campaign is projected in the region of 'Ên Feškhah, a little less than two miles to the south of Khirbet Qumrân, where new Essene installations were detected in 1956.[3]

Meanwhile the exploration of the caves north and south of Khirbet Qumrân, in March 1952, together with subsequent cave discoveries, quite shifted the perspective.

Khirbet Qumrân proved to be the hub of a Hellenistic–Roman occupation spreading nearly two miles north along the cliffs, and some two miles south to the agricultural complex at 'Ên Feškhah. The people of this broad settlement lived in caves, tents, and solid constructions, but shared pottery made in a common kiln, read common biblical and sectarian scrolls, operated a common irrigation system,[4] and, as we shall see, depended on common stores of food and water furnished by the installations of the community center.

The caves yielding manuscripts and identical pottery also radiate out from the center northward and southward. Five of the productive caves,

1.　*Rapport I*, *RB* 60 (1953), pp. 103-6.

2.　Full bibliography is given above, p. 26, n. 1.

3.　Political troubles in the Near East may delay exploitation of the 'En Feškhah ruins. The soundings in 1956, in any case, indicate that the establishment north of the spring is a large one. See *Rapport III*, pp. 576f. On the biblical name of 'En Feškhah, see W.R. Farmer, 'The Geography of Ezekiel's River of Life', *BA* 19 (1956), pp. 17-22. [See now R. de Vaux, 'Fouilles de Feshkha', *RB* 66 (1959), pp. 225-55; and *ADSS*, pp. 60-87.]

4.　See *Rapport III*, pp. 575f. De Vaux's suggestions that the irrigation works are Iron Age constructions, re-used by the Essenes, is almost certainly correct, to judge from parallel Iron Age irrigation works in the Buqê'.

including that containing the remains of an enormous library (Cave IV), lie cut into the south edge of the terrace supporting the settlement, hardly more than a stone's throw from the central building complex.

Finally, explorations to the south toward 'Ain Geddi and westward into the Judaean Buqê', the biblical valley of 'Akôr,[1] have located several Iron II (seventh century BC) sites, but only one site with substantial Hellenistic-Roman remains. This is a site some 15km south of Qumrân, north of 'Ein Geddi, named after its adjacent spring: 'Ein 'el–Ghuweir. In addition to a very large structure, it has a cemetery with burials like those of the Qumrân cemeteries. It probably qualifies as another satellite site of the main Essene site at Khirbet Qumrân like 'Ein Feshkha.[2] If the people of the scrolls were not the Essenes, they were a similar sect, living in the same center and its satellites in the same era.[3]

The history of the community which dwelt at Qumrân can be reconstructed generally, out of the ruins and artifacts uncovered in the five seasons of excavation. Three periods of occupation are marked off by two major destructions within the occupational history of the site. The character of the life of the settlement's occupants in each period may be read in the architectural function of the structures built, as well as determined by their contents; and the dates of the periods are certified by the coins, pottery, and other artifacts sealed in undisturbed strata.

The Essene settlement was built on the shattered foundations of an Israelite fortress which had lain deserted since the sixth century BC. The first major period (Level I) consists of two phases, (a) the brief temporary installations which were replaced by (b) the elaborate central buildings which fix the permanent lines of the Essene settlement. Period Ia consists in large measure of archaeological bits and tatters found covered by or built into the subsequent main building phase: some lines of walls, a cistern or two (one a re-used Iron Age cistern), two pottery kilns underneath a Period Ib cistern. It cannot be reconstructed in detail, and its date and duration are difficult to fix with precision.

1.   This identification was suggested first by M. Noth, *ZDPV* 71 (1955), pp. 42-55.

2.   See P. Bar Adon, 'Another Settlement of the Judean Desert Sect at 'Ain el-Guweir on the Dead Sea' [Hebrew with an English Summary], *Eretz-Israel* 10 (1971), pp. 72-89. Full publication of Bar Adon's explorations of the west bank of the Dead Sea will appear in a forthcoming issue of *'Atiqot*. Provisionally see Zvi Greenhut. 'The City of Salt', *BAR* 19 (1993), pp. 32-43.

3.   Contrast the view of Alan Crown and Lena Cansdale, 'Was It an Essene Centre', *BAR* 20 (1994), pp. 24-35, 73-78.

The exact date of the foundation of the settlement is, of course, a datum we should very much like established, for it bears directly on problems of Essene history within the sectarian scrolls. We can at least set limits between which the beginning of constructions at Qumrân must fall. Copper coins are one excellent clue for establishing the date of strata. At Qumrân, after five seasons, the series of copper coins recovered begins in the reign of John Hyrcanus I (134–104 BC) [one coin identified to date], mounts sharply in the reign of Alexander Jannaeus (103–76 BC) [143 examples], and then declines in the remaining days of the Hasmonaean era (76–37 BC) [ten examples].[1]

How is this coin index to be used? Two principles operate in opposite directions. On the one hand, coins circulate for some period of time. The appearance of coins of Antiochus VII (Sidetes) and John Hyrcanus do not necessarily require us to fix the foundation of the community in their reigns; certainly we cannot go lower, however, than the early reign of Jannaeus for the beginning of the settlement. The coins of Jannaeus are much too numerous. Indeed it is highly probable that the *main* building phase of Period I commenced no later than the reign of Alexander Jannaeus.

On the other hand, the foundations of settlements are notoriously difficult to date archaeologically, for some years pass before a litter of debris, coins included, accumulates and this circumstance is exaggerated in the present instance, since the first phase (Ia) is small, and underwent extensive rebuilding and the establishment of a larger community before many years had passed. It is not improbable, therefore, that the foundation of the community dates well before the reign of Jannaeus, though we can scarcely go earlier than the beginning of Hyrcanus' reign or the end of Simon's reign.

The first major period of communal occupation prospered and grew until Herodian times. Then the community center was destroyed by earthquake early in Herod's reign; a crevasse opened through the center of the community buildings, and the eastern side of the complex dropped some fifty centimeters below the western with the shifting of the ground on which the buildings were founded. Archaeological evidence combines with historical notices in Josephus to indicate that the cataclysm in question was the great earthquake of 31 BC in which some

---

1. Five silver coins of Antiochus Sidetes (138–129 BC) carry us back into the end of Simon's reign. However, silver coins are notoriously misleading in attempting to establish a *terminus ante quem*.

thirty thousand men of Judaea died.[1]

Reoccupation of the site was not immediate. It may have lain abandoned during the remainder of Herod's reign (37–4 BC). The second period of occupation began with the repairing and partial rebuilding of the old settlement during the early years of Herod's successor, Archelaus (4 BC–AD 6), to judge chiefly from the evidence of coins.[2] The fundamental plan of the site was not changed, and the function of most of the installations was not altered. There can be no doubt that the same community which had abandoned the site resettled it.

The desert settlement continued to thrive, without apparent interruption, through the years of Jesus' ministry and the turbulent days of the Roman procurators in Judaea, until the dark days of the first Jewish revolt against Rome (AD 66–70). The community buildings of Qumrân were destroyed under armed attack during the Jewish Revolt. The walls of Period II are mined through; the building ruins were sealed in layers of ash from a great conflagration; and in the blackened debris of the main fortification are the telltale iron arrowheads used by the Roman legionaries.

Actually we can reconstruct in some detail the occasion of the end of the settlement.[3] The last caches of first revolt coins from Period II date

1. De Vaux, *Rapport II, RB* 61 (1954), pp. 231ff.; Josephus, *War* I, 370-72; *Antiq.* XV, 121-47.

2. Archaeological data suggest a gap. Coins of Herod are proportionately few (10 coins) in relation to the length of his reign. A treasure of 561 silver coins hidden in three jars was found below the floor level of Period II in locus 120, above the debris of Ib. Most are of Tyrian stamp, tetradrachms, spanning in date the first century BC, the latest according to Seyrig and De Vaux falling between the years 9–8 BC and 1 BC–AD 1. Presumably the coins were buried at the time of the rebuilding of the site—whether by someone holding out wealth from the common treasury on entrance to the community (cf. Acts 5.1-6), or by an embezzling 'bishop' (that is, *mĕbaqqēr* or *pāqîd*). De Vaux's alternate hypothesis, that the hoard belongs to the era of abandonment, seems less likely (*Rapport III*, pp. 568f.).

3. We do not know the extent to which the Essenes engaged in the war with Rome. Certainly the sect was girded to take up arms in the final Holy War as we know from the liturgy of the apocalyptic war (1QM, 4QM), as well as from hints of military organization (after the pattern of the priestly prescriptions for the battle camp in the desert [Numbers]) in earlier works. Philo's remarks about their refusal to traffic in the weapons of war (*Quod omnis probus liber sit* XII, 78) simply reveal the other face of apocalypticism, its quietism vis-à-vis the present world. The sect refused to soil its holiness in secular violence and the seeking of worldly gain. However, the

from the second and (a few) from the third year of the First Revolt.[1] We know from Josephus that Vespasian rested his forces, including the Fifth, Tenth, and Fifteenth Legions, in Caesarea in the summer of 67 after the first phase of his Galilean campaign.[2] The Fifth and Fifteenth Legions wintered in Caesarea, the Tenth in Scythopolis (Bethshan).[3] In the early spring of 68 Vespasian took up his campaign to reduce Judaea and Peraea. The Tenth Legion (*Fretensis*) under Trajan, father of the future emperor, crossed Jordan into Peraea; Vespasian marched eastward from

war against Rome may have lent itself to interpretation among the Essenes as the beginning of the final Holy War; certainly in other circles of Judaism apocalyptic fanaticism motivated the suicidal revolt. At all events, the Essene retreat at Qumrân was defended to the end, presumably by some Essene stalwarts. And from Josephus we learn of a certain John the Essene, appointed general of Jewish forces in northwest Judaea in the early stages of the First Revolt (*War* II, 566; III, 11).

Milik (*Découvertes*, Appendice) suggests Zealot influence in the War scroll and in the late Essene movement; the evidence he calls upon, however, can be sufficiently explained by the apocalypticism of the sect—early and late. On the other hand, compare Hippolytus, *Refutatio omnium haeresium*, IX, 26.

1. For a discussion of the complex evidence of the coins, see *ADSS*, pp. 33-38.
2. Josephus, *War* III, 409, 412; cf. III, 65; De Vaux *Rapport II*, pp. 232-33.
3. Josephus' evidence on the place of wintering of the Tenth Legion, is, on first look, confused. In *War* III, 412, he seems to say that the Fifteenth Legion was sent to Scythopolis, two legions (apparently the Fifth and Tenth) were quartered in Caesarea. However, in *War* IV, 87, we are told that in the fall of 67 the Tenth Legion was sent to Scythopolis while Vespasian returned to Caesarea with the other two legions (apparently the Fifth and Fifteenth). The latter text seems confirmed by Josephus, *War* IV, 450, where it is said explicitly that Trajan, commander of the Tenth Legion (cf. *War* III, 289) joins Vespasian's forces only after the latter comes to Jericho. Evidently the text of *War* III, 412, which reads τὸ δέκατον δὲ καὶ πέμπτον εἰς Σκυθόπολιν, '...and the Fifteenth to Scythopolis', must be corrected, πέμπτον 'Fifth' to πεμπτόν 'sent', 'dispatched'; '...and the Tenth dispatched to Scythopolis'. Then our evidence is unequivocal, and De Vaux's treatment of the movements of the Tenth Legion is to be corrected accordingly (see *Rapport II*, pp. 232, 3).

Mr. John Strugnell, in discussing the above problem with the writer, has suggested two further points to support or nuance the solution I have proposed. One may argue also that since Titus is in command of one legion (cf. Suetonius, *Titus* IV, 3), and had his winter headquarters in Caesarea, the case is substantiated for the Fifteenth wintering in Caesarea, the Tenth in Scythopolis. We know that the Fifth under command of Cerealius stayed in Caesarea (*War* III, 310), and that Titus took command of the Fifteenth in Alexandria (III, 8, 64, 65; on III, 8, see the edition of Thackeray [Loeb, II], p. 576, n. 2). Unless there was a shift of command of which we have no indication, therefore, it appears that Trajan and the Tenth Legion are left at Scythopolis (cf. Schürer, *Geschichte*[3] I, p. 610, n. 31).

Caesarea, striking first south, then north, reducing Judaea. In June, AD 68, Vespasian led his troops from the pass at Shechem (later Neapolis) down into Jericho, where he was joined by the forces of Trajan come from Peraea. Most of the population fled before the Romans; in any case Vespasian subjugated Jericho, leaving troops behind to garrison the territory. In an interesting aside Josephus tells us that Vespasian investigated the Dead Sea and tested its strange powers of buoyancy by throwing bound prisoners into the sea to see if they would sink or float.[1]

The center at Qumrân was destroyed, no doubt, by a contingent of Vespasian's troops in the early summer of 68. The coins from the coastal cities dated 67–68 are grim confirmation. x

Whether the Essenes in whole or in part fled their settlement with the approach of the Romans, or were trapped in Qumrân and slaughtered, we cannot know with certainty.[2] At all events the Essenes were prevented from carrying away their manuscripts, with the result that their library, abandoned in nearby caves, survived. Ironically, had the community survived, the manuscripts no doubt would have perished.

The third period of Khirbet Qumrân belongs to a Roman garrison, presumably a forward post to protect Jericho against the centers of guerrilla resistance southward in the desert of Judah. The soldiers sliced up some of the common rooms of the main building of the complex into barracks, utilizing only the most easily fortified portion of this building, leaving the remainder of the site in ruins. The elaborate water system of the earlier settlement, not being required by the small company, was by-passed by a crude canal dug helter-skelter through Period II installations[3]

1.   Josephus, *War* IV, 451; 476, 7; cf. De Vaux, *Rapport II*, p. 233.

2.   See p. 60, n. 3 above. There is some likelihood that the Essenes, at least in part, put up resistance. Certainly someone resisted the Romans, using Qumrân as a bastion. And Josephus has special occasion to underline Roman persecution and torture of the Essenes during the Revolt (*War* II, 152). Finally, had they abandoned Qumrân completely, prior to the imminent threat of Roman troops, they no doubt would have removed their MSS with them. The caves immediately surrounding the center, especially Cave IV, can under no circumstances be described as carefully chosen hiding places.

3.   The Roman canal cuts through the SW corner of loc. 77, cuts the walls of loc. 86. The destruction of 86/89, the 'pantry' of the great common room of the community (77) is dated by De Vaux to the end of Period Ib; Milik has suggested that the locus, with its more than 1080 pieces of 'tableware', was not sealed in debris until the Roman conquest, since the hall, loc. 77, continued in use; and an inscribed bowl from 86/89 seems clearly to be dated paleographically to the first century AD.

to connect with a single cistern in the southeast. The post was maintained for some few years, being abandoned toward the end of the first century. Save for squatters in the time of the second Jewish revolt (AD 132–35), the site was not again occupied until archaeologists pitched their tents alongside the ruin in 1951.

The communal life of the Essenes is vividly reflected in their settlement at Khirbet Qumrân. In the first main period of their settlement (Ib) they built an imposing central building, originally square in shape, 37.5 meters (about 124 feet) to the side. To the west, alongside a deep ravine, is a smaller building complex, no doubt the earliest of the substantial structures of the Essene community. Later in the period the constructions were extended to the south of both the western complex and the main building. The eastern side of the central complex is defended by a long line of wall which branches at a slight angle from the northeast side of the central building, forming a triangular area immediately southeast of the central building; the defense wall continues south of the buildings, however, to the precipitous bank of the *wâdī*, sealing off the settlement's exposed flank.[1]

In the northwest quadrant of the main building was a fortified tower to lend security to the community. Their isolated location in the desert, within striking distance of razzias from the southern desert, required such defenses. In the northeastern quadrant were a large community kitchen and storage magazines; in the southeastern a cistern (abandoned after a crevasse caused by the earthquake split it from end to end!), and facilities for washing. The quadrant to the southwest contains rooms for small convocations, study, and, perhaps, for the community's records. The function of one room in particular, is intriguing. A long central chamber in this quadrant, measuring 13×4 meters (about 43×13 feet), contained in the debris of the second period, fallen from the second floor a narrow plaster table, about 5 meters (about $16\frac{1}{2}$ feet) in length, as well as two other shorter tables. Associated was a low bench of equal length. Both originally had been built as permanent fixtures, the table fixed into the plaster floor of its room, the bench into the wall alongside. These are evidently the appurtenances of the ancient scriptorium of the

---

1. No amount of descriptive detail can call up an adequate picture of the community center. The reader is directed to the superb plans drawn by Père Coüasnon, *Rapport III*, Pl. III (see end-paper plan).

community.[1] Mingled in the debris were also two inkpots, one still containing traces of dried ink.

In the scriptorium many of the scrolls must have been penned, almost certainly those copied by scribes whose work turns up repeatedly on scrolls from several caves. It is not unlikely, moreover, that the library of the community found in Cave IV nearby was normally housed in this quadrant of the main building.

To the west and south of the central building is the maze of water channels and cisterns which connects to an aqueduct, still well preserved, which led water from a dam at the foot of the waterfall of the Wâdī Qumrân. Seven major cisterns, and at least six small pools, settling basins, baths, or the like, have been cleared. While all may not have been in use at the same time, it is nevertheless an astonishingly large water system and is capable of serving a substantial community through the long arid seasons normal to this part of Palestine.

The elaborate water system of Qumrân, especially the step cisterns, has produced much fanciful speculation. To those acquainted with Essene habits of baptism, but unacquainted with cistern types in Roman Palestine, the pools seem admirably designed for bathing rites.[x] Unfortunately the pools are typical examples of water reservoirs well known from other sites.[2] On the other hand, two or three small pools are probably baths, including the shallow pool at the entrance way to the settlement. One suspects, however, that the demands of the community for water to be used for drinking and other mundane purposes, as well as water for the ordinary rites of maintaining ritual purity, stressed especially in the priestly practices of the Essenes, is sufficient explanation for the size of the water system. Probably the ritual baptisms called for the living waters of the Jordan not far distant; possibly the waters of ʻÊn Feškhah nearby would have sufficed. In any case, we do not believe they immersed themselves in their drinking water.

On the south side of the central building is a great hall, 22 × 4.5 meters ($72\frac{1}{2}$ × 15 feet). Its floor and walls were plastered. Plaster pillars supported a roof, probably of thatched palm. However, the pillars are found in the eastern extremity of the hall only, and in an annex on the southwestern end of the building. This asymmetrical plan is explained by

---

1. See *ADSS*, pp. 29-33. Compare the views of P. Donceel-Voûte, ʻ"Coenaculum"—La salle a l'étage du *locus* 30 à Khirbet Qumrân sur la Mer Morte', *Banquets d'Orient. Res Orientales* 4 (1993), pp. 61-84.

2. See A. Parrot, *RHPR* 35 (1955), pp. 61-67; De Vaux, *Rapport III*, pp. 539-40.

a round, stone pavement at the western end of the hall, the podium of a reader, expositor, or presiding officer. This hall is clearly the main assembly hall of the community.✗

There is evidence also that in this room the Essenes gathered to celebrate their sacred common meals. This is suggested first of all by arrangements for washing the hall, including a side canal from the aqueduct to lead water to the hall, and planned drainage.[1] Striking confirmation comes from finds in the annex on the southwest corner of the hall, which has proved to be the pantry for the commons. In this room, sealed in by the debris of the Roman destruction,[2] more than 1080 pieces of pottery were uncovered by the excavators: plates and bowls, serving dishes, water decanters, wine flasks, and drinking cups, the 'tableware' of the community.✗

The western quarter, after the completion of the main building in Period Ib, was used chiefly for storage and domestic industries. Two heavy mills of basalt were discovered in position; silos for storing grain, the communal bakery, and what appears to have been a forge were among the other installations uncovered.

The community pottery works was uncovered in the triangle on the southeast of the main building, and proved to be one of the best-preserved establishments of its kind ever found in Palestine. It includes a pit, water outlet, and a walled plaster platform for kneading, cleaning, and drying clay; a platform, presumably for the potter's wheel; a great kiln for baking large pots, another for small vessels.

One rather curious find calls for special mention. In many open areas of the settlement, especially in the court to the north of the western quarter, and in the esplanade to the south of the settlement, the excavators came upon burials of animal bones. The condition of the bones certified that the animals had been slaughtered and eaten: sheep, goats, cattle. The burials were not a means of sanitary garbage disposal. The burials are inside the community enclosure; the bones were neatly placed in jars, or between large sherds of jars, and were carefully buried individually in a large number of deposits. Certainly the bones are the remains of the sacral feasts of the community. They raise acutely, moreover, the question as to whether the Essenes carried on a sacrificial cultus at Qumrân, a question to which we shall return.✗

All these details dredged up by spade and trowel admirably illustrate

1. *Rapport III*, p. 542.
2. See p. 63, n. 1 above.

the life of the community of which we read in classical texts dealing with the Essenes and in the scrolls themselves. ✗

2. *The Old Sources and the New Scrolls*

We have seen that as Khirbet Qumrân has revealed its communal facilities—its enormous water system, its scriptorium, and banquet hall; its common workshops, stores, and agricultural adjuncts; and indeed, its network of caves for the living and tombs for the dead—the possibility that it could be identified with anything other than the Essene 'city in the wilderness' described by Pliny and Dio Chrysostomus,[1] has become increasingly remote. Similarly, fresh analyses of the classical sources, especially Josephus, in the light of the expanding literature from Qumrân have shown that there are few discrepancies between the accounts of the Essenes in the sources and the sectarian literature of Qumrân which are not easily explained by the exterior view or Hellenizing tendency of the classical writer.[2] And we may say further that most of the discrepancies commonly observed by scholars during the early controversy over the identity of the sect of Qumrân exist, not between the sources and the texts, but between former scholarly interpretations of the sources and the texts.

Our chief older sources for the life and practice of the Essenes are Philo Judaeus and Flavius Josephus, to which may be added the short notice of Pliny the Elder.[3] The various accounts of the Essenes in the Church Fathers depend wholly on these sources and consequently are of no independent value. An exception, in probability, is the extended

1.   Pliny, *Naturalis historia* V, xv, 73; *Dio apud Synesium*, 39 (ed. Migne).

2.   Attention may be called to B.J. Roberts' apt statement, 'The Qumrân Scrolls and the Essenes', *NTS* 3 (1956), p. 58; 'Whereas previously one argued for or against the identity according to the extent of disagreement between the scrolls and the sources, the scrolls now become the yardstick by which Philo and Josephus are measured.' Cf. R. Marcus, 'The Qumrân Scrolls and Early Judaism', *Biblical Research* I (1956), pp. 28-31.

3.   Philo, *Quod omnis probus liber sit* XII–XIII (75-91), quoted in full by Eusebius, *Praep. evang.* VIII, 12; *Hypothetica* (*Apologia pro Iudaeis*), quoted by Eusebius, *Praep. evang.* VIII, 11 (cf. Loeb edition, XI, 437-43); Josephus, *War* II, 119-61; cf. I, 78; III, 567; III, 11; V, 145; *Antiq.* XIII, 171-73; XV, 371-79 (x, 4-5); XVIII, 18-22 (i, 5). For the older secondary literature on the Essenes, see Bauer, 'Essener', in Pauly-Wissowa, *Real-Encyclop. d. kl. Altertumswiss.* Supplement-band IV, cols. 386-430.

passage in the *Refutatio omnium haeresium* of Hippolytus.[1] While on the whole it reproduces the information given by Josephus in *The Jewish War*, exhibiting identical wording regularly, as well as taking up subject matter in the same order, the passage adds and subtracts in detail and occasionally contradicts Josephus. With the control afforded by new data from the scrolls, we can now show that in some instances the special readings of Hippolytus may be authentic and, in a few cases, may be superior to Josephus. It would seem to follow that Hippolytus and Josephus (and perhaps Philo as well) drew on a common written source.[2]

While Josephus regularly describes the Essenes as one of the three orders (τάγματα) of the Jews, along with the Pharisees and Sadducees, we must recognize, as Schürer has observed, that in the case of the Essenes we deal with a sect which in structure differs radically from the two main branches of Judaism.[3]

1. *Refutatio omnium haeresium* (ed. Wendland) IX, 18-28.
2. See M. Black, 'The Account of the Essenes in Hippolytus and Josephus', in W.D. Davies and D. Daube (eds.), *The Background of the New Testament and its Eschatology* (Cambridge, 1956), pp. 172-75; and especially Morton Smith, 'The Description of the Essenes in Josephus and the Philosophumena', *HUCA* XXIX (1958), pp. 273-313.
3. *Geschichte*[3] II, p. 559. Ralph Marcus has called the Essenes 'gnosticizing Pharisees' (*op. cit.*, pp. 25-40), and Saul Lieberman, especially, has underlined the parallels between the societies (*ḥăbūrôt*) of the Pharisees and the Essene communities ('The Discipline in the so-called Dead Sea Manual of Discipline', *JBL* 71 [1952], pp. 199-206). Such parallels are expected in groups which almost certainly have common roots in the Hasidic movement of the Maccabean age. As a priestly movement, they also have some features in common with the Sadducees (cf. R. North, 'The Qumrân "Sadducees"', *CBQ* 17 [1955], pp. 164-88). Recent discoveries, notably the study of the Halakhic epistle, make clear that the legal law of the sect has much in common with the Pharisees. See below, Chapter 6. These parallels indicate at most, however, that the Essenes were more deeply rooted in the Judaism of the second century BC than scholars had supposed on the basis of reconstructions of Philo and Josephus. That which places a gulf between the Essenes and the mainstream of Judaism is their apocalypticism, or more precisely, their formation of apocalyptic communities. In no case can the Pharisees, much less the Sadducees, be called apocalyptists, and by no stretch of the imagination can their associations be said to be the *Sitz im Leben* of an apocalyptic literature.

The only plausible ground for hesitation in making a definite identification of the Qumrân sect with the Essenes—once the date and the provenience of the scrolls were established and the life of the Qumrân community was reconstructed—has been the argument that since Palestine 'swarmed' with obscure sects in the first century AD,

The older sources stress that the Essenes separated themselves physically from other Jews, and in so far as possible eschewed all contact with non-Essenes.[1] The separatist tendency of the sectaries is not fully explained in our sources, but one is led to believe that it is to be attributed to the desire to attain moral perfection as well as ritual purity by dissociation from the corruption of the world. This and other apparently ascetic or alien motives in a Jewish 'party' confused earlier scholars.

The Qumrân texts emphasize no less the obligation of the sectarian to avoid all pollution by the children of darkness. The Qumrân community retreated into the desert 'to separate themselves from the abode of perverse men'.[2] The motivation of the group, partially obscured in Philo and Josephus by Greek thought forms, proves to root profoundly in older Judaism, specifically in the priestly laws of ritual purity coupled with a thoroughgoing apocalypticism.[3] To be sure, the community

one must exercise caution in assigning our sect to a known group. This argument has only apparent relevance to our problem. When the Damascus Document alone was known, one could well suppose that an obscure or unknown sect was responsible for its composition. Now that an extensive library is known, the perspective is quite changed. The Qumrân sect was not a small, ephemeral group. Its substantial community at Qumrân persisted some two centuries or more. Moreover, it was not restricted to Qumrân, but, as we know from its documents, counted its camps and settlements in the villages of Judah. Its own sectarian literature is enormous, and of profound and direct influence on Jewish-Christian and Christian movements of the first century AD and later.

The enumeration of various minor divisions and ephemeral groups which allegedly proliferated in Judaism is no longer pertinent, therefore, to our discussion. Our task is to identify a major sect in Judaism. And to suppose that a major group in Judaism in this period went unnoticed in our sources is simply incredible. The people of the scrolls belonged to the Essene party; see further below in Chapter 6.

   1.   See Philo, *Quod omn. prob. lib. sit*, 76; and especially Hippolytus, IX, 26.

   2.   1QS 8.12-13; cf. 5.13-20; 9.3-11, 12-21, especially 19-20; etc.

   3.   The term 'apocalypticism' or 'the apocalyptic' will be used frequently. I do not use the term as an adjective confined to the genre of the apocalypse. By doing so form critics have failed to see the forest for the trees. We need a term to apply to a movement of several centuries which combined certain features of wisdom and late prophetic eschatology in a new synthesis, and produced an immense literature, legal, exegetical and wisdom, as well as eschatological, mythic and cosmological. The apocalypse was at home in this movement, a charismatic genre, and serves as a good tag for the movement, but should not be made the defining or limiting genre. Perhaps it will be useful at the outset to delineate its main motives.

The apocalyptic movement may be succinctly described as the late Jewish attempt to revive Old Testament doctrines of history. In a world filled with a rich mixture of isolates itself to achieve a form of perfection and shuns contact with temptation, living in rigorous simplicity. Their retreat, however, is to be understood, not in a framework of nature-spirit dualism of Greek type, but in the ethical or 'spirit-spirit' dualism of apocalypticism. They go into the desert for a season, to be born again as the New Israel, to enter into the New Covenant of the last days.[1] They await in the desert the Second Exodus (or Conquest), 'preparing the way of the Lord', disciplining themselves by the rule of the ancient Wars of Yahweh

ideas, many of Hellenistic, Iranian, and ancient oriental origin, the apocalyptic impulse to recapture the old prophetic understanding of the history of salvation results in fact in the creation of a new theology of history obsessed with 'last things'. Prophecy became eschatology.

Apocalypticism sees world history in the grip of warring forces, God and Satan, the spirits of truth and error, light and darkness. The struggle of God with man, and of man with sin, evil, and death becomes objectified into a cosmic struggle. The world, captive to evil powers and principalities which have been given authority in the era of divine wrath, can be freed only by the divine might. But the day of God's salvation and judgment dawns. The old age has moved to its allotted end and the age of consummation is at hand, the age of the vindication of the elect and the redemption of the world. Current events signal the approach of the end. The final war, Armageddon, has begun. The Messiah is about to appear 'bringing a sword'. The Satanic forces, now brought to bay, break out in a final, defiant convulsion, manifest in the persecutions, temptations and tribulations of the faithful. In short, the apocalypticist lives in a world in which the sovereignty of God is the sole hope of salvation, and in the earnestness of his faith and the vividness of his hope he is certain that God is about to act. The faithful will be given the gift of salvation.

Such apocalyptic themes find their way into various forms of literature, as we shall see. Characteristic, however, as the term 'apocalyptic' makes evident, is the apocalypse, a book of revelations of things to come in the last days. Daniel and Revelation are canonical examples; the Enoch literature and the Testaments of the Twelve Patriarchs are non-canonical representatives of the genre.

The apocalyptic literature is featured by fantastic visions, calculation of times, and veiled references to contemporary history. The mythological imagery and astrological motives of the ancient Near East, including dualistic themes from Iran, strongly color the language of visions and can be recognized in the speculations about angels and spirits, and preoccupation with calendrical observations. Myths of creation are turned to the use of eschatology, to point to the struggle issuing in the 'new creation'. The national Messiah of Israel, a 'historical' savior, is transformed into a transhistorical warrior (and ultimately into a cosmic redeemer). Yet with all these transcendental and mythological elements, the main impulse of the apocalyptic is the Old Testament understanding of the history of salvation. The diverse borrowings are wholly informed by the Judaic spirit.

1.   Cf. *CD* 4.2-4; 6.18-19; 8.21; and especially 1Q34 [bis] II, 5-8 (*DJD I*, p. 154).

to be ready to fight the final war of God.

Our old sources are thus confirmed but also supplemented by the new. And the Essenes prove to be an apocalyptic community, a *Heilsgemeinschaft*, imitating the ancient desert sojourn of Mosaic times in anticipation of the dawning Kingdom of God.[1] They are priestly apocalyptists, not true ascetics.

We are not to think of the Essenes as a community restricted to the desert of the Dead Sea. Philo reports that they lived in villages and in many-membered 'communities', ὅμιλοι.[2] The latter term suggests that Philo, like Pliny, knew of independent associations like the principal Essene center at Qumrân, called in the texts the *yáḥad*.[3] Josephus no doubt distorts the situation in stating broadly that they settled in large numbers in every town.[4] But he agrees with Philo in numbering the Essenes at four thousand.[5]

Our new scrolls as well make abundantly evident that the community of the desert by no means exhausted the membership of the sect, and laws are laid down to govern the 'community', *yáḥad*, the 'camps' *mahănôt*, and the 'congregation', *'ēdāh*. The last-named term is clear. It applies to the totality of the camps, that is, (sectarian) Israel.[6] The precise range of meaning of the first two terms is not as clear.

The term *yáḥad*, 'community' seems to apply to the community par excellence; i.e., the principal settlement in the desert. The Qumrân settlement is probably unique, not only in being the original 'exile in the

---

1. In the War scroll (1QM), the camp of the Sons of Light (that is, the sectarians, Israel-in-truth) is ordered precisely after the prescriptions for the priestly arrangement of the Mosaic camp of the desert in Num. 2.1–5.4; 10.17-28; etc. (1QM 3.12–4.11). The law of the camp (Num. 5.1-4) is kept (1QM 7.3-7). The victory of God in the final war is compared with the first Exodus (1QM 11.8). The typology of the Mosaic camp lies close to the surface in *CD* (20.26 quotes Deut. 2.14 of the Mosaic camp) and 1QS and 1QSa. The typology of the second Exodus appears in the use of Isa. 40 (1QS 8.12-14) and Ezek. 20 (1QS 6.2 *mgwryhm*: cf. Ezek. 20.38, 1QM 1.3 *mdbr h'mym*: cf. Ezek. 20.35), etc.

2. *Hypothetica* XI, I.

3. R. Marcus goes so far as to suggest that the term ὅμιλος in Philo is a direct translation of *yáḥad*, 'Philo, Josephus and the Dead Sea *Yahad*', *JBL* 71 (1952), pp. 207-9. Rather, I think, the term refers to the 'camps', *mahănôt*, and is not an attempt at direct translation. See p. 71, n. 2 below.

4. *War* II, 124.

5. *Quod omn. prob. lib. sit*, 75; *Antiq* XVIII, 20.

6. *CD* 14.3-6, 10-12. Cf. 1QM 3.13; 4.9.

desert', the home of the founder of the sect, but also in following a celibate rule.[1] It is possible, but not probable, I think, that more than one community could be termed the *yáḥad*. In the Damascus Document, for example, the term *yáḥad* seems to be used only of the old community, the 'Community' of the founder, while the term 'camp' is regularly used of the various settlements, the units of the inclusive *'ēdāh*, 'congregation'.[2]

'Community', *yáḥad*, is also used more generally, especially in the Rule of the Community (IQS), of the 'community of God', especially with eschatological overtones: Israel of the New Covenant.[3]

There are hints that at least some of the 'camps' were secular, and following 'the order of the earth', entered into marriage contracts.[4]

There is finally an order of the 'cities of Israel'; whether this rule is to be sharply distinguished from the rule of the camps is doubtful.[5]

---

1. See 1QS 1.1, 12, 16; 3.2; 5.1, 2, 7-8; 6.18, 21, 22; 7.6, 20, 24; 8.11, 12, 16-17, 19; 9.2, 19. On the place of celibacy in the sect, see below.

2. On the use of *yáḥad* in *CD*, see 20.1, 14, 32. Both the term 'camp' and *'ēdāh* belong to the priestly terminology of the desert organization of Israel (cf. Num., *passim*). So too the 'Prince of the Congregation', *neśî' hâ'ēdāh*, is taken from priestly and Ezekielian contexts to apply to the Davidic Messiah (Ezek. 34.24; 37.25).

Contrary to the impression given by Gaster (*The Dead Sea Scriptures* [Garden City, New York, 1956], pp. 327f.), the term *yáḥad* is not used in the plural in any of our texts. On the other hand, 'camps' is frequent, and certainly is a unit organizationally in *CD*. The standard quorum of ten applies to the 'camp', *CD* 12.22–13.3. In 1QS 6.2-8 one may recognize in prescriptions for a quorum of ten, etc., provision for more than a single *yáḥad*. I think that in fact, however, in the development of Essenism, the term *maḥănēh* replaced *yáḥad* for all but the desert settlement.

Gaster also attributes to Marcus the opinion that Philo's term κοινωνία is a translation of *yáḥad*. Actually, I believe, Marcus only connected Philo's ὅμιλος with *yáḥad*. Gaster's instinct is correct, however, for Philo's frequent use of κοινωνία of the sect, especially in such passages as *Hypothetica* 11, 1, certainly reflects Essene usage. Cf. 11, 14–17; *Quod omn. prob. lib. sit*, 85, etc.

3. See 1QS 2.22, 24, 26; 3.11-12; and especially 5.5-6 and 9.3-11. The translation 'community' is poor in English, since it permits secular connotations or the wide English usage to blur its narrow meaning. The normal theological overtones are made explicit in such phrases as *byḥd 'l, byḥd 'mtw, lyḥd qwdš, bryt hyḥd, lbryt yḥd 'wlmym, lyḥd bryt 'wlm*.

Often, of course, the term *yáḥad* means simply 'fellowship', 'communion', and in combination, 'communal' as in such an expression as 'communal council'. (*'ăṣat hay-yáḥad*).

4. See, for example, *CD* 7.6-8 (19.3-5); cf. *War* II, 160-161.

5. There is no hint in the classical sources of Essenes dwelling outside Palestine.

Philo, Josephus, and the Qumrân writings all speak vividly and repeti- tiously of the intimate fellowship and sense of community cultivated among the Essenes. Philo more than once comments on 'their

This raises the vexed problem of the meaning of the term 'land of Damascus' in *CD*. In the expositional portion of *CD*, the expression appears in 7.14-20, an apocalyptic reinterpretation of Amos 5.26-27, along with the phrases, 'the repentant of Israel who went out from the land of Judah and sojourned in the land of Damascus' (6.5); '...those who entered the New Covenant in the land of Damascus' (6.19); and 'all the men who entered into the New Covenant in the land of Damascus' (8.21– 19.33/34). Many scholars have taken the 'land of Damascus' literally to apply to a place of sojourn of at least one order of Essenes, and some have supposed that *CD* preserves the order of the Damascene communities. Cf. the carefully worked- out views of M.H. Segal, 'The Hababkkuk "Commentary" and the Damascus Fragments', *JBL* 70 (1951), pp. 131-47; and J.T. Milik, *Découvertes*, Chap. III. R. de Vaux has suggested that the exodus to Damascus, if literal, may fall in the archaeological gap at Qumrân during the reign of Herod (*Rapport II*, pp. 235f.). De Vaux himself is quite tentative. The view has been taken up by others and argued more strongly (cf. C.T. Fritsch, 'Herod the Great and the Qumran Community', *JBL* 74 [1955], pp. 173-81).

I believe we are now in a position to dispense with De Vaux's suggestion. An unpublished copy of *CD* from 4Q cannot be dated later than the Hasmonaean period, and is almost certainly pre-Roman. Composition of *CD*, in any case, must be pushed back into the late second century BC, or better, perhaps, the early first century BC. This dating should have been evident already on the basis of internal data. For example, the Kittî'îm, normally the Romans in the Qumrân scrolls composed late (the *pešārîm* and 1QM; see below), play no role in *CD*.

I am increasingly inclined to those views (a shift from my earlier published opinion) which hold that the 'land of Damascus' is the 'prophetic name' applied to the desert of Qumrân. As the Essenes interpreted the Prophets (and Law for that matter) in apocalyptic fashion, they discovered esoteric titles for themselves, for their contemporaries, for their place of sojourn preceding the end, etc., all alluded to in the biblical materials. 'The land of Damascus', the place of exile in Amos 5.25-27 is understood eschatologically, and is evidently such an esoteric designation, parallel to the 'desert of the peoples', another 'prophetic name' of their place of retreat taken from Ezek. 20.35 (1QM I, 2-3).

A number of arguments can be called upon to support this view. First of all, there can be no doubt that *CD* was popular at Qumrân, surviving not only in eight MSS in the main library (4Q) but also appearing in private collections (6Q; cf. M. Baillet, 'Fragments du document de Damas. Qumrân, grotte 6', *RB* 63 [1956], pp. 513-23). The number of appearances is higher than that of Pentateuchal MSS (except Deuteronomy) or of Jeremiah and Ezekiel, for example, so that it is difficult to suppose that the work is not 'at home' in Qumrân. If the Damascus sojourn is to be understood literally, the entire community must have taken part. In no case can *CD* be indescribable community' (κοινωνία)[1] and speaks specifically of their shared treasury, quarters, and clothing, as well as their common meals.[2] Josephus, similarly, is impressed with their common life, their self-appointed poverty and community of goods,[3] and describes their communal meals in considerable detail.

From the Qumrân texts we learn both of the motivation for the communism of the sectarians and of the detailed prescriptions governing communal use of property. 'All who dedicate themselves to the truth of God shall bring all their knowledge and strength and wealth into the Community of God...';[4] 'communally they shall eat and communally

---

the document of a splinter Essene order condemned by the main group (*pace* Segal). Again, it may be noted that the Damascus references are only in expositional material, not in the 'rules'. In the latter sections of the work (which at Qumrân is a single work, contrary to the theory of Rabin), the legislation applies to the 'cities of Israel' (12.19), an awkward designation for 'Damascene camps', and references to the 'city of the sanctuary' (12.1-2), and provision for carrying out sacrifices (12.19ff.; etc.) suggest either that the sectarians of *CD* were near to Jerusalem, or had an independent sacrificial cultus (see below).

Finally, the texts in the expository passages are most easily understood if 'Damascus' is the 'revealed' name for the desert settlements of the Essenes. The 'Damascus' references are often in combination with allusions to the formative period of the sect when the 'repentant of Israel' (cf. the 'repentant of the desert') went out and 'entered the New Covenant'. The laws of the 'men of the *Community*' (*yáḥad*) and 'Righteous Teacher' (20.27-34) or 'Teacher of the *yáḥad*' (19.34–20.1) are the stipulations of the covenant which was 'established in the land of Damascus' (cf. 20.12). Again, the Star, the priestly Messiah of 7.18, associated in this context with the Scepter, the royal Messiah, is said to be coming to 'Damascus' (*hab-bâ' damméśeq*). The problems raised are formidable under any principle of interpretation, but they are insurmountable, I think, if 'Damascus' is not taken as referring to the desert retreat in the wilderness of Qumrân.

There are, to be sure, slight differences between certain laws of the *yáḥad* in 1QS and the 'camps' or 'cities' of *CD*. These are explained most easily, I think, not by positing a different, Damascene Essenism, but by (1) recognizing that the various 'orders' (*sĕrākîm*), in 1QS, 1QSa, and *CD* apply, among other things, to groups within the one congregation which follow slightly differing rules; and by (2) allowing for evolution in the sect, especially in the formative phase. *CD* is almost certainly a later composition than 1QS.

1. *Quod omn. prob. lib. sit*, §§ 84, 91.
2. Ibid., §§ 86-91; *Hypothetica* 11, 4-13.
3. *War* II, 122-27.
4. 1QS 1.11-12; cf. *CD* 13.1.

they shall bless and communally they shall take counsel...';[1] 'this is the rule of the men of the Community...that they separate from the congregation of the men of perversion and become a community in doctrine and property.'[2]

Without anticipating too much of what is to be said in a later chapter, we may observe here that the fully communal existence of the Essenes, as in the primitive Church, is a concomitant of an intense preoccupation with the qualities of life to be realized in the dawning New Age: unity (through the Spirit), brotherhood, love of one's fellow, the breakdown of the disparity between the (wicked) rich and the (oppressed) poor. Jesus in his first Beatitude paraphrases, or rather gives an eschatological interpretation to Ps. 37.9(-29). 'The meek shall inherit the earth' is understood in the sense, 'the poor shall inherit the Kingdom of God.' The Qumrân sectaries fully anticipate Jesus' interpretation in their commentary on Psalm 37, explaining that the 'meek who shall inherit the earth' are the 'Congregation of the Poor' (that is, themselves) who will inherit the New Jerusalem, while the wicked of the nations and Israel will be destroyed forever.[3] And their practice of giving their goods to the 'Poor' is directly alluded to in this setting.[4] Thus the practice of a communal economy among the people of the 'New Covenant' is prompted by their conception of the coming 'economy of God'.

Central in the community life of the Essenes is their communal meal.[5]

1.   1QS 6.1-3; cf. 6.17-23; 9.7-8; etc.

2.   1QS 5.1-2.

3.   Cf. Lk. 6.20 (Mt. 5.3, 5); and 4QpPs. 37 (Allegro, 'A Newly-Discovered Fragment of a Commentary on Psalm XXXVII from Qumrân', *PEQ* 1954, pp. 69-75) I.8-10; II.1-2; and especially II.10-11. It should be noted—to avoid misunderstanding—that the Kingdom-to-come is in the (transfigured) earth, not in 'heaven', both in the Jewish and early Christian understanding. 'Heaven' in the phrase 'Kingdom of Heaven' is, of course, simply a circumlocution for 'God', a device now documented in the scrolls as well as other Jewish literature.

4.   See Gaster's translation of 4QpPs. 37 A.II, 8-13 (*Dead Sea Scriptures*, p. 260).

5.   K.G. Kuhn in an article, 'The Lord's Supper and the Communal Meal at Qumrân' (an expansion of his older article, 'Uber den ursprünglichen Sinn des Abendmahles und sein Verhältniss zu den Gemeinschaftsmahlen der Sektenschrift', *ET* 10 [1950–1951], pp. 508-27) now published in K. Stendahl (ed.), *The Scrolls and the New Testament* (New York, 1957), pp. 65-93, has made detailed comparison of Josephus' account and the passages of the Rule of the Community and Congregation (1QS 6.4-6; 1QSa II, 11-22). His study is important for revealing the peculiarity of Essene practice over against other Jewish meals.

Josephus describes their practice in considerable detail, underlining the mystery and sacredness of the meal. Baths precede the meal. In special garments they enter a private hall. All uninitiated are prohibited entrance. In Josephus' words, 'they proceed to their dining room as to some holy precinct'.[1] They take their seats in silence. None partakes of food prepared by priests[2] until 'the priest' says a blessing.[3] These meals are daily, at midday and in the evening.

These notices parallel the legislation and rubrics for the meal in the Qumrân *Rule*. For example, the Rule of the Community states, 'the novitiate shall not touch the banquet[4] of the Many until his completion of a second year among the men of the Community.'[5] Both in Josephus and the Rule, the novitiate, after a first year within the community,[6] is permitted to draw nearer to its communal life, but admission to the common meal is the final step, taken only after the full two-year term of the novitiate.

The full significance of the common meal of the Essenes becomes clear in the rubrics preserved in the so-called Rule of the Congregation.[7] The heading of the section reads, 'This is the rule for the whole congregation of Israel in the end of days...'; that is, for the eschatological community.[8] Here are excerpts of the order itself:[9]

1. *War* II, 129.
2. *Antiq.* XVIII, 22.
3. On the order of the blessings in Essene, Pharisaic, and Christian meals, see Kuhn, 'Lord's Supper'.
4. The Hebrew term *mšqh*, which may mean simply 'wine', like biblical *mšth*, designates the festal meal which includes wine. More frequently the term *thrh*, literally 'purity' is used of the ritual purity of the inner community, including the food of the meals. But to judge from certain passages (for example, 7.19-20), the *thrh* extends to matters of purity beyond the food of the cultic meals.
5. 1QS 6.20-21.
6. *War* II, 138. Josephus adds to the two-year novitiate an additional year outside the community as 'postulant'. Milik has argued that this datum may be harmonized with the two-year novitiate of 1QS, the candidate passing through three stages in his approach to full membership. I am rather inclined to the view that Josephus here errs in interpreting his source. His first year is equivalent to the first degree of 1QS, and the two-year period of testing is equivalent to the (one-year) second degree of 1QS. The failure of Josephus to distinguish between the last two years suggests that he had conflated a first degree and a two-year total into a three-year period (*War* II, 137-42).
7. 1QSa II, 11-22; cf. 1QS 6.4-6.
8. 1QSa I, 1. It must be borne in mind, at all times, that the 'apocalyptic

[This is (the order) of the ses]sion of the 'Men of the Name who are [invited] to the Feast'[1] for the communal council[2] when [God] sends[3] the Messiah[4] to be with them:[5]

community' was at once the future congregation of the elect and the 'present' sect whose life was conceived as a foreshadowing of the New Age. To fail to grasp fully this eschatological ethos of the sect can only lead to misinterpretation of its texts. For this reason Gaster's translation of the text in question (*Dead Sea Scriptures*, pp. 307-10) is flat and distorted. J. Van der Ploeg's study, 'The Meals of the Essenes', *JSS* (1957), pp. 163-75, must be criticized on similar grounds. Cf. R.E. Brown, 'The Messianism of Qumrân', *CBQ* 19 (1957), pp. 78f; and K. Stendahl, 'The Scrolls and the New Testament, an Introduction and Perspective', in *The Scrolls and the New Testament*, pp. 1-17.

9. Cf. Cross, 'Qumrân Cave I', *JBL* 75 (1956), pp. 124f.

1. The phrase is taken from Num. 16.2 and typologically reinterpreted. Its precise meaning is not clear. The term translated 'feast' (*mw'd*) means 'appointed time', and regularly in our texts means a 'set feast', or, better, 'cultic' convocation.

2. *'ăṣat hay-yáḥad*. This is frequently used in the technical sense 'full-fledged members of the community'.

3. Reading *ywly<k>* for *ywlyd* in the text. Cf. Cross, 'Qumrân Cave I', p. 124, n. 8. Gaster's remarks on this reading and his suggested emendation must be rejected categorically (*Dead Sea Scriptures*, p. 279). In the first place, the understanding of the text as a liturgical anticipation of an eschatological (Messianic) meal in no way depends on the reading. In the second place, the first three letters are clear beyond cavil. The ink is not faint; the leather is blackened, and photographing is made difficult. Those who have had access to the original—and no one is happy with the reading—have without exception agreed that *ywlyd/k* is paleographically fixed. If we have *ywlyd* (or *ywlyk*, J.T. Milik's emendation), followed by a subject which must fit in a space of two letters (the following *'t* is preserved only in the top of an *aleph*), the restoration of the editor's (*'l*) is difficult to avoid.

To be sure the restoration suggested here is not certain; rather it is awkward. But Gaster's restoration is wrong.

Yigael Yadin has resurrected a variant form of Gaster's emendation: *yw'dw* (Gaster: *yw'd*) in his article, 'A Crucial Passage in the Dead Sea Scrolls', *JBL* 78 (1959), pp. 238-41. The writer, in the summer of 1959, after reading Yadin's paper in manuscript, had new enlarged infrared photographs of the section in question prepared, and then removed several layers of leather (from other 'pages') adhering to the back of the section, which hitherto had made a fully clear photograph impossible. The removal was not wholly successful, causing some damage. But the photographs are sufficiently clear, I believe, to bring an end to any further debate on the actual reading. The first three letters are *ywl*[ ]. The fifth letter, *dalet* is virtually certain. No letter follows *dalet*; *yod* is best for the fourth letter: *ywlŷd*. It may be after all that the reading is to be accepted, and the form taken to be a double causative: 'cause to be born'.

4. I.e., the Royal Messiah. Cf. Cross, 'Qumrân Cave I', p. 124, n. 9.

[The Priest][1] shall enter [at][2] the head of all the congregation of Israel and all the fa[thers of] the Aaronids...and they shall sit be[fore him each] according to his rank.

Next the [Messi]ah of Israel [shall enter], and the heads of the thou[sands of Israel] shall sit before him [ea]ch according to his rank...

[And][3] they shall sit before the (two) of them, each according to his rank...

W[hen th]ey solemnly meet together [at a tab]le of communion[4] [or to drink the w]ine, and the common table is arranged [and the] wine [is mixed] for drinking, one [shall not stretch out] his hand to the first portion of the bread or [of the wine] before the priest; for [he shall b]less the first portion of the bread and the wi[ne and shall stretch out] his hand to the bread first of all. Nex[t] the Messiah of Israel shall [str]etch out his hand to the bread. [Next] all the congregation of the Community [shall give tha]nks (and partake), each according to his rank.

And they shall act according to this prescription whenever (the meal) [is arr]anged, when as many as ten solemnly meet together.

The common meal of the Essenes is hereby set forth as a liturgical anticipation of the Messianic banquet. This is clear on the one hand from the roles of the Priest and the Messiah of Israel in the protocol. But it is especially clear when the final rubric (ll.21-22) is compared with the elaborate protocol. That is, in the 'taking of seats' at the meal, the whole of (true) Israel is arranged before the two Messianic figures, the priestly class before the Priest, the laity before the Messiah; in the rubric, however, we are told that this prescription is to be carried out *whenever* the meal is arranged, when as many as *ten men* meet together. Obviously this applies to the current practice of the sect.[5]

5.   The phrase is parenthetical. No doubt in the assemblies of the Essenes the lay head and the priestly head of the community (the types of the Messiahs to come) stood in the stead of the Messiahs of Aaron and Israel.

1.   Restoring *hkwhn* as in l.19.

2.   Restoring *[b]rw'š*. See Cross, 'Qumrân Cave I', p. 124, n. 7.

3.   Restoring *[w]yšbw*.

4.   Text: *[lšl]hn yhd*. The translation 'communion' is technically correct, though it may carry too many connotations in English. Cf. the next line, where I translate *hšwlhn hyhd*, 'the common table', which errs in the other direction since 'common' carries too few religious connotations.

5.   It would not be surprising if in the gathering of all the camps for the annual festival of covenant renewal at Pentecost, one finds the *Sitz im Leben* of the elaborate protocol. For the annual ceremony of the (New) Covenant, see 1QS I, 1–II, 12, etc.; J.T. Milik has established the date of the festival by a combination of an unpublished text with Jubilees 6.17 (*Découvertes*, Chap. IV).

The motif of the banquet already appears in the Old Testament in passages which lend themselves to apocalyptic exegesis, and in eschatological dress reappears in the intertestamental and especially New Testament literature. Perhaps the most important of the Old Testament passages is Isa. 25.6-8, which reads:

> On the mountain the Lord of Hosts shall prepare for all peoples
> A banquet of rich food, a banquet of old wine;
> Fat and marrowy viands, old and refined wine.
> On this mountain he shall swallow up
> The veil (of mourning) which enwraps all peoples,
> The mantle (of grief) which covers all the nations.
> He shall swallow up Death forever;
> [He] shall wipe tears from every face;
> His people's reproach he shall remove from the whole earth.
> For the Lord hath spoken.

The familiar passage Isa. 55.1-5 also received interpretation, rightly or wrongly, as the banquet of David *redivivus*.[1] And a whole kaleidoscope of ideas, the streaming of the nations to the exalted mountain of Zion,[2] the feeding of the flocks (the children of Israel) on the 'height of Israel',[3] the healing and nourishing river issuing from the New Temple on its 'very high mountain',[4] were woven into an apocalyptic fabric.[5] By Hellenistic and Roman times the eschatological banquet and its associated themes became frequent in apocalyptic writing, and are amazingly frequent in the New Testament.[6] It comes as no surprise, therefore, to discover these motives were at home among the Essenes.[7]

1.   So in Rev. 22.17; cf. Ezek. 44.3.
2.   Cf. Isa. 2.2-4 (Mic. 4.1-4), Ps. 74-12-17, especially v. 14, and Isa. 60. For use of the latter passage at Qumrân, see 1QM 12.10-18 which may be, as Milik and others have suggested, a Messianic hymn.
3.   Cf. Ezek. 34.14-16.
4.   Cf. Ezek. 40.2; 47.1-12.
5.   A full discussion of the theme, 'the Banquet of Salvation on the World Mountain' is given in the third chapter of J. Jeremias' volume, *Jesu Mission für die Völker* [*Franz Delitzsch–Vorlesungen* 1953] (Stuttgart, 1956).
6.   In the New Testament, see especially Mt. 8.11 f.=Lk. 13.28f; Rev. 19.9; Lk. 14.15-24 (cf. Mt. 22.1-14); Lk. 22.30. Cf. 1 Enoch 62.14. Specifically Eucharistic passages utilizing the themes of the Messianic banquet will be dealt with below in another connection.
7.   Another example in the Qumrân literature, hitherto missed, is found in 4QpPs. 37 II, 10-11. It appears that 37.11 is taken by the expositor as alluding to the eschatological banquet. In any case, the phrase *hr mrwm yśr'l* is pregnant with

The classical sources on the Essenes, because of their apologetic purposes and Hellenizing tendencies, largely conceal the apocalyptic overtones of Essene thought. Nevertheless there are hints of this theological pattern in all our sources.

Josephus, for example, describes the Essenes as the most 'fatalistic' of the sects in Judaism.[1] Translated from the Greek frame of reference, this characterization points to the predestinarian doctrine typical of apocalyptic thought. In a world captive to the powers of darkness, salvation is the gift of God to His elect, achieved by His new creation. In the section of the Rule of the Community dealing with the doctrine of the Two Spirits[2] (to which the sons of light and darkness are allotted from creation), we find a rigorous predestinarian formulation which teeters on the edge of determinism.[3] And even as the predestinarian doctrine of the Essenes recalls the (milder) Pauline doctrine, so a sectarian doctrine of 'justification by grace' appears in their writings as a corollary of predestination, adumbrating the classical Pauline statement of salvation by faith.[4]

Josephus also takes note of the esoteric nature of their teachings,[5] their interest in angels,[6] their thorough knowledge of the sayings of the

eschatological meaning, recalling the theme, 'banquet on the holy mountain'. The phrase is found in Ezek. 20.40 (a favorite Essene passage for typological exegesis) parallel to *bhr qdšy*. Perhaps we should reconstruct...*hr mrwm yšr['l bhr] qwdšw yt'ngw*... The expression also appears in Ezek. 34.14-16, another passage which played an important role in eschatological symbolism. Again the term *yt'ngw*, 'take exquisite delight', 'make merry', is associated with the language of the eschatological meal. Note its use in the key passage Isa. 55.2 as well as in Ps. 37.11.

We noted above parallels between Jesus' interpretation of Ps. 37 in eschatological terms in the first Beatitude (Lk. 6.20 and parallel), and that of the Essene 4QpPs. 37. The 'poor' are to inherit the Kingdom in the New Age. We should observe at this point also that in the second Beatitude, Jesus seems to continue his exposition of Ps. 37, alluding, like 4QpPs. 37, to the eschatological banquet: 'Blessed are ye that hunger for ye shall be filled' (Lk. 6.21).

1.   *Antiq.* XIII, 172. The term εἱμαρμένη is used.
2.   1QS 3.13–4.26.
3.   See the excellent discussion of Kuhn, 'πειρασμός—ἀμαρτία—σάρξ im Neuen Testament und die damit zusammenhängenden Vorstellungen'. *ZTK* 49 (1952), pp. 200-22.
4.   On the scrolls and 'justification', see the excellent article of S.E. Johnson, 'Paul and the Manual of Discipline', *HTR* 48 (1955), pp. 157-65.
5.   *War* II, 141.
6.   *War* II, 142.

prophets[1] and 'the writings of the ancients',[2] and their practice of prediction.[3] Each of these characteristics of the sect's doctrine and practice, especially the appearance of prophecy among its members, points directly to its apocalyptic structure.

Philo tells us that the Essenes turn their backs upon all philosophy, logical and natural, save that which treats of God and creation, and are much concerned with the ethical branch of philosophy. Translated into another idiom, he is saying that they are interested only in biblical revelation and law. That Philo must be understood so is shown in the succeeding passage where he describes the convocations of the sect in terms strongly reminiscent of the discipline set out in the Rule of the Community.[4] In their convocations, arranged by rank, the sectaries read their Scriptures aloud. One proficient in their interpretation expounds the lection typologically,[5] according to ancient tradition. Philo here records precisely the setting in life of the commentaries of Qumrân.[6] These are collections of typological or apocalyptic expositions of biblical passages, for the most part from the Prophets, the citation of a text alternating with its interpretation. No doubt a body of traditional exegesis developed in the sect, being put down in written form in the so-called commentaries (*pĕšārîm*) of Qumrân.

Hippolytus adds a clear apocalyptic note in attributing to the Essenes a doctrine of world judgment, resurrection of the body (as well as immortality of the soul), eternal punishment of the wicked, and the destruction of the (old) world in a cosmic conflagration. The last-mentioned doctrine is especially distinctive, and is confirmed in the new scrolls.[7]

It is quite impossible within our limits to pursue all of the details in which our classical sources complement and correspond to sources from Qumrân caves. This correspondence can be illustrated by citation of details of community organization, offices and trial procedures, or of common practice in such matters as sanitary regulations,[8] the use of

1.   *War* II, 159.
2.   *War*, 136.
3.   *War* II, 159; cf. *War* I, 78: II, 113; III, 351-54; *Antiq.* XV, 371-79.
4.   Philo, *Quod omn. prob. lib. sit*, 80-82.
5.   *Ibid.*, 82. We have translated διὰ συμβόλων, 'typologically'.
6.   Cf. 1QS 6.6-13.
7.   Hippolytus, *Refutatio* IX, 27: cf. 1QH 3.19-36; Black, *op. cit.*, p. 175. (The same doctrine is attributed to the Pharisees by Hippolytus).
8.   As we have seen, the sect lives by the rules of 'Holy War' associated with the

oaths,[1] the rites of lustration and baptism.[2] On the one hand we can point to verbal reminiscences in Josephus of theological clichés in the Qumrân texts,[3] and on the other hand to the prohibition of spitting in assembly recorded by both Josephus and the Rule of Qumrân.

There are also apparent discrepancies between the Essenes of the classical sources and the people of the scrolls, which require fresh examination.[4]

There is the matter of celibacy. Did the Essenes marry? Philo is

desert era and the Conquest; cf. Josephus, *War* II, 137; 148-49; Deut. 23.10-14; Num. 5.1-4; 1QM 7.3-7. On the 'Essene pickaxe' mentioned by Josephus, cf. R. de Vaux, 'Une hachette essénienne?' *VT* 9 (1959), pp. 399-407.

1. Josephus, *War* II, 135; *Antiq.* XV, 371; Philo, *Quod omn. probl. lib. sit*, 84; *CD* 15.1-5; Mt. 5.33-37; 23.16-22; Jas. 5.12.

2. See Josephus, *War* II, 129, 138 (cf. 149, 150; *Antiq.* XVIII, 19). In the Qumrân texts, see especially 1QS 5.8-23. The passage describes the procedure of initiation into full membership (ll.8, 20, 23), including the oath, covenant, baptism, and separation in matters of goods, labor, food, or even religious discussion. In ll. 10-13 an instruction is given to have the candidate take upon himself covenant obligations; there follows a denunciation of those who insincerely enter the covenant. In ll. 13-14 there follows a warning against the candidate who is baptized without repentance: '[Such a candidate] shall not enter into the water [and as a result] to come into contact with the Purity of the holy men: for they are not purified (thereby) except (*kî 'im*) they repent from their wickedness.' In 1QS 2.25–3.12, there is another list of warnings to him who refuses to enter the covenant or who does so without faith, obedience, and repentance, in which the efficacy of the covenant ceremony or any baptism or lustration (even with 'seas or rivers!') of itself, *ex opere operato*, is sharply denied.

Cf. K. Stendahl, 'ΑΞΙΟΣ im Lichte der Texte der Qumran-Höhle', *Nuntius* 7 (1952), cols. 53-55; N.A. Dahl, 'The Origin of Baptism', *Interpretationes ad Vetus Testamentum pertinentes Sigmundo Mowinckel septuagenario missae* (Oslo, 1955), pp. 36-51.

M.H. Gottstein in his article, 'Anti-Essene Traits in Dead Sea Scrolls', *VT* 4 (1954), pp. 141-47, has failed to recognize the distinction between the efficacy of baptism in the case of one who is repentant and has a holy spirit (1QS 3.7), *ex opere operantis*; and baptism as an *opus operatum*. Gottstein can show at most that the texts of Qumrân reject the latter conception of baptism. The Qumrân sectarians are 'baptist', however, both in their general ideas of purity and in the actual practice of the rites of baptism and lustration. The only question which remains open is whether or not their rite of baptism on entry into covenant was annually repeated in the covenant renewal ceremony. 1QS 2.25–3.12 suggests that it was.

3. For example, in the initiates' oath (*War* II, 139-41), we read '...that he must always hate the unrighteous and take the side of the righteous', and 'that he must love the truth always and denounce the false'. Compare 1QS 1.9-11; 4.23-25, etc.

4. *War* II, 147; 1QS 6.3.

unequivocal in stating that they were a celibate order.[1] Josephus says that they shun marriage but do not reject the institution as such. He attributes to them as a motivation the desire to guard themselves 'from the wantonness of woman'.[2] This seems a convincing enough reason for the practice of celibacy...but one suspects it originates, not in Essene theology, but in Josephus' Hellenistic imagination.[3] Elsewhere Josephus records that one order (τάγμα) of Essenes did in fact marry, while otherwise keeping to the Essene rule.[4]

The evidence from Qumrân is in part ambiguous. It is certain that one order within the sectarian community married.[5] In descriptions of the 'congregation' (*'ēdāh*), women and children are named.[6] There is also data, however, which suggests that the Qumrân 'community', (*yáḥad*), at least, was largely celibate.[7] The large central cemetery of Qumrân, containing about one thousand tombs, seems to contain only male burials. In adjuncts to the central cemetery, skeletons of women and children have been found.[8] It is possible that the outlying cemeteries are later in date, and that the older celibate community later became mixed,[9] or we may suppose that within the environs of the desert of Qumrân was an order of married Essenes alongside a larger celibate community.

---

1. *Hypothetica* 11, 14-17. Philo attributes two reasons for their celibacy, its threat to a fully communal life, and the wickedness of woman. In the latter case Philo indulges himself in a diatribe against womankind which tells us more about Philo than about the Essenes.

2. *War* II, 120-21.

3. The late Professor Marcus has observed *à propos* of the Hellenizing distortion of Josephus, 'I have long suspected, for example, that Josephus has misled us by presenting the great majority of Essenes as celibates while indicating that only a small group of them practiced marriage for the purpose of procreation. This may actually be a reversal of the true situation or at least a gross exaggeration, since it is difficult to believe that even the most heterodox Jews would have disregarded one of the cardinal and widely accepted principles of Judaism, based on God's first commandment to mankind, "increase and multiply"' ('The Qumrân Scrolls and Early Judaism', p. 28).

4. *War* II, 160-61.

5. See above, p. 71, n. 4.

6. Cf. 1QSa I.4, 9-10.

7. Professor Herbert May has reminded me of the expression *prwt zr‘* in 1QS 4.7, in the list of the blessings of the Spirit in the 'world' (*tbl*). Cf. *CD* 4.21–5.11; 7 (=19): 6-8.

8. De Vaux, *Rapport III*, pp. 569-72.

9. So Milik, *Découvertes*, Appendice. See also De Vaux, *ADSS*, pp. 45-48.

This area of Essene life can best be understood, not by positing a sect of marrying Essenes alongside a celibate sect, but by recognizing an ambiguous attitude toward marriage integral to the structure of the Essene faith. While a genuine asceticism has no place in Judaism, there are two streams in Judaism which have dualistic tendencies. One of these is an extremely ancient one, rooted in the priestly distinctions between ritual purity and pollution, 'physical' holiness and 'physical' sin. Certain sexual acts render one unclean so that he may not approach holy things. This is especially vivid in the laws of 'Holy War', where all sexual life is suspended, women excluded from the camp, since God's Spirit (or his holy angels) is present in the camp. The second stream is the late developing apocalyptic movement which assimilates certain elements of Persian ethical dualism to the prophetic understanding of history as a drama of divine warfare culminating in the victory of God. In this tradition the 'normal life' of the old age is qualified. The faithful live in a crisis which marks the death of the Old World, the birth of the New Creation. It is a time of trial, and therefore of an 'abnormal' discipline of the flesh.

At Qumrân these streams come together in a priestly apocalypticism which energizes the dualistic tendencies of both traditions. We have already noted that the rigorous rules of Holy War obtain in the daily regimen of the Qumrân community. Ritual purity is maintained by the community as a whole. The community takes the posture of a priesthood standing in the presence of God.[1] This disciplined life, moreover, is set in an apocalyptic understanding of history. The trumpet has sounded for God's final Holy War. The men of the Essene community are mustered for battle, rank on rank, poised to march side by side with the 'holy ones', the angelic armies of God.[2]

The Essene in his daily life thus girds himself to withstand the final trial, purifies himself to join the holy armies, anticipates the coming conditions in God's inbreaking kingdom. This is the situation which prompts counsels against marriage, at least for some. In the new age he will live eternally in the presence of the holy ones,[3] the angels of God, and even in the very presence of the Holy God. In this new age the righteous live like the angels without need of procreation, and preserve

1. Cf. 1QSb III, 22-IV, 28; and Exod. 19.6, 15.
2. See especially, 1QM 12.1-5.6-10.
3. See, for example, 1QS 11.7-8; 1QH 3.19-23; 6.12-14; 7.29-31; and especially 11.10-14; cf. 1QM 7.6; and Col. 1.12.

themselves in perpetual 'purity' before the throne of God.

The attitude toward marriage in the primitive Church springs from the same theological milieu.[1] In Lk. 20.34-36 is the saying, 'The sons of this age marry and are given in marriage; but those who are worthy to have a lot in that new age, and in the resurrection of the dead, neither marry nor are taken in marriage, for they no longer can die, because they, like the angels, are sons of God being sons of the resurrection.'[2] Paul's teachings on marriage, that he who marries does well, that he who remains unmarried does better, since 'the appointed time has grown very short', are cut from the same theological fabric.[3]

Both in the New Testament and at Qumrân we discover counsels against marriage in *this* decisive moment when *this* world is passing away. In neither community is to be found a theoretical ascetic doctrine of universal validity. Rather we may call Essene (or New Testament) practice an 'apocalyptic' asceticism. It is this apocalyptic asceticism which explains the confusing statements of Josephus and clarifies the ambiguities in the data from the texts and cemeteries of Qumrân.

To be sure, the apocalyptic asceticism of the Essenes and early Christianity was unstable. In its first contacts with Greek paganism, especially Platonic forms of thought, the eschatological tension was lost. The precipitate was Docetic and Gnostic asceticism, as well as those more orthodox forms of piety out of which monasticism sprang. In any case we cannot with felicity speak of Qumrân as a 'monastery', or of Essene sectaries as 'monks'.

Before the discovery of the texts of Qumrân, it was generally held, on the basis of passages in Philo and Josephus, that the Essenes rejected sacrifice.[4] Philo, in commenting on their piety, remarks that their 'extraordinary devotion to God' is shown 'not by sacrificing animals, but by determining to render their own minds holy'.[5] This can be taken to mean that the Essenes repudiated the sacrificial system. It need not be. The conviction that 'obedience is better than sacrifice, hearkening (to the voice of the Lord) than the fat of rams' (1 Sam. 15.22) is shared by prophet and priest in old Israel, and might have been expressed by a

---

1.   I suspect that certain of the New Testament passages here cited are shaped not merely by *an* apocalypticism, but by priestly, that is, Essene apocalypticism.

2.   Cf. Mk 12.25; Mt. 22.30 (parallels); and Mt. 19.10-12.

3.   1 Cor. 7.

4.   See, e.g., Schürer, *Geschichte*[3] II, pp. 568f.

5.   *Quod omn. prob. lib. sit*, 75.

pious Jew of the later period, whatever his party. In other words, Philo's comment would be appropriate if the Essenes (1) rejected the Temple cultus on principle, or (2) insisted only that God's ethical and ritual laws be observed as a prerequisite of valid sacrifices.

The texts of Qumrân leave no doubt that their authors' objections to the cultus of Jerusalem fall under the second alternative.[1] The founder of the sect was a priest, evidently of the legitimate Zadokite line,[2] and the community was dominated by priests who expected to return to the Temple to reinstitute orthopraxy in the days of the Last War.[3] Meanwhile they assert that the sanctuary is defiled,[4] the reigning priesthood false. Nevertheless they preserve and prepare documents pertaining to the priestly service.[5]

There are two additional data to be considered. Josephus writes, 'When the Essenes send their gifts[6] to the Temple, they do <not> offer sacrifices owing to a difference in rites of purity which they practice, and therefore being excluded[7] from the common precinct (of the Temple), they offer sacrifices by themselves.'[8] On the face of it, this text suggests

---

1.   An excellent study of the problem of sacrifice at Qumrân, admirably summarizing the then-known data, is that of J.M. Baumgarten, 'Sacrifice and Worship among the Jewish Sectarians of the Dead Sea (Qumrân) Scrolls', *HTR* 46 (1953), pp. 141-59.

2.   1QpHab. 2.8; 4QpPs. 37 II, 15; 1QM 17.2-3.

3.   1QM 2.1-6. For the role of the future chief priest and priests generally, see 1QM, *passim*; 4QPs. 37 II, 10-11; 4Q Testimonia, 14-20; 1QSb II-V, 19; etc.

On the passage pertaining to sacrifice in 1QS 9.3-6, see J. Carmignac, 'L'utilité ou l'inutilité des sacrifices sanglants dans la "Règle de la Communauté" de Qumrân', *RB* 63 (1956), pp. 524-32 (with postscript by J.T. Milik, p. 532).

4.   1QpHab. 12.7-9; 8.8-13; *CD* 20.22-24; cf. 6.11-14; etc.

5.   On 4Q *Mišmārôt*, see Chapter 1, p. 46, n. 1; laws pertaining to sacrifice are preserved in *CD* 9.13-14; 11.17-21; 16.13.

6.   Greek, ἀναθήματα; Heb. *ḥērem*. Such could be given to the Temple without the donor entering into the cultus or recognizing the legitimacy of the priesthood; the *ḥērem*, unqualified, seems to have been used for repair or ornamentation of the Temple; cf. Lk. 21.5.

7.   On the meaning of εἰργόμενοι in Josephus, see Marcus, 'Pharisees, Essenes, and Gnostics', *JBL* 73 (1954), p. 158.

8.   *Antiq.* XVIII, 19. εἰς δὲ τὸ ἱερὸν ἀναθήματα στέλλοντες θυσίας <οὐκ> ἐπιτελοῦσι διαφορότητι ἁγνειῶν, ἃς νομίζοιεν καὶ δι᾽ αὐτὸ εἰργόμενοι τοῦ κοινοῦ τεμενίσματος ἐφ᾽ αὑτῶν τὰς θυσίας ἐπιτελοῦσιν. The attempt to read the last phrase 'conduct worship separately' (cf. Baumgarten, *op. cit.*, p. 155) while the *same* expression, in the *same* sentence is translated 'offer sacrifices' seems quite out

that the Essenes carried on animal sacrifice privately. Josephus' testimony might simply be dismissed were it not for the appearance at Qumrân of meticulous burials of animal bones.[1] Though it is somewhat difficult to visualize at Qumrân the maintenance of an independent sacrificial cultus by a hyperorthodox sect, I am inclined to think that our evidence now suggests that this was the case.[2]

However the latter question may ultimately be answered, there can be no doubt that Josephus and the Qumrân manuscripts are in essential agreement as to the sectarian attitude toward sacrifice and the Temple. Similarly other apparent discrepancies melt away when older constructions of the classical authorities are re-examined, and when it is remembered that the theological categories of the Essenes are crudely translated into philosophical categories by both Philo and Josephus in writing for the Greek reader.[3]

of the realm of probability. It is better simply to deny the accuracy of Josephus' statement (so Marcus, *op. cit.*, p. 158, n. 2) if one cannot bring himself to suppose the Essenes actually conducted separate sacrifices.

1. See above, pp. 90f.; De Vaux, *Rapport III*, pp. 549f.

2. Warrant for a sacrificial system may be found in a special interpretation given in *CD* 3.18–4.4 to Ezek. 44.15 by the sectarian author. The passage of Ezekiel is slightly changed, apparently for sectarian purposes. In any case the sect is identified with 'the priests and the Levites and [sic!] the sons of Zadok who kept the office of my sanctuary when the children of Israel went astray from me, they shall bring me fat and blood'.

Again, it must be noted that the Essenes did in fact institute and practice an independent calendar of feasts.

Mr. John Strugnell has suggested to me that a rationale for the establishment of an altar at Qumrân could be derived from the sect's patterning itself after the Mosaic camp of the wilderness, where sacrifice was in fact carried on.

The Essene practice would not be wholly without a parallel of sorts in this period. Onias, the hereditary high priest in the time of Maccabees established a temple and cultus at Leontopolis (Josephus, *War* I, 31, 33; VII, 422-35).

3. Josephus' reference to the morning prayers of the Essenes deserves some comment. His text reads, 'They show piety to the Deity in an unusual fashion; before the sun comes up they do not speak of profane affairs, but pray certain traditional prayers to him as if invoking (the sun) to rise' (*War* II, 128). Apparently the antecedent of (εἰς) αὐτόν 'him' is τὸν ἥλιον 'the sun' rather than τὸ θεῖον, 'the Deity'; otherwise the sentence is awkward. On the other hand can we suppose that Josephus really thought the Essenes worshipped the sun? Hippolytus in the parallel passage gives no hint of heterodoxy (*Refutatio* IX, 21). Our manuscripts include a liturgical papyrus containing among other things the sunrise prayer (unpublished; cf. Hunzinger, 'Le travail d' édition...' p. 67), and in 1QH there is an interesting

In the foregoing discussion we have restricted ourselves to points raised by the older sources and to data from the scrolls which bear directly on the older sources. Hence Philo and Josephus have called the tune. Our purpose has been to show how the older sources and the newer texts are mutually illuminating, how they at each point confirm the identity of the people of the scrolls with the Essenes, how the Essenes emerge from our sources a sect of priestly apocalyptists. The classical sources, however, have sharply limited our picture of the Essenes and their history, and we must now turn to a broader examination of the Qumrân manuscripts themselves to piece together more fragments of their life and history.

reference to prayers at specified periods including sunrise (12.4-7). While the sun is determinative in fixing the times of the day and year at Qumrân, so that their calendar is purely solar, there is, of course, no hint of sun worship in these prayers or elsewhere in the Qumrân literature.

Probably Josephus' comment is to be understood as a reference to the unorthodox orientation of the Essene in prayer, facing the rising sun. The Jew normally faced toward the Temple (cf. Dan. 6.10, etc.). Daniélou ('La communauté de Qumrân et l'organisation de l'Eglise ancienne', *RHPR* 35 [1955], p. 108) has noted that early Christian practice follows the Essene custom over against the orthodox. Strugnell has suggested to me that εἰς αὐτόν should be translated 'toward it' (the sun), from the usage of the preposition with εὐχάς, supporting Daniélou's interpretation.

Chapter 3

THE RIGHTEOUS TEACHER AND ESSENE ORIGINS

The library found at Qumrân contains no document which can be called properly a historical work. Historiography was not an interest of the sect's authors. Nevertheless, the scrolls, especially the class of documents inexactly called biblical commentaries, contain many allusions to contemporary events, both in the inner history of the sect, and in the political history of Syria–Palestine. Beginning with the publication of the Damascus Document in 1910, and especially with the publication of the Habakkuk Commentary in 1950, scholars have attempted to reconstruct the history of the sect from data found within the scrolls themselves. For the most part these attempts at synthesis have failed, and the number of theories evolved almost equals the number of scholars who have put their hands to the task. In the search for the archvillain of the sect, for example, the 'Wicked Priest', scholars have found candidates ranging from pre-Maccabean times down into the Roman era and even later. No Hasmonaean priest-king has been left unturned in his grave.

There is little purpose in reviewing the theories and debate which marked the early discussion of the history of the sect.[1] Much of the

---

1. Surveys of the sundry views held by scholars of the historical *cadre* of the scrolls may be found in the following: M. Burrows, *The Dead Sea Scrolls*, pp. 123-33; K. Elliger, *Studien zum Habakuk-Kommentar vom Toten Meer* (Tübingen, 1953), pp. 226-74; H.H. Rowley, *The Zadokite Fragments and the Dead Sea Scrolls*, pp. 31-61; and G. Vermès, *Les manuscrits du Désert de Juda* (Tournai, 1953), pp. 67-108. Among the recently published reconstructions, see G. Vermès, *loc. cit.*; L. Toombs, 'The Early History of the Qumran Sect', *JSS* 1 (1956), pp. 367-81; J.M. Allegro, 'Further Light on the History of the Qumrân Sect', *JBL* 75 (1956), pp. 89-95 (cf. *The Dead Sea Scrolls*, pp. 94-100); T.H. Gaster, *The Dead Sea Scriptures*, pp. 24-28; J.T. Milik, *Découvertes*, Chap. III and Appendice; and C. Roth, 'A Solution to the Mystery of the Scrolls', *Commentary* 24 (1957), pp. 317-24. Reformulations of earlier constructions include the recent studies of I. Rabinowitz, 'Reconsideration of "Damascus" and "390 years" in the "Damascus"

labor during the early phase of the inquiry consisted of simple guess-work guided by too vague and too few allusions in the extant texts to achieve secure results. That this is true should be evident in the sheer variety of theories spawned in scholars' imaginations. Moreover, much of the early study has fallen to philologians who, following the traditional methods of literary analysis, have failed to train themselves in the relatively new disciplines in the fields of archaeology and especially paleography. The unfortunate result has been that a steady stream of historical studies has been published based on premises excluded by archaeological and paleographical data. On the other hand, many of these prematurely obsolete reconstructions have contained extremely important philological advances and cannot be ignored. Finally, the field has been developing with extreme rapidity. To the veiled allusions of the first published texts have been added now explicit references by name to known historical figures. The analysis of new materials for paleography has made crucial progress in several areas. And with each season of excavation at Qumrân, archaeological controls on the interpretation of the texts become tighter and tighter.

1. *Prolegomena to the Study of the Commentaries*

At the outset some word must be said concerning the character of source materials in the scrolls with which we must labor in any attempt

("Zadokite") Fragments', *JBL* 73 (1954), pp. 11-35; (cf. E. Wiesenberg, 'Chronological Data in the Zadokite Fragments', *VT* 5 [1955] pp. 284-308); A. Dupont-Sommer, 'Quelques remarques sur le Commentaire d'Habacuc à propos d'un livre récent', *VT* 5 (1955), pp. 113-29; H.H. Rowley, 'The Kittim and the Dead Sea Scrolls', *PEQ* 88 (1956), pp. 92-109 (cf. '4QpNahum and the Teacher of Righteousness', *JBL* 75 [1956], pp. 188-93). [For some of the more recent literature, see Chapter 6. Oddly enough, despite the establishment of the dates of the scrolls by palaeography, now a most precise discipline in this period, and by carbon$_{14}$ dating which agrees with the paleographical dates, certain scholars are still producing provocative hypotheses placing the *floruit* of the persons and events alluded to in the scrolls in Christian times. Such views, in my opinion, are impossible and do not deserve serious attention. Other views, taken up anew recently, which attempt to separate Qumrân from the sectarian library and associated artifacts found in the caves, I find bizarre. Examples of such views may be found in the following works: R.H. Eisenman, *James the Just in the Habakkuk Pesher* (Leiden: E.J. Brill, 1986); B.E. Thiering, *Redating the Teacher of Righteousness* (Sydney, Australia: Theological Explorations, 1979); and Norman Golb, 'The Dead Sea Scrolls: A New Perspective', *The American Scholar* 58 (1989), pp. 177-207.]

to work out the details of Essene history. Our sources consist chiefly of expositions of biblical prophecy, or of biblical material reckoned as prophecy by the Essenes. These include (1) commentaries, *pěšārîm*, which expound extended passages or entire biblical books verse by verse; (2) collections of 'prophetic' testimonia, sometimes with expository comments appended to each, sometimes without; and (3) historical exposition utilizing a patchwork of biblical citations to interpret in 'prophetic' language the meaning and sequence of historical events of the past and future.

The technique of exposition in all these sources grows out of the presuppositions of apocalypticism, and can be rightly understood only within the categories of this special type of eschatological thought. Two major assumptions characterize apocalyptic exegesis. All biblical prophecy is normally taken to have eschatological meaning. The 'prophets', Moses as well as Amos, the psalmist as well as Jeremiah, speak regularly in open or veiled language of the 'last days'. Their predictions are not to be understood in simple terms of near future or even remote future, but apply to the crisis of the ages, the final times when the historical epoch turns into the transhistorical epoch. Secondly, it must be understood that the apocalyptist understood himself to be living in these days of the final crisis, at the end of days and the beginning of the New Age, so that the events of his own times were recognized as precisely those events forecast by the prophets of old as coming in the last days.[1]

By perusing the Scriptures, the Essenes were able to find detailed descriptions of the events of current history; the central figures of their sect and of their times were hidden in veiled prophetic allusions. The life of their own sect, its origin, purpose, vicissitudes, and glorious destiny all had been laid out in the predictions of the ancients. To be sure, it could be read only by 'those who had eyes to see'. Essene exegesis was necessarily pneumatic, based on the gift of special eschatological 'knowledge'. The secrets of the prophets had to be discovered by inspired interpreters.

The tradition of Essene exegesis was initiated directly, no doubt, by the founder of the sect, the so-called 'Righteous Teacher' (*môrēh haṣ-*

---

1.   Cf. K. Elliger, *Studien zum Habakuk-Kommentar vom Toten Meer*, hereafter *SzHK*, pp. 150-64; W.H. Brownlee, 'Biblical Interpretation Among the Sectaries of the Dead Sea Scrolls', *BA* 14 (1951), pp. 54-76. Elliger succinctly summarizes the hermeneutical principles: (1) prophecy is eschatology and (2) the present is the end-time.

ṣédeq).[1] It is said of him in the Habakkuk Commentary[2] that he spoke of 'all the events which were to come upon the last generation', for 'God placed (him) in the [midst of the "congregation"] to expound all the words of his prophets by whose agency God has related all which is to come upon his people and [his congregation].' In another passage we read,[3] '...God has informed (the Righteous Teacher) of all the secrets of the words of his servants the prophets.' No doubt the founder himself was heavily indebted to earlier apocalyptic materials, especially to Daniel. At all events, certain set forms of exposition and a traditional body of biblical exposition grew up, stemming from the pattern laid down in the early period. This was transmitted and supplemented, no doubt, in the regular study of scholars of the community, and particularly in the regular sessions of the sect mentioned in our sources, where Scripture was read and systematically expounded by those who had become the experts of the community. In a later era the body of traditional exegesis was put into writing in the commentaries and related documents which have come into our hands.

Such a construction of the literary background of commentary materials is necessary to explain certain features of the works. In the first place, there is a consistent treatment of biblical expressions throughout them,[4] despite the fact that their hermeneutic technique lends itself to extreme subjectivity in dealing with Scripture. The commentaries are based on communal and traditional exposition, therefore, and are not merely the result of individual flights of fancy. In the second place, virtually all commentaries and testimonia[5] appear in manuscripts written

---

1. The title probably includes the ideas of 'righteousness' and 'legitimacy'. However, I cannot agree with those scholars who take *ṣédeq* to be an objective genitive, 'one who teaches righteousness', though, obviously the 'Righteous Teacher' teaches righteousness. Cf. T.H. Gaster, *The Dead Sea Scriptures*, p. 5. One may note the parallel title, 'righteous or legitimate Messiah', *mᵉšîᵃḥ haṣ-ṣédeq*, 4Q Patriarchal Blessings 1. 3; *šm h'mt*, 'trustworthy name', 1QpHab. 8.9; etc.

2. 1QpHab. 2.5-10.

3. 1QpHab. 7.4-5.

4. There is, to be sure, an occasional unevenness in treating a 'prophetic' expression. For example, the 'staff', *mhqq*, of Gen. 49.10 is differently interpreted in 4Q Patriarchal Blessings and in *CD*. In the former (1.2) it is the royal covenant, i.e., the covenant of David; in *CD* 6.7, the term is equated with *dwrš htwrh*, the priestly office. See below, Chapter 5, p. 164, n. 1.

5. An exception is 4Q Testimonia inscribed by the same scribe who prepared 1QS as well as a number of other manuscripts, biblical and non-biblical, found in

in late hands, from the second half of the first century BC and the first half of the first century AD. We have shown elsewhere[1] that there are strong reasons to believe that most of the commentaries are autographs. The argument is quite simple. Biblical works and non-biblical works reappear again and again in the caves, sometimes in as many as ten or fifteen copies of a single work. This duplication (or multiplication) of copies among the various caves is significantly absent in a single category of literature: the commentaries. In light of the large number of such works now known, especially from Cave IV, it is difficult to avoid the conclusion that such works were rarely if ever copied, and hence are mostly original works. If this conclusion is valid, it has important implications for dating: the date of the script of a commentary will indicate normally its date of written composition. The deduction to be drawn is that a corpus of traditional exegesis was put into writing only toward the end of the sect's life.

These factors suggest, and inductive examination will show, that the commentaries refer to events over a considerable period of history. The allusions to the history of the sect thus cannot all be fitted into the era of its formation. They must be spread out over at least two generations, and probably longer.

Two other comments, both in the nature of warnings, need to be made *à propos* of Essene apocalyptic exegesis. In the nature of the apocalyptic interpretation of history, events are described from within the context of the elect community. The important events in the history of salvation are the events which involve the sect. From the point of view of the critical historian, this means that major political events, Pompey's conquest of Jerusalem, the death of a king, are judged significant according to their direct bearing on the life of the sect, while insignificant events, the rebuke of an Essene leader, the disturbance of a festal celebration, become turning points in world history. In the commentaries the inner history of the sect is bewilderingly mixed with external political events.[2] In the second place, apocalyptic exegesis

Qumrân caves. His hand belongs preferably to the first quarter of the first century BC.

1. 'Qumrân Cave I', *JBL* (1956), pp. 123f.

2. Some attempt has been made on the part of scholars to distinguish between purely historical commentary and purely eschatological, or between commentaries dealing primarily with external history and those dealing primarily with internal history. Such distinctions involve categories foreign to the apocalyptic mind, and can be applied to Essene materials only by forcing and distortion.

involves a certain form of typology.[1] A prophet like Moses, a messiah like David, a priest like Aaron or Zadok, are expected. There is to be a new desert sojourn, a new Exodus, a new covenant, a new gift of 'the height of Israel', a new Holy War. Figures bearing titles from prophecy, the Righteous Teacher, the False Oracle, the Wrathful Lion, and a dozen others appear 'in the last times'. Apocalyptic typology often takes an ancient figure and projects it into the eschatological future. Such typology, however, never breaks down into allegory, nor even into a *series* of types. For example, the 'Messiah of Israel' in apocalyptic exegesis can never apply to a series of future Davidic kings. The 'prophet like Moses' does not mean the 'continuing prophetic office'. The 'New Age' never grows old to be supplanted by a new 'New Age'. In similar fashion, the 'Righteous Teacher', the 'False Oracle', the 'Lion of Wrath', are not titles designating 'offices' to be filled by a series of appropriate figures. Thus while some of these figures (places, etc.) may have ancient prototypes, in their eschatological role they are to appear in the final age...finally.[2]

From these rather extended comments on the nature of the material in our texts, we are led to draw certain methodological conclusions. Theoretically the allusions in biblical commentaries can be utilized in reconstructing the history of the sect. On the other hand, the elusive character of the data suggests that we can achieve sound historical results only by utilizing outside controls to limit the framework within which our sources operate. Concretely this means that we must approach the problems relating to the historical interpretation of our texts by first determining the time period set by archaeological data, by paleographical evidence, and by other more objective methods before applying the more subjective techniques of internal criticism.

Paleography, the science of dating documents by typological analysis of their scripts, is perhaps the most precise and objective means of determining the age of a manuscript. As early as 1937 the main lines of

---

1.   See Chapter 2, p. 71, n. 5.

2.   For these reasons we cannot accept the proposals of Reicke, ('Die Ta'āmire–Schriften und die Damaskus-Fragmente' *ST* 2 [1948], pp. 45-70) and most recently Gaster (*The Dead Sea Scriptures*, pp. 25-28) to apply a systematic typological exegesis. We must attempt to delineate and adopt the apocalyptic categories of Essene exegesis, avoiding the pitfalls of various types of 'Hellenizing', whether they be 'historicizing', the employing of systematic typology (actually a form of allegorizing), or the utilizing of late rabbinic forms of exegesis.

the development of Aramaic and Jewish scripts from the fifth century BC to the time of the First Revolt were fixed by W.F. Albright's epoch-making study of the Nash Papyrus.[1] In the interval between his programmatic paper and the discovery of the first scrolls of Qumrân the steady increase of epigraphic materials in Aramaic and Hebrew further confirmed his results, so that Jewish paleography had become an established science at the time of the discovery of the scrolls. Immediately upon the publication of the scrolls the specialists in epigraphy and paleography, notably Albright himself, Solomon Birnbaum, Sukenik, and John Trever, fixed the dates of the several scrolls within fairly narrow limits.[2] These dates have since been confirmed by each new development in the field.

The discovery in 1952 of some four hundred fragmentary manuscripts in Cave IV, all dating before AD 70, as well as the discovery of documents of the first and second centuries AD in the region of Wâdī Murabba'ât, some with date formulae, have made possible rapid new advances in our knowledge of early Jewish paleography and in the precision with which the scrolls can be dated. A typological sequence of scripts including several hundred specimens of Jewish script, a number of them precisely dated on non-paleographic grounds as well as some hundreds of scripts from epigraphic sources, has now been established, extending in time from the late fourth century BC to the late second century of the Christian era.

In 1955 the writer published a first study growing out of his early efforts to systematize the new wealth of data for paleographical analysis.[3] Three major periods within the evolution of the script were defined and dated: (1) Archaic, ca. 200–150 BC, (2) Hasmonaean, ca. 150–30 BC and (3) Herodian, ca. 30 BC to AD 70. Relative dating within these periods offers no problem, thanks to the extremely swift evolution of the script.[4] Absolute dates are more difficult to fix,

1. 'A Biblical Fragment from the Maccabaean Age: the Nash Papyrus', *JBL* 56 (1937), pp. 145-76.

2. For bibliography, see S.A. Birnbaum, *The Qumrân (Dead Sea) Scrolls and Palaeography* [*Supplementary Studies of the ASOR* 13-14] (New Haven, 1952); and F.M. Cross, 'The Oldest Manuscripts from Qumrân', *JBL* 74 (1955), pp. 147-72.

3. 'The Oldest Manuscripts from Qumrân', especially pp. 163ff.; in 1961 I published my monograph, *The Development of the Jewish Script*, a much more substantial work (*DJS*).

4. The speed of the evolution can be estimated by the fact that in a period of less than *two centuries*, from the early Archaic to the early Herodian period, the

especially in the Archaic period. However, manuscripts can be firmly dated in the Hasmonaean and Herodian periods within half centuries, and in the case of certain types of scripts we are able to date to the generation with some degree of probability.[1] Jewish paleography in this period is fast approaching the degree of precision achieved by Greek paleographers in a later era.

The dating of the sectarian manuscripts from Qumrân gives extremely important data for fixing the general framework within which we must look for the setting of Essene origins. While biblical manuscripts range in date from the late third century BC to the middle of the first century AD, all extant copies of sectarian works fall in the Hasmonaean and Herodian periods. The earliest manuscripts of the *Rule of the Community* include two copies which are best dated in the first quarter of the first century BC, and one papyrus copy in a proto-cursive script which, while more difficult to date, is earlier still.[2] Obviously none of these was copied before the founding of the community. And it is unlikely that even the oldest of them is the autograph copy.[3] Similarly, other sectarian manuscripts, including the Damascus Document,[4] appear first in copies

evolutionary shifts in the *formal* script are more radical than in the whole of the evolution of the next *millennium*. This means that we can date Qumrân texts within one century with the same typological precision—to make a rough proportion—with which we can date medieval MSS within half a millennium. Moreover, the essentially archaizing book hands of the Middle Ages raise special problems for the paleographer which have parallels at Qumrân only in the case of the so-called Paleo–Hebrew script.

1. The dating of a script to a single generation, in the case of individual manuscripts, cannot be converted automatically into an absolute dating. Despite the speed of evolution in this period, allowance must be made for the *floruit* of a conservative scribe extending beyond his generation. However, in the case of a group of scripts belonging typologically to a certain generation, we can assume methodologically that the majority of the group were copies within the normal span of the generation.

2. One of these is the well known 1QS; the other two are unpublished. The early Hasmonaean papyrus copy is tentatively designated 4QS^e.

3. In the case of 1QS, we can demonstrate its distance from the autograph. (1) Its text exhibits characteristic copyist's errors, as can be shown most easily by comparison with other texts; and (2) in col. V it presents an expanded text (cf. Milik, 'Le travail d'édition...' p. 61). Similarly, in another MS (4Q Testimonia) copied by the same scribe there is a quotation of an older sectarian work (4Q Psalms of Joshua, cf. Strugnell, *ibid.*, p. 65; Allegro, *JBL* 75 [1956], p. 186f.).

4. In *CD* 16.3-4, an older Essene work, perhaps Jubilees, is referred to.

which can be no later than the first half of the first century BC.[1]

Certain conclusions must be drawn. The absence of sectarian manuscripts of the Archaic period suggests that the composition of the early sectarian works probably did not commence until the second half of the second century, BC. To be sure, this is an argument from silence, but it is suggestive.

The relative paucity of biblical manuscripts from the Archaic period points in the same direction. The first main period of the sect's life can hardly be pushed earlier than about 150 BC.

The paleographical dates for the earliest extant copies of the *Rule* are much more instructive. They fix an ironclad *terminus ante quem* for the composition of early Essene works, and hence for the foundation of the sect. We cannot go later than the reign of Alexander Jannaeus for extant copies of this work, and the time of composition must almost certainly be pressed back before 100 BC to permit the textual development and parenetic expansions which characterize our earliest copies. Further we should postulate a certain interval between the decisive events which created the sect and sent it and the Righteous Teacher into exile in the desert, and the composition of the systematic discipline of the community. The Essene *Rule* is not a programmatic work written before the founding of the sect; it reflects the discipline of the first community in the wilderness of Qumrân at a time when its practices had been systematically worked out.[2] Similarly the Damascus Document was composed sometime after the death of the Righteous Teacher (which is referred to twice), yet before the Roman conquest of 63 BC as is shown both by paleographical evidence and internal evidence. In short, paleographical analysis of the texts now sets limits within which we must look for the events which gave rise to the sectarian movement: the

---

1.　Certain works appear mostly in Herodian scripts (the commentaries), and some only in Herodian scripts (1QM). The latter fact tends to support the contention of Y. Yadin (see his thorough study, *mgylt mlḥmt bny 'wr bbny ḥwšk mmgylwt mdbr yhwdh*) and others who maintain that 1QM reflects a knowledge of Roman military practice at the end of the first century BC.

2.　Certainly the Righteous Teacher is not responsible for the *Rule* in its extant form; he may be the author of an earlier work from which the two textual forms found at Qumrân were expanded.

upper limit, while not certain, is suitably drawn about 150 BC; the lower limit, which I should regard as definitively fixed, falls not far from 100 BC; in other terms from the priesthood of Jonathan (160–142 BC) to the reign of Alexander Jannaeus (103–76 BC).

We can also attempt to limit the historical range within which Essene origins fall by analysis of the archaeological evidence for the foundation of the community center of Khirbet Qumrân. In the second chapter we argued that on the basis of the coin series and related data we must fix the date of the earliest installations no earlier than the reign of Simon (142–134 BC), no later, probably, than the reign of John Hyrcanus I (134–104 BC).

It can be argued that the foundation of the community need not be coeval with work of the founder of the sect, or with the crucial events which led to its separation from the body of Judaism. However, such an argument can stand only with the greatest difficulty. All evidence points to the assumption that the Teacher led his flock into the desert, and certainly our earliest sectarian documents presume the existence of the settlement in the wilderness.

Methodologically, we should begin our study of the commentaries by seeking out the most explicit historical allusions, first of all, and relating them, if we can, to the history of the sect.

In a commentary on Nahum (4QpNah.) there is an exposition of Nahum 2.12-13 in which names are named without the usual veil of a biblical sobriquet and events are brought together in such fashion that we can, I think, place them in a known historical context.[1] The key readings are as follows: (1.2) '[This is to be interpreted as referring to Deme]trius, the Greek king who attempted to enter Jerusalem at the advice of "Those who Seek Flattery"[2]...'; (1.3) '...the Greek kings from Antiochus until the accession[3] of the rulers of the Kittīyîm'; and (1.6-7)

---

1.   The document was published by J.M. Allegro in *DJD V*, pp. 37-42.

2.   The phrase *dwršy hhlqwt* 'seekers of flattery' is a designation taken from the "prediction" of Dan. 11.32 where it is said that 'those who act wickedly against the covenant, he (Antiochus Epiphanes) will pervert with *flattery*'. Presumably the term applies in the Qumrân texts to Jews with Hellenistic leanings, no doubt a broad category from the sectarian point of view.

3.   *'md* regularly has the technical sense, 'to take office'. Cf. the usage of *m'md*, 'station, office'.

'...This is to be interpreted as referring to the "Wrathful Lion"...[1] [ ]
who hangs men alive...'

The exposition deals with a very small unit of Scripture and in all
probability deals with a single series of events. On this assumption we
must look for a setting in the framework set by the text itself, in the era
of the Greek kings between Antiochus and the establishment of Kittaean
rulers in the East. The Antiochus in question is probably Antiochus IV,
Epiphanes (175–163 BC), though a later important Seleucid such as
Antiochus VII, Sidetes (138–129 BC), is not excluded. The Kittaean
rulers seem clearly enough to be the Roman rulers who arrive on the
scene beginning with Pompey, who conquered Jerusalem in 63 BC.[2] In

1.   The designation 'Wrathful Lion' is most suitably applied to the Judaean
opponent of Demetrius, and it seems clear enough, despite breaks in the text of ll.5-8,
that he is responsible for the crucifixions mentioned. Admittedly, however, this
construction depends finally on one's interpretation of the whole.
2.   Aemilius Scaurus, governor of the Syrian province in 62 BC which included
Judaea, is mentioned by name (*'mylyws*) in an unpublished calendar from Cave IV,
along with Šĕlāmṣîyôn (Alexandria 76–67 BC) and other known historical figures.
J.T. Milik, who will publish the document, was kind enough to show the text to the
writer in the summer of 1956. [Recently published is a prayer for King Jonathan,
certainly to be identified with Alexander Jannaeus (103-76 BC). See Esther Eshel,
Hanan Eshel, and Ada Yardeni, 'A Qumran Composition Containing Part of Ps. 154
and a Prayer for the Welfare of King Jonathan and his Kingdom', *IEJ* 42 (1992),
pp. 199-229.]
      The identification of the Kittîyîm (pronounced in this period *Kittî'îm*) with the
Romans, both in 4QpNah. and 1QpHab., and normally at least in IQM, appears to me
to be established. The documents all date to the Roman period. And we have argued
that they were *composed* in the Roman period on grounds quite independent of the
Kittîyîm problem. In my opinion, the reading in 1QpHab. 9.4-5 ('This is to be
interpreted as referring to the last priests of Jerusalem who gathered wealth and riches
from the spoil of the peoples whose wealth and booty is to be given into the hand of
the Kittaean army') must refer to Pompey's conquest. Cf. 1QpMic. 11.12-13;
4QpNah., 11. Any remaining doubts are dispelled by the Nahum *péšer*.
      Professor Rowley argues with erudition, however, against the identification (see
most recently, 'The Kittim and the Dead Sea Scrolls', pp. 92-109). Behind his argument is a strong inclination to assume that identification of the Kittîyîm with the
Romans disqualifies the view that Essene origins are pre-Roman. This is not the case,
I think, any more than the mention of an Antiochus disqualifies a post-Maccabean
date for the beginnings of the sect. The Righteous Teacher and the Wicked Priest are
never directly associated with Antiochus, the Kittîyîm, or with the Wrathful Lion for
that matter. Juxtaposition of the mention of events of sectarian beginnings and the mention of the Romans in 1QpHabakkuk in exposition of different sections of Habakkuk

this framework we must look for (1) an attempt by a Greek king named Demetrius to enter Jerusalem, preferably in an attack on a Judaean prince who (2) crucified men alive.

Of the Greek kings named Demetrius, Demetrius III (Eukairos), is the most suitable candidate.[1] His adversary was Alexander Jannaeus, the priest-king of Judaea from 103–76 BC. Josephus records that an open civil war broke out in Jannaeus' reign, continuing for six years (93–88 BC) during which a reported fifty thousand Jews were killed. In 88 BC the desperate enemies of Jannaeus called upon Demetrius Eukairos for succor. Demetrius met Jannaeus at Shechem and decisively defeated him. However, Demetrius was not permitted to follow up his victory. The Jews who had asked his help and fought with him suddenly went over to the side of their archfoe, Jannaeus. This strange behavior can be explained, I think, by assuming that Demetrius proposed (perhaps on the advice of Hellenists) to attack the capital and subjugate Judaea once more to the Seleucid crown. Only under such circumstances would there be sufficient incentive to induce Jewish rebels—and even in this case only the more orthodox—to desert to Jannaeus.[2] When Demetrius was forced to retire in the face of Jannaeus' new strength, the latter was successful in stamping out the rebels. In the process we are told that he crucified captives in wholesale lots.[3]

does not prejudice the question of the precise date of the Teacher's ministry; it only illustrates the fact discussed above that the commentaries contain traditions of exegesis developed over a considerable period of time, written down late.

1.   Professor Rowley ('4QpNahum and the Teacher of Righteousness', pp. 188-93) has argued that Demetrius I (Soter) may be referred to in this context. Against his position it must be argued that Demetrius I is not described appropriately as having 'attempted to enter into Jerusalem'. It is true that two of his generals, Bacchides and the infamous Nicanor, were sent to Jerusalem (the king himself did not come), but both entered Jerusalem freely. Indeed both Bacchides and Nicanor used Jerusalem as headquarters for their actions against Judas in the hinterlands. When Nicanor was killed remnants of his army fled to Jerusalem for refuge; and Bacchides fortified the city against Jonathan (1 Macc. 9.52-53). It seems rather unlikely that one would speak of 'an attempt to enter Jerusalem' unless the attempt was against opposition and was not carried out. And if it were a famous *general* who *entered* Jerusalem, why speak of the *king trying* to enter?

2.   J.M. Allegro adopts this proposal for the specific occasion on which Demetrius 'sought to enter Jerusalem' in his publication of 4QpNah., 'Further Light on the History of the Qumrân Sect', *JBL* 75 (1956), pp. 85-95, esp. 92; cf. C. Rabin, 'Alexander Jannaeus and the Pharisees', *JJS* 7 (1956), pp. 3-11.

3.   Josephus, *Antiq.* XIII, 372-83; *War* I, 90-98.

This construction, while theoretical in part, admirably fits our requirements. What does it tell us of the history of the Essenes? The Wrathful Lion and the events of his time discovered in the prophecy of Nahum by the sectarians certainly belong to 'their history', that is, to the 'end of days'. This is the pattern of exegesis in the commentaries. However, we have no way of knowing whether the terrible events in the reign of one of the illegitimate priests of Jerusalem (to speak from an Essene point of view) belong early or late in the history of the sect.[1] There is no mention of the Righteous Teacher in connection with the events, and no reason to connect the Wrathful Lion with the figures of the era of Essene origins such as the wicked priest *par excellence* whose biblical sobriquet seems to be the False Oracle (*maṭṭîp hak-kāzāb*) or more simply the False One ('*îš hak-kāzāb*).[2] Just as we cannot date the foundation of the sect in the Roman era because of references to Pompey's conquest of Jerusalem in the Habakkuk Commentary or the mention of Aemilius Scaurus in the calendar from Cave IV, so we are not obliged to date the beginning of the movement in the time of Jannaeus. On the other hand we are quite near the minimal date fixed on archaeological and paleographical grounds, and cannot absolutely exclude a date for the rise of the sect in the early reign of Jannaeus.[3]

Our task is much simplified. We have learned something of the problems which are raised in the study of the expository writings of Qumrân and we have limited the scope of our search for the beginnings of the Qumrân sect to the second half of the second century BC.

2. *The Righteous Teacher and the Wicked Priest*

The key to any sound reconstruction of the historical circumstances which gave rise to the Essene movement lies in an adequate explanation of the peculiarly priestly character of the early schismatic community.

In the extended introductory exposition of the Damascus Document are several crucial passages dealing with the origin of the sect. In one of these (*CD* 3.18–4.4)[4] the sectarian author discovers in 1 Sam. 2.35 and

---

1.   Cf. H.H. Rowley, 'The Kittim and the Dead Sea Scrolls', p. 94.
2.   See below, p. 116, nn. 4 and 5.
3.   Josephus' testimony to the prophecy of Judas the Essene (*Antiq.* XIII, 311-13; *War* I, 78-80) in the reign of Aristobulus I (104–103 BC) argues strongly for a pre-Jannaeus date for Essene origins. Cf. Milik, *Découvertes*, p. 60.
4.   See above, Chapter 2, p. 86, n. 2.

Ezek. 44.15 prophecies of the origin of his sect. The passage reads as follows:

> And God in his wondrous secret counsels made atonement for their trans-
> gression and forgave their iniquity, and he built for them a 'faithful (priestly)
> house'[1] the like of which has never arisen, formerly or lately. Those who
> hold fast to (this house) shall live forever, and all human glory is theirs,
> even as God promised them through Ezekiel the prophet, saying, 'the
> priests and the Levites and [*sic!*] the sons of Zadok who kept the office of
> my Sanctuary when the children of Israel went astray from me, they shall
> bring me fat and blood.' The 'priests' are the repentant of Israel who went
> out from the land of Judah...and the 'sons of Zadok' are the chosen of
> Israel, the 'Elect of the Name'[2] who shall arise in the end of days.[3]

The founder of the sect, the Righteous Teacher, was himself a priest. The
'opposite number' of the Righteous Priest was the Wicked Priest, the
archpersecutor of the sect. The priests of Qumrân regarded the
Jerusalem sanctuary as defiled, its priests false, its calendar unorthodox.
In the end of days the Essene (Zadokite) priesthood would be re-estab-
lished in the New Jerusalem, the false priesthood overthrown for ever.
Meanwhile, the Essene community is organized as an ideal priestly
theocracy. Priests dominate its councils, take precedence in its protocols;
a priestly Messiah overshadows the royal Messiah in visions of the New
Age. The whole life of the community is shaped in the interest of
Priestly objectives. In short the Essenes are a counter-Israel organized by
a counter-priesthood, 'true' Israel led by the 'legitimate' priesthood.[4]

All this suggests that the origin of the Essene movement must be
sought for in the struggle of rival priestly houses, the one hyperorthodox
and presumably legitimate, the other less orthodox but successful in
gaining control of the high priesthood and Jerusalem cultus.[5] The
founders of the sect would thus be found among priests whose authority

---

1. Cf. 1QS 8.9, where a parallel expression recalling 1 Sam. 2.35 is used of the
sect.

2. A favorite biblical sobriquet of the sect taken from Num. 16.2; cf. 1QSa II, 2,
11, 13. Probably the expression 'the Name' is not to be understood in its sense in
Num. 16.2, but as reference to the divine name (cf. 1QS 6.27).

3. Cf. 1QS 5.2, 9; 1QSa I, 2, 24; II, 3; 1QSb III, 22-23, etc.

4. If the conclusions drawn at the close of Chapter 2 are correct, we may add that
the Essenes also instituted a counter-sacrificial cultus.

5. This view, by no means new, is worked out most persuasively by Vermès and
Milik. See G. Vermès, *Les manuscrits du Désert de Juda*, pp. 78-89; and J.T. Milik,
Découvertes, Chap. III.

was lost, whose orthodox convictions were flouted, whose hopes for establishing a faithful theocracy in Israel had turned to despair, but who turned for comfort and new hope in an apocalyptic priestly community.

Within the chronological framework we have established, there is little difficulty in discovering the occasion for the birth of a dissident priestly sect. The history of the Maccabees is the story of the decay of the ancient line of Zadokite high priests, and the rise of a vigorous new house of reigning priests.

The last of the great high priests of the old Zadokite (Sadducean) line was a priest of the Oniad family, Simon II, who died about 200 BC.[1] Ben Sira sings the praises of Simon in Ch. 50 of Ecclesiasticus, ending with the pious hope that the 'covenant of Phinehas', that is, the high-priestly office,[2] will never pass from him or his descendants.[3] Ironically enough his line failed in his sons Onias III and Jason. The Oniad house was divided over the confused politico-religious issues of the day. Onias III, who had succeeded his father Simon, was pro-Egyptian by political persuasion and is pictured as defender of the ancient faith. In any case he opposed the strong policy of Hellenization imposed by Antiochus Epiphanes (175–163 BC). His brother Jason, whether out of personal ambition or because of genuine pro-Syrian sympathies we cannot be certain, allied himself with the Syrian party and was willing, even eager, to expedite the process of Hellenizing Jewry. In Jason's struggle for power he finally approached Antiochus, offering him a sum of money to recognize him as high priest in his brother's stead. Jason's move, however, set an ominous precedent. In the past the Greek kings had not interfered, normally, with the regular succession of the high priests. The Tobiad clan, long rivals of the high-priestly family for political sway in Judaea, had never dared to challenge directly the right of the Oniads to the supreme office in the land. But when the power to appoint high

---

1. On the question of the identification of Simon with Simon the Just, see the discussion and literature cited by R. Marcus, *Josephus* (ed. Loeb) VII (Cambridge, 1943), Appendix B.

2. Cf. Num. 25.12-13; Eccles. 45.24; and 1 Macc. 2.54.

3. Presumably the Essenes approved of Ben Sira, since a copy of a Hebrew version appeared in Cave II, Qumrân. On the present passage, preserved in the quoted form only in the Hebrew text, and the significant passage in the hymn inserted in the Hebrew version at 51.12 ('Give thanks to Him who elects the sons of Zadok to be priests' [51.12.ix]), see J. Trinquet, 'Les liens "sadocites" de l'Ecrit de Damas, des manuscrits de la Mer Morte, et de l'Ecclésiastique', *VT* 1 (1951), pp. 287-92.

priests passed into the hands of Antiochus at the instigation of an Oniad, the Tobiads were quick to see an opportunity to break the power of the Oniad family. Their protégé was a certain Menelaus, the son of a Temple official, but not of Zadokite family.[1] Within four years of Jason's accession to office Menelaus succeeded in capturing Antiochus' appointment to the high priesthood. The strife between the rival houses led by Jason and Menelaus shortly became open civil war, and in the resulting chaos Antiochus found opportunity to carry out his fearful massacres, terminating in the desecration of the Temple in 167 BC, and the complete Hellenization of the city. The stage was now set for the rise of the Maccabees, whose destiny it was to win independence for the Jews, and with it to establish a new high-priestly house.

In the early days of the Maccabean revolt, shortly before Mattathias' death in 166 BC, we hear for the first time of a certain 'congregation of the Ḥasîdîm (Assideans)...all of whom devote themselves to the Law' (1 Macc. 2.42).[2] Nothing is said explicitly in our sources of their origins or destiny. Presumably they included priestly and lay elements of strict faith who found themselves leaderless with the decay of the Zadokite priesthood in the reign of Antiochus. In the warfare between Jason and Menelaus they had no recourse but to stand aloof, since with the victory of either their cause was lost.

The Maccabean uprising gained their support, at least in its early stages. But they never rallied wholeheartedly to the Maccabean cause, it seems, and with the appointment of Alcimus, the successor of Menelaus, were quick to seek a reconciliation with the new high priest.[3] This circumstance is puzzling. Alcimus was the pro-Syrian appointee of the Seleucid throne.[4] We are told, on the one hand, that while the

---

1.   On the ancestry of Menelaus, see 2 Macc. 4.23 (cf. 3.4); Josephus, *Antiq.* XII, 238; and the discussion of H.H. Rowley, *The Zadokite Fragments and the Dead Sea Scrolls*, p. 67, n. 7.

2.   The latter phrase strikes a familiar chord; the Qumrân texts speak of 'those who devote themselves' to the covenant, truth, community, or holiness. Cf. 1QS 5.1, 6, 8, 10, 21, 22; 6.13; 1Q14, X.7; and W.H. Brownlee, *The Dead Sea Manual of Discipline*, p. 7, n. 5, who already makes the combination with 1 Macc. 2.42.

3.   Cf. 1 Macc. 7.15 (vs. 2 Macc. 14.6).

4.   Josephus, *Antiq.* XII, 387; 1 Macc. 7.5-9; 2 Macc. 14.3, 13; cf. *Antiq.* XX, 235. Alcimus was appointed about 162 BC, probably by Antiochus Eupator, confirmed by Demetrius I (Soter). In any case, the conflicts in our sources are not serious ones.

Maccabees actively opposed Alcimus,[1] the Hasîdîm trusted him and sought to come to terms with him because he was 'of the seed of Aaron'. On the other hand, Josephus says flatly that he was not of the house of Onias III.[2] An explanation may be found for this set of circumstances if Alcimus were descended from a collateral branch of the Zadokite line,[3] and hence in some sense a legitimate high priest. At all events, Alcimus betrayed their trust, and they returned to the Maccabean camp.[4]

Probably in the congregation of the Hasîdîm, devoted to the ancient Law and no doubt to the Zadokite priesthood, uneasy allies of the Maccabean warrior priests, we find ancestors of the Essene sectaries who appeared in the desert of Qumrân in the next generation.

Support for this view may be found in an introductory section of the Damascus Document:

> In the epoch of wrath, three hundred and ninety years[5] after he gave them into the power of Nebuchadnezzar, king of Babylon, he visited them and caused a root of planting[6] to sprout from Israel and from Aaron to possess His land[7] and to grow rich with the good things of His land. And they came to understand their iniquity and to know that they were guilty men; but they were like blind men or like those who grope for the way twenty years. And God recognized their works, that they sought Him with a whole heart and so raised up for them a Righteous Teacher to make them tread in the way of His heart and to instruct the last generations that which He would do in the last generation against the congregation of the false. (*CD* 1.5-12)

1.   1 Macc. 7.14-16; Josephus, *Antiq.* XX, 235.

2.   *Antiq.* XII, 387.

3.   On Lysias' advice, Antiochus Eupator had Menelaus put to death. Yet the rightful successor, Onias IV, was by-passed. Presumably Lysias sought to conciliate the Jews and re-establish peace by siding neither with the Oniad nor Tobiad houses. *Antiq.* XII, 382-88.

4.   1 Macc. 7.13-17.

5.   On the construction of the phrase, see E. Wiesenberg's 'Chronological Data in the Zadokite Fragments', *VT* 5 (1955), pp. 284-308. While his conclusions appear to me unacceptable, he has collected valuable data bearing on the problem.

6.   A favorite appellation from prophecy (Isa. 60.21; 61.3) applied by the sect to themselves. Cf. 1QS 8.5-8; 1 Cor. 3.9.

7.   The expression (from Isa. 60.21) is understood eschatologically as in 4QpPs. 37.

The scriptural number '390' (Ezek. 4.5) cannot be used for precise calculation.[1] It was a round number of prophecy put to Essene use. Perhaps the era to be spanned is from the Exile to the days of Antiochus Epiphanes.[2] The key figure, however, is the twenty years in which the priests and laity wandered like blind men before the commencement of the Righteous Teacher's ministry. The period of groping, that is, when the forerunners were 'right-minded' but wrong in their discernment of their proper duty, best corresponds to the period in which the Ḥasîdîm were in active support of the Maccabees, roughly from the 160s to the 140s BC.[3]

If these various assumptions are true, then the Righteous Teacher began his ministry late in the reign of Jonathan (160–142 BC) or early in the reign of Simon (142–134 BC), and was a Zadokite priest of Hasidic sympathies. In any case, this construction of events points us precisely toward the period required by the external criteria of archaeological and paleographical analysis: the second half of the second century BC.

The period of troubles for the Zadokite priesthood rose to a crisis after the death of Alcimus (159 BC).[4] No official high priest was appointed, apparently, for a period of some seven years.[5] In this interval Jonathan together with his brother Simon gained control of the land outside Jerusalem, alternating between times of consolidation and periods in the field against the armies of Demetrius I; apparently a kind of rump government was established at Michmash with Jonathan at its head, while the Hellenistic party ruled in Jerusalem. In 152 BC Jonathan's fortunes shifted abruptly. Alexander Balas, the alleged son of Antiochus IV, appeared in Syria claiming Demetrius' throne. In the ensuing struggle Demetrius and Alexander began to bid for the support of Jonathan and his army, with the result that Jonathan first was enabled to seize Jerusalem and refortify the city and Temple (on the bid of Demetrius), and then by deftly shifting to the support of Alexander, to win appointment as high priest of the Jews. At the Feast of Tabernacles

1. Cf. the discussion and literature cited by Rowley, *The Zadokite Fragments and the Dead Sea Scrolls*, pp. 62-64.
2. Cf. 4QpNah., 1.3.
3. Compare J.T. Milik's treatment, *Découvertes*, Appendice.
4. Cf. *Antiq*. XII, 413; 1 Macc. 9.54-57.
5. Josephus, *Antiq*. XII, 414, 419, 434, states that Judas was made high priest by the people, and was high priest three years. In *Antiq*. XX, 237, however, there is a statement to the effect that there was a priestly interregnum of seven years. Finally 1 Macc. seems to place the death of Alcimus after that of Judas.

in 152 he formally was invested with the robes of his office.

This was the initial step in the usurpation of the high priesthood by the new Hasmonaean house. No doubt Jonathan's readiness to accept the Syrian king's appointment to the high priesthood confirmed the fears and crystallized the opposition of the Zadokite elements of the Hasîdîm, as well as some strict lay members belonging to this wing of Judaism. However, Jonathan's appointment to office followed the pattern initiated by Jason and Menelaus. He was charismatic leader of his people in the war for independence not yet won—a Syrian garrison still resided in Jerusalem—but *de facto* high priest, not by will of his people but by appointment of their suzerain.[1] It was not yet wholly clear, from the point of view of the Zadokite priesthood, that a new high-priestly dynasty was being established once for all...though the handwriting on the wall can be read by the historian. The final and decisive step was to be taken by Simon, Jonathan's successor.

Meanwhile, Alexander and Demetrius passed from the Syrian scene, and two new rivals, Demetrius II and Tryphon, the latter as the ostensible protector of Alexander Balas' young son, Antiochus VI (145–142 BC), fought for supremacy over the Seleucid empire. Jonathan again advanced the interests of Jewish independence by playing one off against the other. However, Tryphon turned on Jonathan finally and by treachery captured him at Ptolemais. When word came from Ptolemais of his brother's captivity Simon at once took leadership and hastened to complete the walls of Jerusalem, fortifying the city in anticipation of Tryphon's attack.[2] After an attempt at negotiation of the release of Jonathan in which Tryphon proved false, Simon opposed the Syrian with the Jewish army. Tryphon chose prudently not to attack frontally but, circling, took his forces home to Syria through Trans-Jordan, murdering Jonathan en route (142 BC).

The lot had fallen upon Simon to bring to a completion the work of his warrior brothers. Simon is glorified as the 'man of counsel' of the five Maccabean brothers in 1 Maccabees; and while Judas is appointed in the blessing of his father to be the captain in fighting the battle of the people, Simon is named 'father' of the brethren, and indeed is

---

1.   Jonathan did not dare claim for his family the full right to the high-priestly office though he functioned as high priest. This suggests that Zadokite opposition to the Hasmonaeans had not yet been broken.
2.   1 Macc. 13.1-11.

mentioned first.[1] This reflects, of course, the major role of Simon in the eyes of this historian. Simon, the last of the brothers, was finally to achieve for the first time full independence for his people; he was to be established as the founder of a new high-priestly line.

Simon immediately upon Tryphon's withdrawal set to work fortifying his entire realm.[2] He offered recognition and support to Demetrius II, the rival of Tryphon, in exchange for full freedom from taxation, full recognition of Jewish control of all fortified sites in Judaea, forgiveness for all unpaid tribute and taxes, amnesty for all past disloyal acts against the Seleucid crown.[3] Demetrius, in his desperate need for support, had no alternative but to award all the privileges demanded by the Jews. Apparently Simon was recognized at this time by Demetrius as high priest.[4]

According to 1 Maccabees, a new era was established in Israel, dating from the first year of Simon (142 BC). Actually the full independence of Judaea is better reckoned from the following year when Simon succeeded at last in driving out the Syrian garrison from the citadel of Jerusalem, a quarter century after its establishment by Antiochus IV.[5] He further fortified the Temple hill alongside the citadel, as well as the citadel itself, and established himself there with his men.[6]

In the third year of Simon's reign, 140 BC, a great assembly was held of 'the priests and people and the heads of the nation and the elders of the country'. The decree of the assembly was engraved in bronze and set up on stelae in Mount Zion. The decree, after the introductory formula, eulogizes 'Simon, son of Mattathias...of the sons of Joarib and his brethren [who] exposed themselves to danger and stood firm against the enemies of their nation so that their sanctuary and their Law might be established and so have greatly glorified their nation.'

> And Jonathan assembled his people and became a high priest to them and was gathered to his people. And their enemies proposed to invade their

1.   1 Macc. 2.65.
2.   1 Macc. 13.33; 14.33-34, 37-38.
3.   1 Macc. 13.34-40.
4.   See 1 Macc. 13.36; 14.38.
      Josephus (*Antiq.* XIII, 213) telescopes the first three years of Simon in such fashion that he is of no help in indicating the conditions under which Simon took up priestly duties.
5.   1 Macc. 13.49-53; cf. *Mĕgillat Ta'anît*, 5.
6.   1 Macc. 13.53; 14.37.

country in order to devastate their country and stretch forth their hand against their sanctuary. Then rose Simon and fought for his nation and he spent much of his own wealth, armed the warriors of his people, and gave them pay. And he fortified the cities of Judaea...

And the people saw the faithfulness of Simon and the glory which he proposed to bring to his nation and they established him as their leader and highpriest because of all these things he had done, and for the justice and faith which he had shown to his people, and because he had striven in every way to exalt his people. And in his days, through his successful conducting of affairs, the (foreign) nations were removed from their country, as well as those (foreigners) who were in the City of David, i.e., those who were in Jerusalem, who had built a citadel for themselves from which they sallied forth to pollute the area about the sanctuary and greatly sully its purity. And he invested [this citadel] with Jews and fortified it for the security of the country and the city, and elevated the walls of Jerusalem. King Demetrius confirmed the high priesthood to him in accord with these events, and made him one of his 'Friends' and gave him great honor...(1 Macc. 14.30-39).

The most important part of the decree now follows in which it is officially affirmed that:[1]

The Jews and the priests were pleased that Simon should be their leader (ἡγούμενος), and high priest forever, until a faithful prophet should arise, and that he should be their general (στρατηγός), and take charge of the holy things (of the sanctuary)...that he be obeyed by all and that all documents in the country be written in his name, and that he be dressed in purple and wear gold.

And none, neither one of the laity nor one of the priests should be allowed to set aside any part of these (decisions) or to countermand orders given by him or to gather an assembly in the country apart from him, or dress in purple and wear a gold ornament. Whoever should act contrary to these (decisions), or set aside any part of these should be liable to punishment.

All the people were pleased to grant Simon the right to act according to these words; and Simon accepted and was pleased to act as high priest and to be the general and governor of the Jews and of the priests and to be the chief of all. (1 Macc. 14.41-47).

---

1.   On the construction καὶ ὅτι at the beginning of 14.41, see F.-M. Abel, *Les livres des Maccabées* (Paris, 1949), p. 260, n. 41. However the syntactical (or textual) problem is to be solved, it is certain that the body of the (original) decree is to be found in vv. 41-47.

Several points in the decree must be examined closely. The decree is more than a mere eulogy of Simon.[1] It officially proclaims that Simon and his sons are established as the progenitors of a perpetual high priesthood 'until a faithful prophet arise' (in the last days). Moreover, the decree has teeth; it warns against opposition to Simon, by layman or *priest*, including a prohibition of private assembly, threatening punishment to anyone who acts contrary to any of the stipulations of the decree. This decree reflects not merely a spontaneous welling-up of gratitude and praise for a hero. It is the decree of an assembly of priests and laity controlled by pro-Maccabean elements which officially recognizes the Hasmonaean dynasty and turns the *de facto* rights and privileges enjoyed by Jonathan into rights *de jure* for Simon's *house*.

Thus in the early years of Simon the high priesthood was irrevocably transferred from the Zadokites to the Hasmonaeans. We cannot expect our primary source, 1 Maccabees, with its overwhelmingly pro-Maccabean bias, to give attention to Zadokite opposition to Simon. No doubt, however, the priestly elements of Zadokite lineage furnished a continuing and steadily mounting opposition from the days of Jonathan's usurpation under the aegis of Alexander Balas until Simon's ultimate election by the priests and the people.

That there was opposition to such a shift from *de facto* to *de jure* status for a non-Zadokite high-priestly house is patent in the threat against those who give a show of disobedience. Probably also we must recognize a tacit acknowledgment that the legitimate priesthood is being set aside in the phrase '...high priest forever, until a faithful prophet arise'. That is, the house of Simon is, in an ultimate sense, provisional, at least until pronounced legitimate over against the Zadokite house by the 'faithful prophet' who will decide such matters in the last days. Simon's house is prepared to rule in the present age and abide by the decision of the eschatological spokesman of God.

With the decree condemning all opposition to Simon, we discern clearly the new high priest's determination to stamp out, indeed to persecute, those who refuse to recognize the full legitimacy of his office. This program, falling in the early years of Simon, seems to give the appropriate occasion for the crystallization of the Essene sect, its persecution and the persecution of its Righteous Teacher, and the exile in the wilderness of Judah. All was now lost from the point of view of pious Zadokite priests. Simon's power and popularity were over-

---

1.   Cf. Abel, *loc. cit.* and the literature cited.

whelming. His exaltation to the high-priestly office was by the election of the priesthood and elders of Israel, and not merely by the appointment of the Syrian suzerain. And Simon had gained hereditary rights to the high priesthood for his seed.

The historical setting of Essene origins seems to be established by the convergence of our several lines of inquiry. The detailed task of seeking out concrete identifications of the main figures and events concealed in the veiled apocalyptic language of the Qumrân texts is more difficult and at best precarious. Nevertheless we propose to attempt tentative reconstructions of the careers of the Wicked Priest and the Righteous Teacher.

Our chief data for reconstructing the career of the Wicked Priest, the adversary of the Righteous Teacher, is found in the commentary on Habakkuk.[1]

Among the important passages for our purposes are the following. In 8.8-13 we read, 'This is to be interpreted as referring to the Wicked Priest (quoting Hab. 2.6) who was called by a trustworthy name[2] when he first took office, but when he ruled over Israel became proud and forsook God and betrayed the statutes (of the Law) for the sake of wealth. He robbed and gathered the wealth of violent men who had rebelled against God, and seized the wealth of peoples, so further burdening himself with guilt. And he engaged in abominable practices, in every manner of impurity.' The information provided is less specific than we should like. We learn that the Wicked Priest before or at the beginning of his rise to power had a good name. Either he was known as trustworthy or, perhaps, bore a name, Simon, which had good associations for the sectarians. The text is too vague to be certain. Further, the priest for the sake of wealth and ambition fattened himself with the loot of violence, most of it, no doubt, taken in wars against neighboring peoples. He appears to be rebuked for not 'devoting' the spoil to God in accord with the laws of Holy War. Most of this data can

1. 1QpHab. 1.13; 8.8-13; 8.16–9.2; 9.9-12; 9.16–10.5; 11.12-15; 12.2-6; 12.7-10.

2. The phrase appears in the Old Testament in contexts where one is called by another's name (cf. Gen. 48.6; Ezra 2.61; cf. 1 Chron. 23.14; Elliger, *SzHK*, p. 198). To be called by a 'trustworthy name' may mean no more than that Simon had a good reputation. On the other hand it may be an allusion to the fact that Simon had the same name as the beloved Simon II (the Just?) celebrated in Ben Sira, the last of the great Zadokite high priests.

be fitted with equal ease to any of the warrior high priests from Jonathan to Alexander Jannaeus. The first phrase, however, if it suggests a change in the status of the priest in the eyes of the sectarians, applies aptly only to Jonathan and Simon. Jonathan began as a military hero, only later accepting the high-priestly office. Simon was a man of counsel, self-effacing during his brothers' turns at leadership. On Jonathan's captivity he provided his substance as well as leadership in saving Jerusalem from Tryphon. Once established in power, however, he arrogated to himself and to his seed the high-priestly office, and affected a royal robe.

Several passages speak of the dreadful end of the Wicked Priest. IQpHabakkuk 9.9-12 is one of the more important of these.[1] 'This is to be interpreted as referring to the Wicked Priest whom, because of transgression against the Righteous Teacher and the men of his party, God gave into the hand of his enemies to bring him low with a mortal blow...' The passage immediately suggests Jonathan's end at the hand of Tryphon.[2] It may be applied also to the death of Simon at the hands of Ptolemy, son of Abubos (Ḥabūb) and his men.

In order to understand better the application of this passage to the peculiar conditions of Simon's demise, as well as to prepare a basis for additional passages shortly to be discussed, a review of the last days of Simon is desirable.

In 140 BC, the year in which the decree confirming Simon in his high-priestly office was set up in Mount Zion, Demetrius was absent in Media fighting the Parthians. He was taken captive by the Parthians, and for a few years the Jews were untroubled by the contenders for the Seleucid throne, living in peace. 'Simon's peace' is celebrated in the ode of 1 Macc. 14.4-15; it was a period in which he consolidated his office and realm; however, the period of peace proved short-lived. In 138 Antiochus VII, Sidetes, brother of Demetrius, was successful in invading Syria, ousting Tryphon, and securing the realm. Almost immediately he

---

1.   1QpHab. 8.16–9.2 also speaks of the horrors of the Wicked Priest's death, almost certainly. For a detailed discussion of some of the problems of the passage, see Elliger, *SzHK*, pp. 202-3. Cf. 9.16–10.5 (?). Regularly the author describes the death in hyperbolic images. The priest is struck down by a divine blow, suffers the pangs of the damned, etc. None of these figures can be made to walk on all fours. In effect all point to a violent death at the hand of enemies, and we can say little more.

On 1QpHab. 11.12-15, and 4QpPs. 37, Pl. 3b ll. 3-4, see below.

2.   So Milik and Vermès.

took steps to reassert Syrian control of Judaea, demanding that the concessions granted by Demetrius (and by himself before he came to power) be given up. Simon, confident in his new strength, refused, and hostilities between the Seleucid power and the Jewish theocracy commenced anew.

Antiochus sent Kendebaios, one of his generals, to re-establish control of the Palestinian coastal plains preparatory to an attack on Judaea proper. Simon countered by sending his eldest two sons, Judas and John Hyrcanus, to oppose Kendebaios. Judas and John were successful in defeating the Syrian general in the plain between Modin and Azotus. Antiochus was forced to seek other means to subdue the Jews under Simon.

1 Maccabees turns abruptly from the defeat of Kendebaios to the tragic death of Simon and his sons. In February, 134 BC, Simon, together with Judas (probably his eldest son[1]) and his youngest son, Mattathias, toured the cities of Judah, evidently reviewing the forts which he had built or which were under construction.[2] No doubt Simon was preparing against the attack of Antiochus Sidetes who struck later in the same year.[3]

In this connection, Simon and his sons descended to Jericho, administered by Ptolemy, son of Abubos. The latter appears to have been of Idumaean stock, more or less Judaized to judge from the fact that he had married into the high-priestly family. The district of Jericho was heavily Idumaean in population in this period, and normally formed a district separated from Judaea proper.[4] Unknown to Simon, Ptolemy had organized a plot of considerable proportions,[5] no doubt with the

---

1.   Cf. 1 Macc. 16.2, 14. In 16.2, Judas is named before John in speaking of the eldest two sons. On the other hand, John has already been appointed governor of Gezer (13.53) and may in fact be the eldest. Josephus, *Antiq.* XIII, 228, speaks of three sons, but in XIII, 247, speaks of another brother, probably in error.

2.   1 Macc. 16.14. ἐφοδεύειν is used here in its technical sense.

3.   Josephus, *Antiq.* XIII, 236. Antiochus reduced Judaea in 134 BC, besieged Jerusalem in 133–32, finally bringing the capitulation of John Hyrcanus and the destruction of the walls of Jerusalem. Cf. *Antiq.* XIII, 236–47; *War* I, 61 cf. 1 Macc. 16.23.

4.   On Ptolemy's background, and the character of the Jericho 'nome', see Abel, *Maccabées*, p. 280; *Histoire de la Palestine* I (Paris, 1952), p. 205.

5.   1 Macc. is laconic in reporting the character of Ptolemy's plot. We gather from the events that happened immediately following Simon's murder that Ptolemy's attempt to gain hegemony over Judaea was carefully ordered and had considerable

complicity of Antiochus VII,[1] to destroy Simon and his heirs, hoping to supplant Simon at Antiochus' appointment.

Ptolemy's opportunity came on the occasion of Simon's visit to the fortress of Doq, built on a high peak guarding Jericho.[2] 1 Maccabees (16.15) notes that the small fortress was built by Ptolemy. Presumably it was part of Simon's general program of fortifying Jericho carried out by Ptolemy as commanding officer, *strategós*, of Jericho. Ptolemy held a great banquet for Simon and his sons, having secreted certain of his men in the fortress. When Simon and his sons were drunk Ptolemy's men murdered Simon, and later his two sons.[3] Simon's remaining son, John Hyrcanus, was warned in time to protect himself against Ptolemy's assassins. His forces remained loyal so that he was able to overpower Ptolemy's partisans and assume the high priesthood before turning to face the armies of Antiochus Sidetes.

These events could well be described in Essene tradition in the words, 'God delivered him into the hand of his enemies to bring him low with a mortal blow.'[4]

Three other passages, two in the Habakkuk roll, one in the so-called

---

support outside of Jerusalem. Men were dispatched to Gezer to kill the remaining heir, John Hyrcanus; others were dispatched to take possession of Jerusalem; letters were sent to the generals of the army of Simon to win their allegiance (1 Macc. 16.19-20).

1.   The fact that Ptolemy immediately dispatched word of his *coup* to Antiochus Sidetes (1 Macc. 16.18), and asked for immediate assistance, suggests prior connivance on the part of Antiochus VII. Ptolemy could not hope to overthrow the popular and powerfully entrenched Maccabean party without backing from some quarter. No doubt he looked for support from dissident Hellenistic elements in Judaea, including the Idumaean faction. Ptolemy could not seek aid openly, however, and remain in Simon's confidence. It is thus even more likely that he acted with previous assurances of support from Antiochus.

2.   For the location of Doq on the 'Mount of Temptation', site of the later Byzantine monastery Δουκα, see Abel, *Géographie de la Palestine* II (Paris, 1938), 307; *Maccabées*, p. 281.

3.   Cf. *Antiq.* XIII, 228-39; 1 Macc. 16.16.

4.   In the late commentary to Ps. 37, in a fragment expounding Ps. 37.32-33 (*JBL* 75 [1956], Pl. 3b), the Wicked Priest is said to be given 'into the hands of violent foreigners' (*'rysy gw'ym*), apparently, though the reading is not completely certain. The phrase can be applied specifically to Ptolemy and his men; more likely, however, in this instance it must be taken more generally, including the Seleucid role in the affair.

Testimonia of Cave IV, are most easily connected with the circumstances of Simon's death.

The Testimonia Document[1] lists biblical prophecies relating to the chief figures expected by the sect in the last days. The first quotation speaks of the 'prophet like Moses'.[2] The second quotation, from Num. 24.15-17, concerns the Star of Jacob and the Scepter of Israel, the priestly and royal Messiahs respectively, expected by the sect.[3] The third quotation relates to the priesthood, quoting Deut. 33.8-11, including the phrase 'and taught thy judgments to Jacob, thy Torah to Israel'. This may refer again to the priestly Messiah, but much more probably refers to the Righteous Teacher.[4] The fourth and final quotation is taken from the sectarian Psalms of Joshua,[5] quoting the curse of Joshua upon Jericho in Josh. 6.26, 'Cursed before the Lord be the man that rises up and rebuilds this city [ ]. At the cost of his first born shall he lay its foundation, and at the cost of his youngest son shall he set up its gates' (RSV). The exposition (from the Psalms of Joshua) continues: 'and behold an accursed man, a son of Belial[6] has come to power to be a trapper's snare to his people and ruin to all his neighbors...' The context is broken,[7] and in the next line the two sons of the accursed man are

---

1.   The list is published as Document IV in Allegro's article, 'Further Messianic References in Qumran Literature', pp. 182-87 and Plate; cf. N. Wieder, 'Notes on the New Documents from the Fourth Cave of Qumran', *JJS* 7 (1956), pp. 71-76. [See now *DJD V*, pp. 57-60.]

2.   The quotation is from the 'Samaritan' recension of Exodus at Exod. 20.21 as first pointed out by Msgr. Patrick Skehan; cf. R.E. Brown, 'The Messianism of Qumrân', *CBQ* 19 (1957), p. 82.

3.   In the traditional exegesis of the sect, the Star and the Scepter are distinguished; cf. *CD* 7.19-20; Test. Levi 18.3. Milik's interpretation, that the citation applies only to the royal Messiah is wrong (*DJD I*, pp. 121 f.).

4.   The actual title of the Righteous Teacher is taken from Hos. 10.12 and Joel 2.23 (modified; cf. *CD* 6.11). However, Deut. 33.10 is most aptly applied to the Righteous Teacher (cf. Gaster, *op. cit.*, p. 5).

Allegro's reading *wy'yrw* should be corrected to *wy'wrw* (*ywrw* of MT); it is merely an orthographic aberrancy of familiar type.

5.   See C. Newsom, 'The "Psalms of Joshua" from Qumran, Cave 4', *JJS* 39 (1988), pp. 56-73.

6.   The text reads *'rwr 'yš bly'l* corrected to read *'yš 'rwr 'yš bly'l*. The original reading was probably *'yš 'rwr bn bly'l*.

7.   We should probably reconstruct: *w'md* (l. 25) [*w'*]*wmd*[*ym bnyw 'mw lh*]*ywt šnyhm kly ḥms*, 'and he rose to power, (l. 25) and his sons rose to power with him becoming instruments of violence'.

mentioned: '(so that) the two of them becoming violent instruments, and they have rebuilt the [city?]...and set up a wall and towers for it to make a stronghold of wickedness []...horrors in Ephraim and Judah []...[and they shall] commit sacrilege in the land...[bl]ood like water [...] on the battlements of the daughter of Zion and in the district of Jerusalem.'

The passage assuredly applies to an archenemy of the sect, and presumably therefore to the Wicked Priest. The application of the passage to Simon and his older and younger sons Judas and Mattathias, and their deaths in Jericho imposes itself. The slaughter in Jerusalem and its environs described in the last lines reflects the attack of Antiochus Sidetes upon Judaea in 134–132 BC immediately following Simon's death.[1]

Further support for the identification of the Wicked Priest with Simon is found in IQpHabakkuk 11.12-15: 'This means the priest whose dishonor was greater than his honor. For he did not circumcize the foreskin of his heart but walked in ways of drunkenness in order to quench (his) thirst. But the cup of God's wrath will swallow him up...!' The drunken high priest not merely drinks in carousals, the cup of wrath swallows him. The comment admirably fits Simon's drunken demise.[2]

One more passage requires our attention, IQpHabakkuk 11.4-8: 'This

---

1.   One looks in vain for another historical setting for the passage. J.T. Milik (*Découvertes, ad loc.*) has tried to make Jonathan and Simon the 'two sons', and apply the building of the city not to Jericho, the original context, but to Jerusalem, alluded to in the last lines. The difficulties here are obvious. The patriarch Mattathias had no part in the building, and himself was scarcely the villain of the sect. Moreover, it is awkward to apply a Jericho prophecy to Jerusalem, even given the methods of exegesis used by the Essenes.

But if one grants that the curse is reapplied to Jerusalem, which is certainly not impossible, we still must identify Simon with the accursed one, his two sons with the 'vessels of violence'. Jonathan, Simon, and John Hyrcanus all built the walls of Jerusalem and otherwise fortified the city. Simon, however, is not only associated with the fortification of the cities outside Jerusalem, but also with the rebuilding of the 'City of David', i.e., the citadel and its environs. On Simon's building operations, cf. 1 Macc. 13.10; 13.33; 13.52; 14.33; 14.37; Josephus' elaboration of 1 Macc. 13.52; 14.37 may not be historically sound (*Antiq.* XIII, 215-17; *War* I, 50), but must also be taken into account. Moreover, Simon's adult sons who share rule with him defeat Kendebaios, jointly administer his projects of fortification, and otherwise stand beside their ancient father. Finally the blood bath in Jerusalem in our text appears to follow on the heels of the building projects, and hence only can be the attack of Antiochus Sidetes following Simon's death.

2.   So already G. Vermés, *op. cit.* pp. 99-100.

means the Wicked Priest who pursued after the Righteous Teacher to overwhelm him (or swallow him up) in the fierceness of his wrath at his house in exile.[1] And in the season of the festival of rest, the Day of Atonement, he suddenly appeared before them to overwhelm them and to make them stumble on the fast day, their sabbath of rest.' The attack of the Wicked Priest on the Righteous Teacher and his fellows[2] is made at the Teacher's establishment in exile. It falls on the *sectarian* fast day, not the orthodox one as is clear (1) from the fact that the religious calendar of the sect differs as we know from calendrical texts, and (2) from the fact that the priest is not presiding at his duties at the Temple.[3] If indeed the Wicked Priest attacked the sectarians in exile, it follows most naturally that he appeared *at Qumrân*. To be sure, it is quite conceivable that the sect hid elsewhere before constructing their permanent installations at Qumrân. But following the more obvious connection, we can apply our archaeological dating of the beginning of the community center to the question of the identity of the Wicked Priest. The last years of Simon fall just within the upper limit for the foundation of the settlement of Qumrân.

A cycle of texts speak of the Wicked Priest (or possibly of another enemy roughly contemporary with the Wicked Priest) under the biblical appellation, the False Oracle,[4] or more simply the False One.[5] The title is taken from Mic. 2.11, and is regularly combined in sectarian exposition with Ezek. 13.8-12.[6] A typical example of this complex combination of texts is found in IQpHabakkuk 10.9-13, commenting on Habakkuk 2.12: 'the interpretation of this [passage] relates to the False Oracle who caused the assembly[7] to go astray in building a city of vanity in blood and establishing a congregation in falsehood...their work will be in vain

---

1.   *'byt glwtw=l-byt glwtw* (Segal, Yeivin, *et al.*).
2.   Cf. 1QpHab. 12.2-10 and 4QpPs. 37 (to vv. 32-33) for other allusions to the Wicked Priest's persecution of the Teacher and/or his party.
3.   Cf. S. Talmon, 'Yom Hakkippurim in the Habakkuk Scroll', *Biblica* 32 (1951), pp. 549-63 [reprinted in Talmon, *The World of Qumran from Within* (Jerusalem and Leiden: Magnes and Brill, 1989), pp. 186-99]; Milik, *Découvertes*, Chap. III.
4.   1QpHab. 10.9-13; *CD* 4.19-20; 8.2-13 (especially 12-13).
5.   1QpHab. 2.1-10; 5.9-12; *CD* 20.14-15; cf. the 'Scoffer' or 'Scoffers' (Isa. 28.14), *CD* 1.13-21; 20.11 (14-15).
6.   See *CD* 4.19-20; 8.2-13; and especially 1QpHab. 10.9-13.
7.   The term is *rabbîm* which may mean 'multitude' or more technically 'democratic assembly' (frequent in the texts of Qumrân).

because those who reviled and reproached the Elect of God will enter into fiery judgments.' How literally the commentator wishes the phrase 'building a city' to be taken is hard to determine,[1] but taken literally or figuratively, Jonathan and Simon both qualify, and perhaps John Hyrcanus as well. At all events, the main point is that the False Oracle leads the assembly to build a false congregation, a faithless Israel over against the Essene elect.

In other contexts we hear of those who, following the False One, deal treacherously against the New Covenant, and refuse to listen to the inspired words of the Righteous Teacher;[2] and of the house of Absalom which refuses to help the Righteous Teacher against the False One who 'rejected the Law in the midst of their whole congre[gation]'.[3] All of these passages may reflect the public occasions upon which the Righteous Teacher opposed the 'building' of a false high-priestly house, and its concomitant, a false congregation. And if this is the case, probably the Wicked Priest is identical with the False Oracle or False One. If not, the latter is to be identified with the Wicked Priest's successor or predecessor, that is with John Hyrcanus or Jonathan.[4]

In the course of our discussion we have spoken often of the Essene Master. A systematic reconstruction of his career is quite impossible. For all our labors, he remains a shadowy figure. We do not know even his name. There is no hint of his identity in our older sources. The Essene commentaries hide him under his scriptural title, the Righteous Teacher. They mention him fairly frequently,[5] but usually in very general contexts.

1. Similarly the expression 'builders of the wall' taken from Ezek. 13.10 may or may not be taken literally in *CD* 4.19; etc.

2. 1QpHab. 2.1-10; cf. *CD* 20.11, 14-15.

3. 1QpHab. 5.9-12. On the identity of 'Absalom's house', cf. 1 Macc. 13.11; 11.70; and D.N. Freedman, "The House of Absalom" in the Habakkuk Scroll', *BASOR* 114 (1949), pp. 11-12.

4. Abbé Milik has proposed to distinguish the two figures, identifying the False Oracle with John Hyrcanus. His chief evidence is that John had a reputation as a prophet (cf. Josephus, *Antiq.* XIII, 288-98, 300; etc.). The identification is quite attractive. Most likely the Righteous Teacher's ministry continued into Hyrcanus' reign, and, in any case, the two may have come into direct contact before John's accession to the high priesthood. Of course John, like Jonathan and Simon before him, engaged himself in refortifying Jerusalem (1 Macc. 16.23).

5. 1QpHab. 1.13; 2.2; 5.10; 7.4; 8.3; 9.9/10; 11.5; *CD* 1.11; 6.11; 20.1, 14, 28, 32; 1QpMic. 10.6; 4QPs. 37 II, 15 (Ps. 37.23b-24a); 4QpPs. 37.32-33 (?); 4QpPs. 37.14-15 (1.4).

We have noted that the Righteous Teacher was a priest, a fervent supporter of the Zadokite high priesthood, and hence presumably of Zadokite lineage himself. His ministry probably began sometime late in the reign of Jonathan. He suffered persecution and defeat at the hands of Simon, the Wicked Priest, and perhaps also under Jonathan, and/or John Hyrcanus. He was an inspired interpreter of the Scriptures, one 'who spoke with authority'. He won a following from remnants of the Ḥasîdîm, including, we believe, a radical wing of the Sadducean (Zadokite) party. He was a founder and in effect the author of the Essene faith. When Simon had established himself in the high priesthood 'forever' and persecuted all who would gainsay him, the Righteous Teacher fled, leading his little congregation into exile in the wilderness of Qumrân. There he established his 'eschatological' community, the community of the New Covenant. In exile he was still not secure from the wrath and persecution of the Wicked Priest, who on one occasion, at least, attacked the community on their private Day of Atonement.

We do not know the time or circumstance of the Righteous Teacher's death. It is unlikely that he survived the reign of John Hyrcanus. He may not have lived to hear of Simon's dreadful end in nearby Jericho. Many scholars have argued that he died violently under persecution at the hands of the Wicked Priest.[1] However, if this were the case, it is never stated explicitly. The passage discussed above (IQpHab. 11.4-8) in which it is said that the Wicked Priest pursued the Righteous Teacher to overwhelm him (or swallow him up) comes as close as any to implying that the Teacher was martyred. The Damascus Document speaks twice of the death of the Teacher but uses the passive expression 'from the day the Teacher of the Community was gathered (to his fathers)...'[2] A newly published text bears on the question; unfortunately it is badly preserved. The passage being interpreted is Ps. 37.33: 'The wicked watches the righteous and seeks to kill him; Yahweh will not abandon him in his hand...' The comment seems to read as follows: 'This is to be interpreted as referring to the Wicked [Pries]t who [...the Righteous

---

1.   A. Dupont-Sommer, the most articulate advocate of a martyr death, has defended his position systematically in 'Le maître de justice fut-il mis à mort?' *VT* 1 (1951), pp. 200-15; and more recently in 'Quelques remarques sur le Commentaire d'Habacuc, à propos d'un livre récent', *VT* 5 (1955), pp. 113-29, a review and answer to K. Elliger's *SzHK*.

2.   *CD* 19.35-20.1; 20.14. The expression normally applies to peaceful death, but may apply to a violent death (e.g., 1 Macc. 14.30).

Teacher?] to kill him...but God will not ab[andon him in his hand...]'
On the basis of the passage being commented upon, we with some
confidence can reconstruct the exposition to apply to the Wicked
Priest's attempt to kill the Righteous Teacher, and God's deliverance of
the Teacher.[1] In light of this text I think we must say that while the
Wicked Priest attempted to take his rival's life, the Righteous Teacher
was spared, perhaps to be killed later by another adversary, perhaps to
die of old age.[2]

1. 4QpPs. 37.32-33 (ll. 1-3). Allegro, 'Further Light on the History of the
Qumran Sect', pp. 94f., attempts to avoid the plain meaning of the passage by
referring the deliverance to eschatological times, having observed that the verb is
future. Two things must be said: (1) the events of the Teacher's ministry are in a
sense 'eschatological', and (2) the tense of the verb is taken from the psalm quoted.
The use of tenses in the commentaries is rarely helpful in interpretation, since
predictions are being expounded, and the writer often shifts his point of view from
that of scripture to that of his own time and vice versa.

2. Dupont-Sommer in his article, 'Le Testament de Lévi (XVII–XVIII) et la secte
juive de l'alliance', *Semitica* IV, pp. 33-53 (cf. *The Jewish Sect of Qumran and the
Essenes* [London, 1954], pp. 38-57) attempts to use the Testament of Levi, especially
Chap. 10: 14-15, 16, and 17-18 to support his view that the Righteous Teacher was
martyred, and, indeed, was identified as the Messianic 'savior of the world'. The use
of 10.14-15, and 16 as witnesses to Essene history could hardly be defended on
methodological grounds even at the time Dupont-Sommer wrote (before the extensive
apocalyptic literature of Cave IV became known). The key elements in these passages
including the conception of the Messiah as a transcendental 'savior of the world', the
slaying of the savior, the subsequent destruction of the Temple and dispersion of the
Jews among the Gentiles, and the second coming of the Messiah, are suspect and
have generally been assigned to the Christian stratum of the Testaments.

At all events we are now in a position to use Qumrân discoveries to lend weight to
the view that the Testaments are indeed Judeo-Christian editions, in part reworked, of
older Essene sources. See below, Chapter 5, p. 145, n. 2 and p. 146, n. 1. Nor can the
elements listed above be discovered in the extensive new apocalyptic materials from
Qumrân. Cf. Chapter 5, p. 183, n. 1.

Similarly we must protest against the method of treatment of Chap. 17 by Dupont-
Sommer. First of all he remarks that the term 'jubilee' here by a 'curious shift
designates the time of a priesthood, of a pontificate, whatever its precise duration may
have been' (p. 38), and proceeds to treat the priesthoods of the seven jubilees as a
series of successive priests. It is possible that underlying the present form of the
document was a list of seven priests, and the formula 'the Nth priest' (vv. [2], 4-7)
was original, 'in the Nth (jubilee)' (vv. 2, 3, 8) secondary. But we can scarcely deal so
cavalierly with the meaning of the term 'jubilee'.

Dupont-Sommer then identifies the seven priests with seven of the Hasmonaean
dynasty. Judas Maccabaeus is the first, called 'annointed' who 'shall rise to save the

The Essenes regarded their Master with a respect which approached adoration. Belief in his teachings was tantamount to salvation.[1] As Moses mediated the Old Covenant to Israel, so the Righteous Teacher instituted the Community of the Renewed Covenant, opened up the meaning of the ancient Scriptures, and established a new discipline in anticipation of the Messianic era. He was in the eyes of his later disciples an eschatological figure predicted in Scripture who was to aid in bringing the New Age to birth.[2]

world'. Presumably the Essene author was unaware that Judas never functioned as high priest. The last of the series is Aristobulus. Hyrcanus II is omitted in the interests of arriving at the number seven. Perhaps Professor Dupont-Sommer would now shift to Hyrcanus II as seventh, omitting Aristobulus.

Actually the chief offense of this construction of the list (ignoring for the moment the fashion in which the Righteous Teacher is related to the chapter) is in the sweeping approval given to Judas and Jonathan by an Essene, that is, a *Zadokite* author. In the writer's opinion such a view is little short of preposterous. Moreover, no adequate explanation is given to the distinction made between the two priests called 'anointed' priests and praised, and the remainder, called merely 'priests' and condemned. Why the sharp line drawn between Jonathan and Simon?

By such procedures the priests of Chapter 17 can be made to fit almost any chronology. As an example, taking up Dupont-Sommer's hypothesis that the list goes back to a series of seven priests terminating in the day of the Righteous Teacher, let us fit it to our own chronology. The two 'anointed priests' will be the revered Simon (see above) and Onias III, both Zadokites. Trouble begins with the 'priest' Jason, mounts with Menelaus. Alcimus is 'possessed by darkness'. So, too, Jonathan and Simon, the latter the worst of the lot. In this construction, the proper succession from Simon to Simon is followed, and an adequate explanation for the judgments upon each by the Essene priesthood is at hand. Such an analysis is at least as plausible as that of Dupont-Sommer.

1.   1QpHab. 8.1-3.

2.   The question of the possible Messianic pretentions of the Righteous Teacher will be raised in Chapter 5.

Chapter 4

THE OLD TESTAMENT AT QUMRÂN

The Essene manuscripts, biblical and non-biblical, contribute new data to several areas of Old Testament study: the history of the Hebrew canon,[1] the development of Hebrew (and Aramaic) dialects, scripts, orthographies, and scribal procedures, and—the fields which will be selected arbitrarily for treatment here—the historical criticism of the Old Testament, and the history of the Old Testament text.

1. *The Scrolls and Historical Criticism*

While the most fruitful fields of study lie elsewhere, the new manuscripts are not without interest for the historian of Old Testament literature. Almost certainly we must cease to date any biblical work belonging to the Former or Latter Prophets (not to mention the Torah), or any extensive pericope within these books, later than the early second century BC. To be sure, This *terminus ad quem* is exceedingly late and merely confirms recent trends in the analysis of the latest materials in prophetic literature. It is none the less a gain to have manuscripts, albeit fragmentary and incomplete, of the books of the Pentateuch, the Prophets, especially the Twelve, dating from the second century BC,[2] which rule out

---

1.   The subject of canon is briefly touched upon by the writer in 'Qumrân Cave I', pp. 122f., and by H.L. Ginsberg in his excellent article, 'The Dead Sea Manuscript Finds: New Light on *Eretz Yisrael* in the Greco–Roman Period', from Moshe Davis (ed.), *Israel: Its Role in Civilization* (New York, 1956), pp. 45-49. See now also, F.M. Cross, 'The Text Behind the Text of the Hebrew Bible', in *Understanding the Dead Sea Scrolls*, ed. H. Shanks (New York: Random House, 1992), pp. 139-155.

2.   The oldest MSS from Qumrân IV include the following (all of which antedate the oldest of the Cave I MSS, 1QIsa^a): 4QEx^f and 4QSam^b from the third century BC; 4QEx^e; 4QDeut^a; 4QIsa^a; 4QJer^a; 4QXII^a; 4QXII^c; 4QJob^a; 4QPsa^a; 4QQoh^a from the second century BC. A fairly large group of biblical MSS belongs to the late second century or early first century BC, none of which is listed here. For illustrations

categorically speculations about extremely late additions to prophetic works.[1] Indeed it is probable that no canonical work postdates the Maccabean age. An exception, at least theoretically, may be made in the case of the Book of Esther, missing at Qumrân. More likely, however, Esther was rejected by the sectaries, as suggested by H.L. Ginsberg,[2] or is missing purely by chance. Ecclesiastes, sometimes dated in the second, or even in the first century BC, by older scholars, appears in one exemplar from Cave IV (4QQoh[a]) which dates ca. 175–150 BC.[3] Since the text of the manuscript reveals textual development, it is demonstrably not the autograph, and hence the date of composition must be pushed back into the third century or earlier. A second-century BC copy of the canonical Psalter (4QPsa[a]), though fragmentary, indicates that the collection of canonical psalms was fixed by Maccabean times, bearing out the current tendency to date the latest canonical psalms in the Persian period.[4]

Psalm studies will be strongly affected also by the appearance in Essene circles of collections of hymns of Maccabean and Hasmonaean date. They include many categories of material of which the Thanksgiving Hymns (1Q and 4QH) are but a single type.[5] Analysis of the literary types, the prosody, and the language and theological motifs of these documents will greatly expand our knowledge of the development of late Old Testament psalmody on the one hand, and will illuminate on the other hand difficult problems in the study of the literary types and prosodic

of the script of certain of the unpublished MSS listed above, and a discussion of the typological sequence of the Qumrân texts, see the writer, 'The Oldest Manuscripts from Qumrân', pp. 147-65.

1.   For example, Dupont-Sommer, as late as 1950, speculated about the possibility of bringing such materials as the Servant Passages of Isa., Dan. 9, Zech. 12, etc., down into the first century BC (*The Dead Sea Scrolls*, p. 96), on the grounds that the Essene Righteous Teacher might be reflected in them. Such speculations were not to be taken seriously by Old Testament specialists for several reasons. But the appearance of second-century copies of each of the above-mentioned passages provides the *coup de grâce* to any such aberrant theories. Here, as elsewhere, the further study of Essene materials themselves disproves earlier hypotheses based on undisciplined examination of Essene literature.

2.   'The Dead Sea Manuscript Finds…' pp. 39-57, especially p. 52.

3.   Cf. J. Muilenburg, 'A Qoheleth Scroll from Qumrân', *BASOR* 135 (October 1954), pp. 20-28; cf. Cross, 'The Oldest Manuscripts from Qumrân', pp. 153, 162.

4.   Other grounds for a Persian dating of the Psalter are given below. Cf. the writer's earlier discussion in *BA* 17 (1954), p. 3; and P. Hyatt, 'The Dead Sea Discoveries: Retrospect and Challenge', *JBL* 76 (1957), p. 5.

5.   Provisionally, see J. Strugnell, 'Travail…' p. 65.

canons of New Testament psalms (especially in the prologue of Luke) and poetry. Preliminary study already indicates that the psalms of the Maccabean period are much developed beyond the latest of Old Testament psalms; their language is neoclassical, not classical; sapiential forms and language have profoundly influenced hymnic style. Older patterns of symmetry (meter) and many classical forms of thought rhyme (*parallelismus membrorum*) have largely broken down or been lost.[1] The hymns are archaistic. They imitate biblical psalms to such an extent that most Essene hymns are patchworks of phrases from the Psalter, and, notably from the Prophets; yet the mood and theological structure differ strikingly from canonical psalms. For suitable parallels one must look to the hymns, especially the apocalyptic hymns, of the Apocrypha and New Testament.

In one rather striking instance, a Qumrân document promises to throw light on oral, or possibly literary, sources lying behind the fixed edition of an Old Testament book. In 1956 J.T. Milik identified and published a few fragments of a Cave IV document, designated the 'Prayer of Nabonidus', after its first line: 'The words of the prayer which Nabonidus, king of Assyria and Babylon, the great king, prayed...'[2] The prayer relates how Nabonidus came down with a 'dread disease by the decree of the Most High God', was 'set apart from men' for a seven-year period in the Arabian oasis of Teima. A Jewish diviner, presumably Daniel—the broken text does not reveal his name—intervenes, speaks of the king's worship of 'gods of gold, bronze, iron, wood, stone, silver...' (Cf. Dan. 5.4).

The document is closely related in language, style and genre to the cycle of tales collected and edited in Daniel 1–6 (so-called Daniel A). It is strongly reminiscent of Daniel 4, the story of Nebuchadnezzar's being driven from men for seven years, during which he learns that the 'Most High rules the kingdom of men...' ending with the snatch of poetry in which the king 'blesses the Most High and praises and honors Him who

1. These tendencies are already at work, of course, in late Old Testament poetry. The failure of New Testament scholars to recognize this development has hindered advances in the analysis of poetic materials embedded in the New Testament, notably in the Gospels.

2. '"Prière de Nabonide" et autres écrits d'un cycle de Daniel', *RB* 63 (1956), pp. 407-15. [A corrected text of the Prayer has been published by the writer, 'Fragments of the Prayer of Nabonidus', *IEJ* 34 (1984), pp. 260-64. This paper contains recent bibliography.]

lives forever'. In fact there is every reason to believe that the new document preserves a more primitive form of the tale. It is well known that Nabonidus gave over the regency of his realm to his son Belshazzar in order to spend long periods of time in Teima; while Nebuchadnezzar, to judge from extrabiblical data, did not give up his throne. Moreover, in the following legend of Belshazzar's feast, the substitution of Nebuchadnezzar for Nabonidus as the father of Belshazzar (Dan. 5.2) is most suggestive. Evidently in an older stage of tradition, the cycle included stories of Nebuchadnezzar (cf. Dan 1–3), Nabonidus (Dan. 4), and Belshazzar (Dan. 5).[1] The change of names, as well as the development of the elaborate details of Nebuchadnezzar's theriomania, is best attributed to the refracting tendencies of oral transmission, in this case the shift of a legend from a lesser to a greater name. It is not necessary to think of the Prayer of Nabonidus as a literary source of the canonical Daniel, or even to give the prayer priority in terms of its written composition. The prayer may simply derive from a parallel, but more conservative line of orally transmitted material.[2]

2. *The Archaic Text of the Old Testament*

The most direct and obvious contribution of the Qumrân scrolls is in the field of Old Testament textual studies.[3] At the outset we may remark that the new scrolls give evidence of the antiquity of the type of textual tradition which has survived in the form of the traditional Hebrew

---

1.   This suggests that in the riddle of Dan. 5.25-28, the kings referred to originally as a mina, shekel, and half shekel, were Nebuchadnezzar, *Nabonidus*, and Belshazzar respectively, as pointed out by D.N. Freedman, 'The Prayer of Nabonidus', *BASOR* (1957), pp. 31-32. Cf. H.L. Ginsberg's discussion, *Studies in Daniel* (New York, 1948), pp. 24-26.

2.   With the publication of the Habakkuk Commentary, scholars duly noted that the work treated only the first two chapters of Habakkuk. Since it is generally accepted that the psalm of Ch. 3 was not composed by the prophet, a number of scholars jumped to the conclusion that prophecy and psalm had not yet been wedded when the commentary was composed. This position cannot hold. The Qumrân commentaries often treat short pericopes, a psalm, a section of chapters, and only rarely the whole of a short prophetic book.

3.   This discussion of the text of the Old Testament at Qumrân is a revised and expanded form of material published in the writer's article, 'The Dead Sea Scrolls', in Vol. XII of *The Interpreter's Bible* (New York-Nashville, 1957), copyrighted by the Abingdon Press in 1957. Copyrighted material is used here by permission.

Bible.[1] Again the scrolls preserve many new readings some of which are superior to received readings, some of which are inferior. Nevertheless, the textual scholar finds the chief interest of the scrolls neither in their testimony to the age of our received text (which has never been seriously doubted), nor merely in individual readings as such. The real importance of the biblical scrolls lies in the data they yield for the reconstruction of the textual history of the Old Testament.

To make this point clear, perhaps it will be useful to glance backward at the state of textual studies before the coming of the Qumrân and Murabba'ât scrolls.

The eighteenth and nineteenth centuries witnessed the assiduous collection and study of extant Hebrew manuscripts, together with the ancient versions into which the Hebrew had been translated. These studies led to the first systematic reconstructions of the history of the Old Testament text. The culmination of this stage of study is found in the works of Paul de Lagarde, who stated categorically that all medieval Hebrew manuscripts were descended from a common ancestor, a single master scroll. This official text, according to Lagarde, could be dated no earlier than the first century of the Christian era. That is, these studies seemed to establish that in the first century CE, the rabbis had fixed an authoritative Hebrew text, chosen arbitrarily from the more or less fluid textual traditions alive in the pre-Christian period, and that this official text in effect destroyed all variant lines of tradition in normative Judaism.[2] Old Testament textual criticism found itself at an impasse.

---

1. That is to say, a proto-Rabbinic recension for certain books is present at Qumrân. As we shall see, this tradition was chosen by the rabbis, who, after further recensional activity, established the base of the *textus receptus*, the traditional consonantal text. See below.

2. See Lagarde, *Anmerkungen zur griechischen Übersetzung der Proverbien* (Leipzig. 1863),. Cf. Reider, *Prolegomena to a Greek–Hebrew and Hebrew–Greek Index to Aquila* (Philadelphia, 1916), pp. 81ff.; H.M. Orlinsky, *On the Present State of Proto-Septuagint Studies (AOS Offprint Series 13)* (New Haven, 1941), pp. 81-91; especially p. 84 and references; R.H. Pfeiffer, *Introduction to the Old Testament* (New York, 1941), pp. 78, 79; B.J. Roberts, *The Old Testament Text and Versions* (Cardiff, 1951), pp. 23-29. [See now M.H. Gottstein's important paper, 'Hebrew Bible Manuscripts: Their History and Their Place in the *HUBP* Edition', *Biblica* 48 (1967), pp. 243-290; reprinted in F.M. Cross and S. Talmon, eds. *Qumran and the History of the Biblical Text* (Cambridge, MA: Harvard University Press, 1975), pp. 42-89.]

Attacks on Lagarde's position show at most that he overstates his case. All

There were only a few hints of the state of the text in the era sealed off by the promulgation of a standard text. The Pentateuch of the Samaritans, having been transmitted along different channels, preserved

medieval manuscripts stem from a single, narrow, recensional base. This is evidenced not only by the early, pre-Tiberian manuscripts from the Cairo Genizah, but decisively now by the appearance of the Murabba'ât fragments, especially the great Minor Prophets scroll (not to be confused with the Greek recension of the Minor Prophets). Medieval variants, whether in biblical manuscripts, or in rabbinic texts (see Aptowitzer, *Das Schriftwort in der rabbinischen Literatur* [*Sitzungsberichte der kais. Akad. der Wiss. in Wien.* Phil.-Hist. Klasse Bd. 153.6, 1906; 160.7, 1908] and H.L. Strack, *Prolegomena critica in Vetus Testamentum hebraicum*, Leipzig, 1873) are for the most part merely orthographic, or secondary, a witness to subsequent development of variant readings which for a number of reasons may coincide with older witnesses, the Septuagint, etc. In the Targums, Aquila, and Jerome, some genuine survivals of readings which predate the official recension of the first century AD are expected, since in each case older materials were used alongside the new standard text.

Part of the difficulty arises from differing presuppositions as to the state of the Hebrew text in the pre-Christian period. For those who presume an extremely conservative development of the Hebrew textual tradition, the variants of the post-Aqiba period loom large. For those who suppose that the pre-Christian period was marked by a Hebrew text which exhibited widely different recensional traditions, the medieval variants appear to be negligible. As we shall see, the pre-Christian Hebrew text exhibits *recensional* variation which differs *toto caelo* from the variation exhibited after the promulgation of the official Hebrew (consonantal) text.

The general reaction against Lagardian positions, therefore, represented today especially by the Kahle–Sperber school (cf. Kahle, 'Untersuchungen zur Geschichte des Pentateuchtextes', *TSK* 88 [1915], pp. 432-39), has gone much too far. The text established by AD 100 appears to be the culmination of rabbinic recensional activity which began perhaps a early in the century, to judge from the Qumrân texts (cf. Cross, 'A New Qumrân Biblical Fragment Related to the Original Hebrew Underlying the Septuagint', *BASOR* 132 [December, 1953], p. 24, n. 36). Barthélemy's Greek recension of the Septuagint is evidence of this early trend. There is no doubt that our copy dates at the latest from the first century AD, and preferably about the turn of the Christian era, and represents an early attempt to *revise the* LXX into conformity with the proto-Masoretic text. (On the dating see Barthélemy, *op. cit.*, p. 19; and C.H. Roberts quoted by P. Kahle, '...Die im August 1952 entdeckte Lederrolle...' *TLZ* 79 [1954], col. 81). It may be noted that in his article devoted precisely to this new recension, Kahle fails to deal with this point, that the scroll is a Jewish revision, *not* translation, which takes the pre-Christian Septuagint as its base. The failure is most curious, since this is easily the most significant characteristic of the text, as well as most damaging evidence against Kahle's theories of Septuagint origins.

The Murabba'ât texts certify that the consonantal base of the *textus receptus* had an alternate form of the text for the Torah.[1] Actually, however, the Samaritan provided little help toward reconstructing the early history of the Hebrew text. This was due not only to its restricted scope, but to certain confusions which attended its early study. Generally it was presumed to be an extremely early branch of tradition separating from the main Jewish line at the time of the early Samaritan rift (fifth century BC). In fact its text is a relatively late branch, going back at earliest to Hasmonaean times.[2] That this was the case has long been likely on historical grounds. It is now clear both on paleographical grounds—the Samaritan script is a derivative of the Paleo-Hebrew script which was revived or became resurgent in the Maccabean era of nationalistic archaism—and on orthographic grounds.[3] The text type found in the Samaritan is difficult to categorize. On the one hand it stands very close to the proto-Rabbinic text. Yet it has a large number of readings in agreement with the Septuagint. Again, it is replete with inferior readings: expansion, transposition, insertion of parallels from other passages or books, readings of a type which must have been introduced at a fairly early date when the text was relatively fluid. They are not the result of specifically Samaritan recensional activity in all probability.[4] In any case

been fixed finally by the days of the First Revolt, and that Lagarde was, after all, right in principle. Indeed the evidence from Murabba'ât indicates that even the principles of orthographic practice (use of vowel letters, *matres lectionis*) became fixed at this time. While minor orthographic variations appear, as well as a few variants of other types, they are no more significant than variants in Tiberian Masoretic manuscripts; the relatively fluid orthographic practice of the Hasmonaean and Herodian periods known from Qumrân has vanished, once for all.

1.   A non-Rabbinic text type also appears in some of the Apocryphal and Pseudepigraphical works, which being rejected by rabbinical Judaism, did not undergo revision. Cf. Kahle, 'Untersuchungen...' pp. 399-410; *The Cairo Genizah* [The Schweich Lectures 1941] (London, 1947), pp. 147-8.

2.   Cf. the writer's remarks in 'A Report on the Biblical Fragments of Cave Four...' p. 12, n. 5a. Contrast Kahle, 'Untersuchungen...'; Roberts, *The Old Testament Text and Versions*, pp. 188-96; and M. Greenberg, 'The Stabilization of the Text of the Hebrew Bible, Reviewed in the Light of the Biblical Materials from the Judean Desert', *JAOS* (1956), pp. 161-63.

3.   That is, Samaritan orthography reflects neither the restricted use of *matres lectionis* characteristic of the third century and earlier, nor the revised spelling principles of the rabbinic text. Rather it exhibits the characteristic full orthography of the Maccabean and especially Hasmonaean eras. Cf. Cross, 'The Oldest Manuscripts from Qumrân', p. 165.

4.   Cf. Kahle, 'Untersuchungen...' pp. 399-410. (See below.)

the Samaritan Pentateuch has been only of limited use in the task of recovering a more primitive form of the Hebrew text of the Old Testament.

The best hope for a break-through into the unknown era before the promulgation of the official textual recension of the rabbis lay in the Septuagint, the standard Greek Old Testament of the early Church, which according to tradition traced its lineage to an Alexandrian translation of the third–second centuries BC. Perhaps by reconstructing the Hebrew underlying this antique version, the textual critics might gain detailed knowledge of the development of the early text, enabling them thereby to reconstruct a more nearly original form of the Hebrew Bible.

This was not an easy path to the pre-rabbinic Bible. Two difficult and complex problems required resolution before the Septuagint could be used confidently to reconstruct an old Hebrew text type. In the first place, Septuagint scholars had to establish the original form of the Old Greek translation (the proto-Septuagint) out of a maze of manuscripts belonging to Christian recensions of the Old Greek, and its daughter versions. This required the grouping of the manuscripts, the versions, and citations in ancient authors into families and then the establishment of the text types belonging to the recensions of the Septuagint known, especially, from Jerome: the Hesychian (Egyptian), Lucianic (Syrian), and Hexaplaric (Palestinian), as well as unknown recensions to be detected by inductive critical procedures. The task was further involved by the presence of contamination of the transmission of the Septuagint by later Jewish Greek texts which had been successively revised back into conformity with the developing Hebrew text. Such recensions include the Greek text of the Minor Prophets partially published by Barthélemy,[1] probably identical with the Quinta of the Hexapla, which revises the Septuagint by a late pre-Christian Hebrew text (closely allied with the proto-Masoretic tradition), and especially Theodotion and Aquila, both of which appear to be based on the earlier Jewish recension, revising it to conform to the authoritative Hebrew text which emerged about AD 100.[2]

---

1.   Bibliography on the Barthélemy recension is listed on p. 34, n. 2, and p. 35, n. 1.

2.   The above description is, of course, oversimple. The number of Jewish revisions of the Septuagint may be larger than the present evidence suggests, and the detailed relationships between such and the 'Three', Theodotion, Aquila, and Symmachus, may be more complex than is suggested by first study. The problems of

Figure 1. Cave IV, Qumrân viewed from the floor of the Wâdī Qumrân. The ruin of the community center is situated above on the marl terrace through which the wâdī cuts. Photograph: F.M. Cross.

Figure 2. Cave IV as it appeared undisturbed in the 1920s before secondary openings were made by Bedouin. The cave may be seen high in the column of marl immediately to the left of the side torrent bed. Photograph: Harvard Semitic Museum.

Figure 3. Khirbet Qumrân and vicinity.

Figure 4. The sites of the caves which produced manuscripts. Caves IV–X are located in the marl terrace adjacent to the community center; Caves I, III, and XI are high in the limestone cliffs.

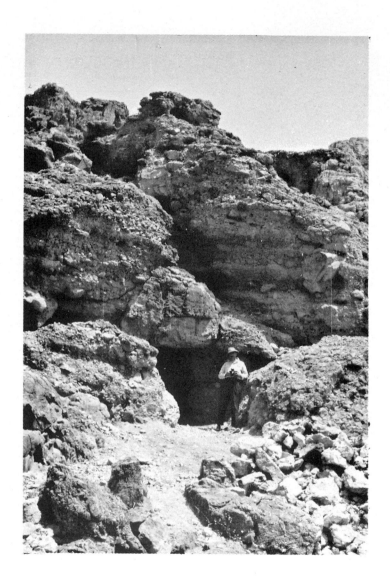

Figure 5. The entrance to Cave XI (after clearance by Ta'âmireh shepherds).
Photograph: F.M. Cross.

Figure 6. Excavations at the northwest tower of community buildings at Qumrân.
Photograph: Jean Starcky.

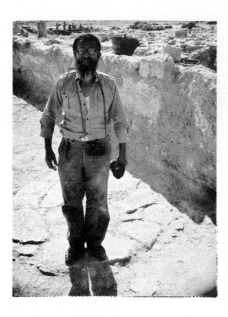

Figure 7. R.P. Roland de Vaux in his excavation togs. He is standing in the commons of the community. Photograph: F.M. Cross.

Figure 8. Five of the seven original members of the international committee preparing and piecing together Cave IV manuscripts. Shown are (from left to right) John Strugnell, John Allegro, Monsignor Patrick Skehan, Claus-Hunno Hunzinger, and J.T. Milik. Missing are Abbé Jean Starcky and Frank Moore Cross. Photo: Jean Starcky.

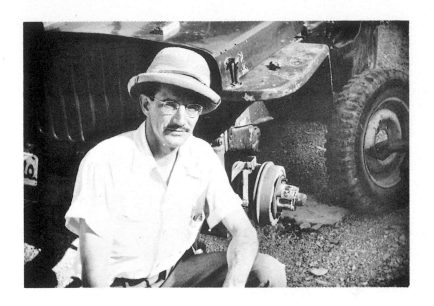

Figure 9. The author, stranded in the wilderness above Qumrân (ca. 1955).

Figure 10. Qumrân Cave IV manuscript fragments in a lot purchased with a
grant of $15,000 from McGill University.

Figure 11. The Psalms Scroll from Qumrân, Cave XI (4QPs^a). The scroll is shown in the condition it was found, before unrolling. Photograph: Israel Antiquities Authority.

Figure 12. Fragments of a Jeremiah manuscript from Cave IV (4QJer[b]). It contains an edition of the text of Jeremiah shorter than that preserved in the Masoretic Text. This shorter text is found also (in translation) in the Old Greek version of Jeremiah. Photograph: Israel Antiquities Authority.

Figure 13. A manuscript of Qohelet (4QQoh^a) dating to *ca.* 175–150 BC.
Photograph: Israel Antiquities Authority.

Figure 14. A fragment of the oldest biblical scroll from Cave I, Qumrân, a manuscript of Samuel (4QSam[b]) dating to *ca*. 250 BC. Photograph: Israel Antiquities Authority.

Figure 15. Samaria Papyrus 2 from the Wâdī ed-Dâliyeh. It records the contract of sale of an 'unblemished' female slave. It dates from December–January, 352–351 BC. Photograph: Israel Antiquities Authority.

Figure 16. Early Aramaic and Proto-Jewish Scripts.

Line 1. The classical Aramaic cursive of the late Persian Empire. From Papyrus Luparensis, *CIS (pars secunda)* I:1, 146 A, B, Tab. XVII. *Ca.* 400 BCE.
Line 2. An Aramaic vulgar cursive of the early third century BCE from Egypt. From the Edfū Papyrus published by Sayce-Cowley, *PSAB* 29 (1907), Pls. I, II.
Line 3. An Archaic proto-Jewish hand of the mid-third century BCE. From an unpublished manuscript of Exodus–Leviticus from Qumrân (4QExod–Levᶠ). The script contains letter forms which eventually evolve into the early Jewish cursive character.
Line 4. An Archaic proto-Jewish formal hand of the mid-third century BCE. From a manuscript of Samuel (4QSamᵇ) published in part by the writer in *OMQ*: 147-172, esp. Fig. 6 and Fig. 2, 1.2.
Line 5. An Archaic proto-Jewish formal hand of *ca.* 200 BCE. From an unpublished manuscript of Jeremiah from Qumrân (4QJerᵃ).
Line 6. An Archaic or Early Hasmonaean semiformal script of *ca.* 175–150 BCE. From a manuscript of Qohelet from Qumrân (4QQohᵃ).
Line 7. An Archaic or Early Hasmonaean semiformal script of *ca.* 175–150 BCE. From a manuscript published by M. Baillet, *DJD* VII: 4Q 504 (DibHamᵃ).

Figure 17. The Evolution of the Formal Hand in the Hasmonaean and Early Herodian Periods.

Line 1. A script transitional between the Archaic (Proto-Jewish) and Hasmonaean periods (*ca.* 175–150 BCE). From a manuscript of Deuteronomy from Qumrân (4QDeut[a]).

Line 2. A typical Hasmonaean script (*ca.* 125–100 BCE). From a manuscript of Deuteronomy (4QDeut[c]). Compare the hand of the great Isaiah scroll (1QIsa[a]) of about the same date.

Line 3. A Late Hasmonaean or Early Herodian hand (*ca.* 50–25 BCE). From a manuscript of Samuel (4QSam[a]).

Line 4. A typical Early Herodian formal script (*ca.* 30–31 BCE). From a manuscript of the Order of the War (1QM).

Line 5. An Early Herodian 'Round' semiformal hand (*ca.* 30 BCE–20 CE). From a manuscript of Numbers (4QNum[b]).

Figure 18. The Development of the Jewish Scripts in the Late Herodian Period.

Line 1. A developed Herodian formal script (*ca.* 20–50 CE). From a manuscript of Daniel (4QDan^b).
Line 2. A Late Herodian formal script (*ca.* 50 CE). From a manuscript of Deuteronomy (4QDeut^l).
Line 3. A Late Herodian formal script (*ca.* 50 CE [–68 CE]). From a manuscript of Psalms from Qumrân (4QPs^b), published by P.W. Skehan, *CBQ* 26 (1964): 313-322 and Plate. This script represents the classic book hand of the First Jewish Revolt, the prototype of the post-Herodian biblical hand.
Line 4. A post-Herodian biblical hand (*ca.* 75–100 CE). From a manuscript of Psalms from the Nahal Hever.
Line 5. A formal Jewish script from a Hebrew contract dated in 133 CE, published by J.T. Milik, *DJD* II, Pls. XXV–XXVI.

Figure 19. Semicursive Scripts from Qumran.

Line 1. A semicursive hand from a manuscript of the Twelve Minor Prophets (4QXII^a). *Ca.* 150–100 BCE.
Line 2. A semicursive script from a manuscript of Daniel (4QDan^e). *Ca.* 100–50 BCE.
Line 3. An unusual semicursive from a non-biblical Aramaic work (4Q530 [Book of Giants ar^b]. *Ca.* 100–50 BCE.
Line 4. A late Hasmonaean semicursive script from a papyrus document (4QpapMMT^e). *Ca.* 50–25 BCE.
Line 5. A hand from a manuscript containing part of the Enoch literature (4QEn ar^g). *Ca.* 50-51 BCE.
Line 6. A script used in an Aramaic papyrus from Cave VI (6Q8), edited by M. Baillet, *DJD* III, Pl. 24.

The task of supplying the materials from which the proto-Septuagint text can be recovered is by no means completed. Progress has been made in the seventy-five years since Lagarde initiated his program, despite pauses to solve unexpected complexities, and occasional loss of faith by some in the very existence of a proto-Septuagint which consisted of more than a congeries of distinct and competing Greek translations. The still incomplete edition of the Larger Cambridge Septuagint, the continuing publication of the great Göttingen edition of the Septuagint, recently at an increased tempo, and the publication of individual studies of which Margolis' *The Book of Joshua in Greek* is the outstanding example, are major advances. Nevertheless the determination of the text of the Septuagint in a given Old Testament passage is one of the most exacting tasks of the biblical scholar, and in some portions of the Old Testament, fortunately decreasing steadily in extent, remains a precarious task at best.

If we can presume that we know what the text of the Septuagint is, a

---

proto-Lucian, proto-Theodotion, Rahlfs' and Katz's 'R' recension, etc., will require complete re-examination in light of the new texts of the LXX from Qumrân, and the new Greek data from the 'undesignated provenience', as well as the Hebrew texts from these finds and from Murabba'ât. (On these texts, see Chapter 1, especially p. 28, n. 3, and p. 29, n. 2).

All the new evidence seems to suggest that these problems will be solved in the general framework of the proto-Septuagint hypothesis formulated by Lagarde and developed by Rahlfs, Montgomery, Margolis, and in the present generation by Orlinsky, Katz, and especially Ziegler. That is to say, the remnants of Greek texts at variance with the standard Septuagint and which appear to be pre-Hexaplaric in date, are now most easily explained as surviving from Jewish revision(s) of the Septuagint. Not only do we now possess such a recension, but we possess the various Hebrew text types reflected by it, by the 'Three' and, indeed, by the proto-Septuagint itself.

For recent discussions of the proto-Septuagint question, see Orlinsky, *On the Present State of Proto-Septuagint Studies* (cf. 'The Septuagint—Its Use in Textual Criticism', *BA* 9 [1946], pp. 21-34); 'Current Progress and Problems in Septuagint Research', in H.R. Willoughby (ed.),*The Study of the Bible Today and Tomorrow* (Chicago, 1947); P. Katz, 'Septuagintal Studies in the Mid-Century...'; 'Das Problem des Urtextes der Septuaginta', *ThZ* 5 (1949), pp. 1-24; J.W. Wevers, 'Septuaginta Forschungen...'; P. Kahle, *The Cairo Genizah*, Chap. II.2; Roberts, *Old Testament Text*...pp. 104-19. [More recent studies include: S. Jellicoe, *The Septuagint and Modern Study* (Oxford: Clarendon Press, 1968); and E. Tov, *The Textual Use of the Septuagint in Biblical Research* (Jerusalem: Simor, 1981); P. Kyle McCarter, *Textual Criticism, Recovering the Text of the Hebrew Bible* (Philadelphia: Fortress, 1986).]

second formidable difficulty appears when the Septuagint comes to be used as a witness to the archaic Hebrew text. Does the Septuagint in a given passage witness to an ancient Hebrew text at variance with the *textus receptus*, or are its divergent readings to be explained away as due to translation procedures? Does the Septuagint reflect in distorted form the *Hebraica veritas* as assumed by Origen and Jerome as well as ancient Jewish scholars, or does it often testify in faithful fashion to a different Hebrew text from the one we have always known?

These questions gave rise to sharp debate in the nineteenth century. The issue was joined between supporters of the antiquity and fidelity of the Masoretic tradition who would explain away the apparently divergent readings of the Septuagint, and those who insisted on laying their Septuagint side by side with the traditional Hebrew Bible—as if the two were variant manuscripts which by comparison could be forced to yield a text superior to both. On the side of the medieval Hebrew text stood such figures as Fränkel and Löhr; in support of the importance of the Old Greek for textual criticism stood Thenius, Lagarde, and the master, Julius Wellhausen. The debate persists into the twentieth century. Indeed the polemic against the trustworthiness of the Septuagint translators and the usefulness of their version as a witness to the pre-Masoretic text had come close to winning the day. How can the critic be sure, said this school of thought, that when the Greek translator departs radically from the received text, the Hebrew manuscript from which he translated also deviates? Could not these deviations be caused by bad translation techniques? Was the Greek a literal and faithful translation of its *Vorlage*? Or was it full of error, paraphrasing, and arbitrary changes? Increasingly scholars have looked upon the Septuagint with a jaundiced eye, and, following the lead especially of H.S. Nyberg, a new conservative respect for the medieval Hebrew text has gained sway.[1]

Then with the discovery of the Qumrân scrolls we were suddenly catapulted over the alleged barrier into the forbidden land. The great Isaiah scroll of Cave I was published first. It proved rather an anticlimax.

---

1.   Cf. H.S. Nyberg, 'Das textkritische Problem des Alten Testaments am Hoseabuche demonstriert', *ZAW* 52 (NF 11), 1934, pp. 241-54; *Studien zum Hoseabuche* (Uppsala, 1935); P.A.H. De Boer, *Research into the Text of I Samuel I-XVI* (Amsterdam, 1938), and sequent studies in *Oudtestamentische Studien I* (1942) and *VI* (1949). Cf. the literature, especially that of the Gehman school discussed by Wevers, 'Septuaginta-Forschungen, II. Die Septuaginta als Übersetzungsurkunde', *ThR* 22 (1954), pp. 171-90.

While it conserved thousands of variant readings, few of its readings were significant, and even fewer superior to the traditional readings. It seemed that the defenders of the traditional Hebrew Bible were vindicated, and that the work of the rabbis in preparing the official text current in the first century AD had had negligible effect on the history of textual transmission. Certainly it was true that the text of Isaiah preserved in the Masora was based on an extremely early textual type, already at home in Palestine in the late second century BC.[1]

There was one ambiguity in this construction of the evidence. Isaiah in the Septuagint is not one of those books where traditional renderings and those of the Greek translation clash. Isaiah in Greek appears to have been translated from a manuscript quite close to the proto-Rabbinic tradition. However, it was difficult to be certain, since the translation of Isaiah is among the poorest in the Greek Bible.[2] What was needed was a group of manuscripts from other biblical books where the Septuagint translation was good, where it was extremely literal when it agreed with Masoretic readings, but where in places it branched radically from this later standard text. This was the case, for example, in the historical books, especially in Joshua and Samuel. It is also true of Jeremiah, where the Septuagint omits or changes the order of large sections of material. Ideally, of course, the scholar needs samplings from the whole Old Testament in order to reconstruct a valid history of its transmission.

The recovery of more than one hundred twenty biblical scrolls from Cave IV came, therefore, as incredibly good fortune. Here at last was the material for sampling the textual types extant in virtually every book of

1. The literature on the Isaiah scroll (1QIsa[a]) is quite extensive. A general discussion may be found in M. Burrows, *The Dead Sea Scrolls*, pp. 301-15, and full bibliographic notes for textual studies of the early finds may be found in his bibliography, pp. 420-35; of the older studies, noteworthy are the contributions of Baumgartner, Beegle, Hempel, Kahle, Loewinger, Milik, and Orlinsky. The most recent discussions dealing with the text of Isaiah at Qumrân are those of W.F. Albright, 'New Light on Early Recensions of the Hebrew Bible', *BASOR* 140 (1955), pp. 27-33; P.W. Skehan, 'The Text of Isaias at Qumrân', *CBQ* 8 (1955), pp. 38-43; M. Greenberg, 'The Stabilization of the Text of the Hebrew Bible...' pp. 163f.; and H.H. Orlinsky, 'Notes on the Present State of the Textual Criticism of the Judean Biblical Cave Scrolls', in E.C. Hobbs (ed.) *A Stubborn Faith* (Papers on Old Testament and Related Subjects Presented to Honor William Andrew Irwin) (Dallas, 1956), pp. 117-31.

2. See J. Ziegler, *Untersuchungen zur Septuaginta des Buches Isaias* (Münster i. W., 1934).

the Old Testament. Here was a substantial basis for the establishment of the archaic, pre-Masoretic history of the Hebrew Bible. Moreover, thanks to the Murabba'ât texts which extend the series from Qumrân down into the second century AD, we have direct evidence for the first time as to just what happened to the text in the crucial era before, during, and after the time when the official text was fixed.

Initial study was directed to the historical books, especially to Samuel.[1] The text of Samuel contained in the three scrolls from Cave IV is widely at variance with that of the traditional Masoretic Bible; it follows systematically the rendering of the Septuagint of Samuel.[2] For example, in the few published fragments of the archaic Samuel text (4QSam^b), there are some thirteen readings in which the Qumrân text agrees with the Greek against the readings of the received text, four readings in which the Qumrân text agrees with the traditional text against the Septuagint. The ratio of readings in agreement with the Septuagint against the Masoretic text is even higher in the large Samuel manuscript (4QSam^a).[3]

It now becomes clear, at least in Samuel, that the Septuagint's divergent text was due less to 'translation idiosyncrasies' than to the type of text which it translated. These manuscripts establish once and for all that in the historical books the Septuagint translators faithfully and with extreme literalness reproduced their Hebrew *Vorlage*.[4] And this means that the Septuagint of the historical books must be resurrected as a primary tool of the Old Testament critic. This is a repudiation of much

---

1.   Cross, 'A New Qumrân Biblical Fragment...' pp. 15-26; 'The Oldest Manuscripts from Qumrân', pp. 165-72.

2.   The older Samuel MS (4QSam^b) often preserves a text superior to both the Septuagint and Hebrew *textus receptus*. The non-specialist can find a translation of one such passage in my article, 'The Oldest Manuscripts from Qumrân', p. 171.

3.   Cf. Cross, 'A New Qumrân Biblical Fragment...'; *passim*; E. Vogt, 'Textus praemasoreticus ex Qumran', *Biblica* 35 (1954), pp. 263-66; and J. Hempel, 'Ein textgeschichtlich bedeutsamer Fund', *ZAW* 65 (1953), pp. 296-98.

4.   The literalness of the Septuagint of Samuel is not, of course, the mechanical and tortured literalness of Aquila. However, the translator reflects systematically in his translation, shifts of tense, the presence or absence of the article, and so on, so far as Greek idiom permits. Study of the method of the translator over against the Qumrân text soon teaches one his technique, so that from his translation his *Vorlage* can be predicted with high accuracy. Save for a very few poetic passages (e.g., the Song of Hannah) where the Greek text probably had a prehistory, paraphrasing is virtually absent from the Septuagint of Samuel, and no evidence is to be found of conscious changes made by the translator on theological or otherwise tendentious grounds.

of the textual theory and method developed and applied to the Hebrew text of Samuel during the last generation.[1]

All this does not mean that the Septuagint in the historical books presents a text which is *necessarily* superior to the Masoretic text. The question of which witness is superior is another problem, to be decided in individual readings. It does mean that the Septuagint reflects accurately a Hebrew textual tradition at home in Egypt in the third–second centuries BC, and that thanks to the Qumrân manuscripts we have the means to control its evidence.[2]

The state of the text in other books of the Old Testament is a more complicated one. Among no less than thirty Pentateuchal manuscripts from Cave IV, Qumrân, at least three sharply defined textual traditions persist.[3] The majority of the texts are allied closely with the proto-Rabbinic tradition. However, the text type underlying the Septuagint is well represented. For example, there is the Deuteronomy manuscript of which fragments of Deut. 32 were published by Monsignor Patrick Skehan. It preserves a text derivative from the Hebrew recension underlying the Septuagint in a passage where the *textus receptus* is defective, so that by comparison of the three texts, a text superior to any one of the witnesses may be reconstructed.[4]

---

1.   Among the studies of the text of Samuel, for example, that which needs least revision in light of the new evidence is Wellhausen's *Der Text der Bücher Samuelis* published in 1871.

2.   In fact comparative studies of the text of Samuel are tending to indicate that the Masoretic text here is based on an extremely narrow and often inferior textual recension. Its text is often defective as the result of systematic revision (see below, n. 57). Textual scholars are accustomed to the fact that a *textus receptus* is normally a conflate text; the reverse is true of Samuel; it is a text characterized by frequent and extensive haplography. On the other hand the Hebrew underlying the Septuagint is a full text, sometimes conflate, frequently original. That the two texts stand at opposite poles in their textual development is a most fortunate circumstance for the critic who wishes to reconstruct their common ancestor and thereby press back to an extremely early form of the Hebrew text.

3.   Cf. Cross, 'A Report on the Biblical Fragments of Cave Four...' p. 12; '*Le travail d'édition...*' p. 56; and the papers of the writer, 'The History of the Biblical Text in the Light of Discoveries in the Judean Desert', *HTR* 57 (1964), pp. 281-99 [= *QHBT*, pp. 177-95]; 'The Contribution of the Qumran Discoveries to the Study of the Biblical Text', *IEJ* 16 (1966), pp. 81-95 [= *QHBT*, pp. 278-292]; and 'The Evolution of a Theory of Local Texts', *QHBT*, pp. 306-20. [Literature on the most recent discussion may be found below in Chapter 6, pp. 177-83]

4.   Skehan, 'A Fragment of the "Song of Moses" (Deut. 32) from Qumrân',

One Exodus manuscript 4QExod[b] (formerly 4QEx[a]) belongs system-atically to the Egyptian textual tradition reflected in the Septuagint;

BASOR 136 (December, 1954), pp. 12-15; cf. Albright, 'New Light on Early Recensions of the Hebrew Bible', p. 32, n. 27.

The textual history of Deut. 32.43 in 4Q, LXX, and MT can be diagrammed as follows:

Original Text

hrnynw šmym 'mw   whbw 'wz (?) lw bny 'lhym
ky dm bnyw yqwm   wkpr 'dmt 'mw
    Shout for joy, O heavens, before him;
        And ascribe might to him, O sons of God;
      For he avenges the blood of his children
        And purges the people's land.

Proto-Masoretic Text

hrnynw [šmym 'mw
whbw 'wz (?) lw bny 'lhym
hrnynw] gwym 'mw
ky dm <'bdyw> yqwm
Etc.
Shout for joy, [O Heavens, before him,
And ascribe might to him, O sons of God;
Shout for joy,] O nations for his people;
For he avenges the blood of his <servants>,
Etc.

Proto-4Q Deuteronomy

hrnynw šmym 'mw
[whbw 'wz (?) lw bny 'lhym
hrnynw gwym 'mw]
whštḥww lw kl 'lhym
ky dm bnyw yqwm
    Shout for joy, O heavens, *before him*,
        [And ascribe might to him, O sons of God;
    Shout for joy, O nations, *before him*,]
        And bow down to him, all ye divine ones;
    For he avenges the blood of his children,
      Etc.

The following points may be observed in v. 43a. The corruption of the MT is best explained on the basis of a text in which one doublet, *hrnynw šmym 'mw* and *hrnynw gwym 'mw*, but only this doublet, appears. As pointed out to me by John Strugnell, though at points it appears to offer a more consistent form of that tradition than the Septuagint itself. For example, in the first five verses of this manuscript, partially preserved on a single fragment, no fewer than six certain variants are to be found, four on the preserved leather, two fixed by reconstruction of the fragment.[1] Four readings are in

LXX μετὰ τοῦ λαοῦ αὐτοῦ is merely a double rendering of '*mw* (a familiar phenomenon in the LXX). The shifts to *gwym* here, and to '*bdyw* in the next bicolon are secondary though perhaps early variants which modernize the primitive diction of the passage. In both cases, therefore, LXX and 4Q are superior to MT.

The text of 4Q presumes a double conflation. Not only is there the doublet underlying the *haplography* of MT, but a second doublet appears. *whšṯhww lw kl 'lhym*, taken from Ps. 97.7 (or its source), no doubt because of its strong resemblance to the original *whbw 'wz lw bny 'lhym* (cf. Ps. 29). On the Greek rendering ἄγγελοι θεοῦ for *bny 'lhym*, cf. Deut. 32.8 LXX, and the text referred to by Skehan, p. 12.

The doubly conflate text presumed by the reconstruction above actually appears, though in a slightly different order, in the LXX.

In v. 43b the loss of *wlmśn'yw yšlm* is best explained as haplography in a (hemi-) stichometric manuscript. However, the entire bicolon *wnqm yšyb lṣryw wlmśn'yw yšlm* is intrusive from Deut. 32.41, two verses earlier, where it is surely original. Here it constitutes not poetic parallelism, but mere tautology. Its introduction may have been occasioned by the combination *yqwm-wnqm*, as suggested by John Strugnell.

1. The first fragment of 4QEx[b] reads as follows (Exod. 1.1-5):

> 1.]'t y'qwb 'byhm 'yš[(v. 1)
> 2.]yśśkr zbwlwn ywsp wbný[(v. 3)
> 3.]ḥmš wšb'ym npš wymt[(vv. 5-6)

> 1.]with Jacob their father, each[
> 2.]Issachar, Zebulun, Joseph and Benj[amin
> 3.]seventy-five persons. And (Joseph) died[

The following variants are significant. In l.1, 4Q adds '*byhm*, 'their father', with LXX (τῷ πατρὶ αὐτῶν). In l.2, 4Q adds *ywsp*, 'Joseph' in his proper position as a son of Rachel (see Gen. 46.19); the reading is found neither in the Greek nor received Hebrew text. However, the phrase *wywsp hyh bmṣrym* ('and Joseph was in Egypt') is omitted in l.3 (between *npš* and *wymt*). In the LXX tradition the phrase is not found at the end of v. 5, but is placed following 'Ασηρ (v. 4). A reconstruction of the text of 4Q indicates that the phrase is lacking also following '*šr*, i.e., where it is inserted in the LXX.

Perhaps the easiest explanation of textual history of these readings is to suppose that the reading *ywsp* in v. 3 together with the omission of the phrase *wywsp hyh bmṣrym* belongs to one textual tradition, the omission of *ywsp* in v. 3 together with the insertion of *wywsp hyh bmṣrym* to another, surviving in the proto-Rabbinic tradition. It is probable that Joseph once appeared in the list in v. 3. Later the agreement with the Septuagint; one is unique, but probably points to an Egyptian text form superior to that used by the translators of the Septuagint; one probably agrees with the Masoretic text against the Septuagint.[1]

There are also manuscripts from Cave IV which ally themselves with that line of tradition of which the Samaritan is a collateral witness. One of these is a Paleo-Hebrew Exodus recently published by Skehan.[2] Another unpublished example is a Numbers manuscript in Jewish ('square') script (4QNum[b]).[3] This latter manuscript, however, is by no means a simple or consistent witness to the Samaritan recension, or even to the proto-Samaritan recension. While it contains expansions

discrepancy was noticed, *ywsp* suppressed, and the phrase *wywsp hyh bmṣrym* inserted. If the phrase is taken to be secondary, then the uncertain position of the phrase, inserted at one point in LXX, at another in MT, is readily explained.

In v. 5, MT reads *wyhy kl npš yṣ'y yrk y'qb*, LXX ἦσαν δὲ πᾶσαι ψυχαὶ ἐξ Ιακωβ. In reconstructing 4Q, it becomes clear that there is insufficient room for the full reading of MT. 4Q like the LXX appears to be shorter. As for the original reading, we cannot speak with any certainty; the reading of MT may be influenced by Gen. 46.26, that of the LXX by Gen. 46.26 or 27.

In 1.3 v. 5, 4Q reads *ḥmš wšb'ym*, 'seventy-five', with LXX (πέντε καὶ ἑβδομήκοντα), against MT *šb'ym*, 'seventy'. The number is based on the LXX tradition which appears in Gen. 46, where (46.20, 27) five additional descendants of Joseph are listed; cf. Deut. 10.10 (LXX), and Acts 7.14. In short, 4Q here represents a recensional reading characteristic of the *Vorlage* of the Septuagint in Genesis and Deuteronomy as well as Exodus.

The LXX of Exod. 1.1-5 may be at variance with MT in three other readings: v. 1 ταῦτα for MT *w'lh*; v. 2 Ιουδας for *wyhwdh*; v. 5 omission of ψυχαί in virtually all witnesses, MT *npš*. It is impossible to be certain of 4Q readings in all but the last of these instances; in v. 5, 4Q reads *npš* with MT, possibly against the tradition of the LXX.

The fragment may be reconstructed as follows:

1. [<>'lh šmwt bny yśr'l hb'ym mṣrymh] 't y'qwb 'byhm 'yš [wbytw]
2. [b'w r'wbn šm'wn lwy <w>yhwdh] yśśkr zbwlwn ywsp wbny[myn dn]
3. [wnptly gd w'šr wyhy kwl npš <ly'qwb?> ḥmš wšb'ym npš wymt [ywsp]

1. The statistics on 4Q Ex[a] 1.1-5 listed in my *Interpreter's Bible* article, p. 655, are incorrect, owing to an unfortunate lapse in which the wrong figures were transferred from my workbook.

2. 'Exodus in the Samaritan Recension from Qumrân', *JBL* 74 (1955), pp. 182-87. [See also, *DJD* XI, pp. 53-130 and bibligraphy.]

3. 'Le travail d'édition...' p. 56. [See recently Nathan Jastram, 'The Text of 4QNum[b]', *MQC* I, pp. 177-98 and references.]

characteristic of this recension[1] and regularly follows less striking Samaritan variants, its contacts with the Septuagint tradition are even more striking. To be sure, the standard Samaritan text frequently agrees with the text underlying the Greek; however, in this manuscript the agreement is far more extensive, and often its text sides with the Septuagint over against both the *textus receptus* and the Samaritan.[2]

The text of Jeremiah is of particular interest. In the recension underlying the Septuagint text it is one eighth shorter than in the Hebrew Bible. Scholars have suggested that the translators simply abbreviated their text for their own reasons. Other scholars have maintained that two ancient recensions are responsible for the differences.[3] From Qumrân comes a fragmentary Hebrew manuscript, which, where preserved, follows the short text of Jeremiah found hitherto only in Greek. In ch. 10, for example, the Septuagint omits no fewer than four verses, and shifts the order of a fifth. The Qumrân Jeremiah (4QJer[b]) omits the four verses and shifts the order in identical fashion.[4] The longer recension is also present at Qumrân.

As for the remaining books of the Old Testament, a number of books

---

1. For example, Deut. 3.21 is inserted after Num. 27.23, a reading otherwise attested only in the Samaritan and Samareitikon. And after Num. 20.13, Deut. 3.23-24 is inserted; the Samaritan is likewise expanded here by the addition of Deut. 3.24.

2. The following are chosen at random: in Num. 35.21, 4Q and LXX add *mwt ymwt hrwṣh* after *hw'* (LXX θανάτῳ θανατούσθω ὁ φονεύων); Num. 26.33 in 4Q and LXX reads *w'lh šmwt bnwt* (καὶ ταῦτα τὰ ὀνόματα τῶν θυγατέρων) *versus* MT and Samaritan *wšm bnwt*.

3. Cf. Orlinsky, *On the Present State of Proto-Septuagint Studies*, p. 85; W.F. Albright, 'New Light on Early Recensions...' p. 28 and references.

4. The fragment of 4QJer[b] cited contains the left portion of a column of text. Ends of lines are preserved with the text of Jer. 9.22–10.18. Lines 5-7 give the reading in question.

l. 5 wbz]hb yyphw bmqbwt	[=MT v. 4]
l. 6]tklt w'rgmn	[=MT v. 9]
l. 7]y'bdw mn 'r''	[=MT v. 11]

Reconstruction demonstrates what can be seen even with a casual comparison of the text with MT and LXX, that with LXX, 4QJer[b] transposes v. 5 after v. 9, and omits vv. 6-8 and 10. It will be noted also that 4Q transposes MT *bmsmrwt wbmqbwt* to read *bmqbwt* [*w<b>msmrwt*] with LXX, ἐν σφύραις καί ἥλοις.

[See J.G. Janzen, *Studies in the Text of Jeremiah*. HSM 6 (Cambridge, MA: Harvard University Press, 1973); and Emanuel Tov, 'The Jeremiah Scrolls from Qumran', *Revue de Qumran* 14 (1989), pp. 189-206.]

are preserved in texts which belong to the proto-Rabbinic family: Isaiah as we have seen, Ezekiel, and the Book of the Twelve (Minor Prophets). It is still premature to discuss the text of many of the manuscripts containing books of the Hagiographa at Qumrân. Study has not proceeded far enough. While many of the manuscripts stand close to the proto-Rabbinic text, some manuscripts appear to present complicated textual problems.[1]

3. *Early Recensions of the Old Testament*

Sufficient materials are available now to permit first attempts to reconstruct in outline the early Hebrew recensions (or local texts) of the Pentateuch, the Historical Books, and perhaps Isaiah and Jeremiah. An excellent beginning has been made by W.F. Albright in his programmatic study, 'New Light on Early Recensions of the Hebrew Bible'.[2] However, the ground is not yet sure, and many missteps will be taken before certain results can be hoped for. The following suggestions, therefore, are provisional; they attempt to comprehend the evidence as presented above.

First of all we may inquire into the history of the Hebrew recension which underlies the Septuagint of Samuel. As in the case of the Pentateuch, so no doubt in that of Samuel, the text type was present in Egypt in the early Ptolemaic period when the Septuagint began to be translated. Albright has argued that behind the translators' Hebrew text stands a recension edited sometime in the fifth–fourth centuries BC in Egypt.

There is, however, other strong evidence which ties this old recension to Palestine. For example, examination of the passages of the large Samuel manuscript (4QSam[a]) which are paralleled in Chronicles gives

---

1.　For a detailed discussion of a manuscript of Lamentations (4QLam[a]), see F.M. Cross, 'Studies in the Structure of Hebrew Verse: The Prosody of Lamentations 1.1-22', in *The Word of the Lord Shall God Forth*, C.L. Meyers and M. O'Connor, eds. Essays in Honor of David Noel Freedman in Celebration of His Sixtieth Birthday (Winona Lake, Indiana: American Schools of Oriental Research, 1983), pp. 129-55. The Cave 4 manuscripts of Daniel have been published by Eugene Ulrich, 'Daniel Manuscripts from Qumran. Part I: A Preliminary Edition of 4QDan[a]', *BASOR* 268 (1987), pp. 17-37; and 'Part 2: Preliminary Editions of 4QDan[b] and 4QDan[b]', *BASOR* 274 (1989), pp. 3-6; and James Muilenburg, 'A Qoheleth Scroll from Qumran', *BASOR* 135 (1954), pp. 20-28.

2.　*QHBT*, pp. 140-46.

direct evidence that the Chronicler often utilized an edition of Samuel closer to the tradition of the Cave IV scroll than to that which survived in the Masoretic recension.[1] This suggests that the text type underlying the Septuagint, which is closely allied to that used by the Chronicler not long after 400 BC in Palestine, is derived from an Old Palestinian recension.[2] Again, the archaic Samuel manuscript (4QSam[b]) obviously reflects at many points a text which antedates both the proto-Rabbinic recension and that underlying the Septuagint,[3] though its affinities are

1.   An example of the interesting affinities between 4QSam[a] and Chron. on the one hand and LXX to Sam. on the other hand is found in a fragmentary column at the end of 4QSam[a]:

2 Sam 24.16b wml'k yhwh hyh 'm grn h'wrnh hybsy <   >
1 Chron. 21.15b   wml'k yhwh 'md 'm grn 'rnn hybsy wyś'...
4QSam[a]   [wml'k y]hwh 'wmd '[m grn 'rw]n' hybsy wyś' [

[2 Sam 24.16b+]
1 Chron. 21.16a...h'rṣ wbyn hšmym whrbw šlwph bydw...
4QSam[a]   ]h'rṣ wbyn [hšmy]m whr[b]w šlwph bydw[

2 Sam 24.17a-MT:...w'nky<   > h'wyty w'lh hṣ'n mh 'św
2 Sam 24.17a-LXX[OL]...w'nky hr'h hr'wty w'lh hṣ'n mh 'św
1 Chron. 21.17a...<   > whr'hr'wty w'lh hṣ'n mh 'św
4QSam[a] [w']nky hr'h hr'ty w'lh h[ṣ'n

Several points are to be noted. 4QSam[a] and 1 Chron. 21.16 preserve a verse which has dropped out of MT by haplography (*wyś' dwyd...wy'mr dwyd*) as well as agree against Samuel in reading *'md/'wmd* for *hyh* in 24.16b=21.15b. In 2 Sam 17a, 4QSam[a] and LXX to Sam. agree against MT Chron. (21.17a) stands closer to 4QSam[a] than to MT Sam. That *hr'ty* is the superior reading is evident. *Resh* and *waw* are virtually identical in the Jewish book hand of the third century BC. The *matres lectionis waw* and *yodh*, probably introduced after the third century, were most easily confused in the late first century BC.

2.   By 'Old Palestinian' we mean the text family current in Palestine at the end of the fifth century BC (i.e., according to our chronology, the time of Ezra). No doubt this text was developed from materials which had passed through the hands of the Exilic, i.e., early Babylonian community. By the 'Babylonian' text, however, we mean the text of the 'continuing' or late Babylonian community which persisted after the Restoration, and after the return of Ezra. This 'Babylonian' text diverged from the 'Old Palestinian' text after the introduction of the latter into Palestine. It is questionable whether we can detect any readings derived from sources surviving in Palestine from pre-Exilic times, though such may explain some of the radical divergences of later local texts.

3.   Cf. Albright, '...Early Recensions...' p. 33; and Cross, 'The Earliest

clearly with the latter. Since the manuscript itself dates from the middle of the third century, and there is no strong reason to suppose that several texts imported from Egypt came to Qumrân,[1] we must conclude that it is a witness to a collateral line of tradition that persists in Palestine from a time antedating the divergence of the Chronicler's Palestinian text of Samuel and the Hebrew textual tradition surviving in Egypt. Perhaps it is easiest to suppose that this Old Palestinian text type derives from the fifth-century Jewish community in Palestine, and that the ancestral Egyptian textual tradition diverged from this Old Palestinian text no earlier than the fourth century, no later than the early third century BC.[2]

We are left with the problem of the origin of the proto-Rabbinic recension of Samuel. No exemplars of its text are found at Qumrân, but there is no reason to suppose that it did not exist in the pre-Christian period. The analogy of other books, Isaiah, Jeremiah, the Pentateuch, warns us that the proto-Masoretic tradition is sometimes old, and not merely the creation of the recensional activities of the rabbis, and that the appearance of one recension at Qumrân does not exclude the presence of another. Moreover, the proto-Rabbinic text of Samuel is clearly the result of systematic revision.[3] Can we suppose it to be a late Palestinian recension which ousted the Old Palestinian surviving both in

Manuscripts from Qumrân', p., 172.

1.   It is not impossible, of course, that a number of the Qumrân texts came from Egypt. There are a number of lines of potential connection between the Essenes and Alexandrian Jewry. The presence of Greek Septuagint manuscripts at Qumrân as well as the manuscripts under consideration could be explained by such contacts.

2.   Albright's evidence for Egyptian influence on the Hebrew tradition used by the Greek translators is most convincing in the Pentateuch. The question as to whether or not the Historical Books underwent recensional work in Egypt, and if so when, perhaps should be left open.

3.   Monsignor Skehan has called an excellent example to my attention. In 2 Sam. 4.1, 2 the MT reads *wyšm' bn š'wl...hyw bn š'wl...* The latter phrase makes no sense whatever; the former is not happy. In both the LXX and 4QSam[a] the reading is *wyšm' mpybšt bn š'wl*, which grammatically makes perfect sense. However, Mephibosheth is an obvious blunder. Ishbosheth is meant in both instances. The reviser of the text did not replace the erroneous reading with the correct one; rather he excised the mistake and left the text standing. In the case of *hyw lmpybšt bn š'wl*, he cut out not only *mpybšt* but also *l* and forgot to replace it before *bn šwl*, leaving nonsense. Precisely the same phenomena, the excising of a mistake and thereby the creation of a defective (and senseless) text appears in 2 Sam. 3.7. Here again LXX and (in part) 4Q preserve the full but corrupt text to which MT is secondary.

Egypt and at Qumrân? The radical divergence of its text as well as its frequently inferior readings speak against such a conclusion. A recension in Palestine should have produced both a better text and a text closer to the Egypto-Palestinian family. We can hardly suppose the proto-Rabbinic recension to be a 'standard' text, while a text superior in many ways, and certainly standard in the day of the Chronicler, is reckoned a vulgar text. If, then, Egypt and Palestine are eliminated as possible localities for the development of the proto-Masoretic text, we may look to Babylon. It is not impossible that the ancestral proto-Rabbinic tradition developed independently in Babylon (after the return of the Exiles) and was reintroduced into Palestine in the Hellenistic period or later.

The evidence for reconstructing the history of the local recensions of the Pentateuch is rapidly accumulating; however, the problems are more complicated, and the recensional distinctions less clear cut than in the case of Samuel.

The Paleo-Hebrew text of Exodus, and especially the Numbers scroll described above, furnish materials for reconstructing the prehistory of the Samaritan recension. As we have seen, the Samaritan recension proper branches off in the early Hasmonaean period.[1] It differs from the 'proto-Samaritan' text at Qumrân only slightly; these differences would include, no doubt, the specifically sectarian readings—by chance the passages in question are not extant at Qumrân—and closer affinities to the proto-Rabbinic tradition. There is not the slightest reason to suppose that the 'proto-Samaritan' is in any sense a sectarian recension. In its textual characteristics it stands between the proto-Masoretic recension and the Egyptian recension preserved in the Septuagint as well as at Qumrân. Contrary to both the Egyptian and the proto-Masoretic traditions, however, it is characterized by free expansion, 'modernizing' revisions, insertion of parallel passages, and the like, most of its changes being transparently secondary. Such a process must have taken some time; these peculiarities are the product of traditional growth, not recensional endeavor.

Similarly, if Albright is correct, the Egyptian influences reflected in the Hebrew underlying the Septuagint suggest that the Old Egyptian recension was made no later than the fourth century.[2] Probably the Egyptian textual tradition and the proto-Rabbinic tradition separated as

1. See above, p. 127, nn. 2-3.
2. Albright, *op. cit.*, p. 30.

early as the fifth century, and the 'proto-Samaritan' cannot have diverged much later.

There can be no doubt that the proto-Samaritan text is Palestinian. If for no other reason, this can be argued from the fact that the Paleo-Hebrew script survives thanks to its transmission in texts of this type. The origin of the proto-Rabbinic tradition is less than clear. Possibly it was a text in use in official circles from the fifth century onward in Palestine, being transmitted independently, though side by side with the developing vulgar text represented in the proto-Samaritan. On the other hand it may be that it is a type which developed outside Palestine in the fourth and third centuries (presumably in Babylon) later being reintroduced—though in no case later than the Maccabean period. This would explain the repudiation of the traditional Paleo-Hebrew script in the rabbinic period (an unexpected development), as well as the influence of the proto-Rabbinic text on the Samaritan (*sensu stricto*) recension.

These details are enough to indicate that the biblical scrolls from Qumrân begin a new period in the study of the text of the Old Testament. Perhaps it is not too much to hope that in proper time, Old Testament scholars will be able to establish a genuinely critical or eclectic text of the Old Testament which would reconstruct a pre-Christian state of the Old Testament. At all events, the new finds will chart new courses by which progress will be made toward a more accurate, more intelligible Old Testament.[1]

---

1   See F.M. Cross, 'Problems of Method in the Textual Criticism of the Hebrew Bible', in *The Critical Study Sacred Texts*, ed. Wendy Doniger O'Flaherty (Berkeley: Berkeley Religious Studies Series, 1979), pp. 31-54.

Chapter 5

THE ESSENES AND THE PRIMITIVE CHURCH

Students of Christian origins have regularly traced the historical continuities which intimately connect Christianity and Pharisaic Judaism.
Thanks particularly to the rich traditional materials preserved by the
later rabbis, we have been able to reconstruct much of Pharisaic faith
and practice in the pre-Christian period, although it has never been
entirely clear how much tradition has shaped the picture of earlier
Jewish practice in the image of the normative Judaism which was
crystallized out of the Pharisaism which alone of the Jewish movements
of pre-Christian times survived the catastrophic Jewish wars against
Rome. Since Pharisaism is the best-known, and certainly the dominant
branch of early Judaism, there has been a natural tendency to equate it
with the Judaism of the first centuries before and after the initiation of
the Christian era, and Christianity has often been seen as its simple
derivative. Jesus himself has been called a renegade Pharisee and, the
New Testament polemic against the Pharisees notwithstanding, with
some justification. Certainly Pharisaism formed a major part of the
Jewish matrix in which Christianity was conceived, and from which it
drew its life and understanding. There can be no doubt that Pharisaism
was an important line along which the heritage of Old Israel was
transmitted to the Jewish-Christian community which claimed to be the
New Israel.

The early Church, however, was not the child of a single parent. Its
lineage must also be traced historically to those sectarian Jewish communities whose life and cult provided the 'setting in life' for apocalypticism. The language of the early Christian community, including that
of the sayings attributed to Jesus, is shot through with the terminology
of the Jewish apocalyptic; and the early Church conceived itself to be
precisely an eschatological community. We do well, therefore, if we are
to understand these motives in her structure and thought, to discover

the faith and forms of the apocalyptic communities which preceded Christianity.

The Essenes prove to be the bearers, and in no small part the pro-ducers, of the apocalyptic tradition of Judaism. As we have seen, an extraordinarily rich and extensive apocalyptic literature appears in the Essene library of Qumrân. Cycles of Enoch literature, Testaments literature, Daniel literature, pseudo-Jeremianic literature, and pseudo-Mosaic literature, as well as a score of apocalyptic types hitherto unknown, have proved to be at home among the Essenes of Qumrân, and hence, presumably, among the Essene cells of Palestine generally. No doubt Essene editions of certain apocalyptic works are based on sources composed in the Hasidic 'congregations'[1] or like communities of the Maccabean or late pre-Maccabean era. Such an explanation evi-dently obtains in the case of the rich Daniel literature at Qumrân,[2] only a portion of which escaped later condemnation by Pharisaic Judaism. In the case of other apocalyptic works it is difficult to determine whether they are properly designated 'Essene' or 'proto-Essene'. The concrete contacts in theology, terminology, calendrical peculiarities, and priestly interest, between the editions of Enoch, Jubilees, and the Testaments of Levi and Naphtali found at Qumrân[3] on the one hand, and the demonstrably sectarian works of Qumrân on the other, are so systematic and detailed that we must place the composition of these works within a single line of tradition. There can be no question here of isolated apocalyptists composing spontaneous works reflecting merely private or individual idiosyncrasies of doctrine or calendar. These works are molded by a common tradition, forged within the life of a continuing community with more or less separatist tendencies.[4] That is to say, much

1.   The Ḥasîdîm in 1 Macc. 2.42 receive the significant designation, συναγωγὴ 'Ασιδαίων, 'congregation of the Ḥasîdîm'. Our best source, as we have seen, distinguishes this 'congregation' from both the Hellenist and Maccabean parties. To what degree they were an organized group in their 'dedication to the Law', we cannot say with certainty. It seems highly probable, however, that in their movement they anticipated the separatist traits of the Pharisees and Essenes, and formed structured congregations or at least loose associations.

2.   Cf. Milik, '"Prière de Nabonide" et autres écrits d'un cycle de Daniel', p. 415; Cross, 'Fragments of the Prayer of Nabonidus', pp. 260-64.

3.   The qualification, *found at Qumrân*, is to be noted. The later editions of Enoch and the Testaments introduce apocalyptic traditions belonging to a different stratum and will be discussed below.

4.   See most recently on the Essene origin of Enoch, the Testaments, Jubilees,

of the apocalyptic literature found at Qumrân originates in Essene or proto-Essene (presumably Hasidic) communities and expresses not only their common speculative interests, but their common 'eschatological existence' as a community.[1]

In some sense the primitive Church is the continuation of this communal and apocalyptic tradition. It is not merely by chance that so much of the surviving literature of apocalyptic affinities was suppressed in normative Jewish circles and survived almost solely in a Christian milieu. And it is most significant that the literary genres featured in the 'Qumrân' apocalyptic remained living literary forms in the Jewish-Christian community at the same time they were dying in Judaism at large. The direct use of Essene or proto-Essene materials in Christian compositions, and, indeed, the publication of Christian compilations of Essene or proto-Essene sources can now be documented impressively.[2]

etc., R. Marcus, 'The Qumrân Scrolls and Early Judaism', pp. 9-17. Cf. H.H. Rowley, *Jewish Apocalyptic and the Dead Sea Scrolls* [Wood Lecture, 1957] (London, 1957), *passim*; and H.L. Ginsberg, 'The Dead Sea Manuscript Finds...' pp. 45-49.

1. It is worthy of note that the Qumrân library has not produced works composed in Jewish circles hostile to the sectarians. For example, there is no trace of the strongly pro-Maccabean histories of the Maccabees. See further below, n. 1, p. 182.

2. For example, the early Enoch literature is directly quoted in the New Testament, and had strong influence on several books, notably Revelation (cf. Charles, *Apocrypha and Pseudepigrapha* II, pp. 180ff). Again, it seems increasingly clear, from provisional examination of the documents of Cave IV, that those views are correct which insist that the received editions of 1 Enoch and the Testaments of the Twelve Patriarchs came from Jewish-Christian hands which supplemented and reworked (rather than merely interpolated) Essene editions. On the (Judeo-) Christian origin of the Testaments, see M. DeJonge, *The Testaments of the Twelve Patriarchs: A Study of Their Text, Composition, and Origin* (Manchester, 1954), who goes much too far, in my opinion; Milik's review of DeJonge (in light of Cave IV materials), *RB* 62 (1955), pp. 297-98; and 'Le Testament de Lévi en araméen', *ibid.*, pp. 398-406, especially pp. 405-6. Cf. Braun's discussion and citation of older literature, 'L'arrière-fond judaïque du quatrième évangile et la Communauté de l'Alliance', *RB* 62 (1955), p. 5, n. 4. Milik has recently identified a second source of the Christian edition of the Testaments at Qumrân, fragments of a Testament of Naphtali, which adds weight to his analysis.

On the Qumrân Enoch literature, see J.T. Milik, *The Books of Enoch: Aramaic Fragments of Qumrân Cave 4* (Oxford: Clarendon Press, 1976).

Another illustration is the doctrine of the 'Two Ways' found in the Rule of the Community (1QS). The theme is implicit in the Gospel of John (cf. Braun, *op. cit.*,

The full import of the continuities which bind together the earlier apocalyptic communities of Palestine with the primitive Christian community cannot be indicated, however, by reference to the survivals of Essene literary materials in Christian circles or the borrowings of Essene or Hasidic themes in Christian literary composition. We have known some of the Jewish apocalyptic writings from ancient times, of course, and these, together with more recently discovered works belonging to the same tradition, have played an increasingly important part in scientific New Testament studies. It is a commonplace of New Testament research today that the Jewish apocalyptic exerted a profound and direct influence on earliest Christianity. The new finds will extend our knowledge of this literature greatly, to be sure, and give us fresh means to analyze and describe its development[1] as well as its

p. 18), and this and like Essene formulations are found in the Didache, the Epistle of Barnabas, and elsewhere. Cf. J.-P. Audet, 'Affinités littéraires et doctrinales du "Manuel de Discipline"', *RB* 59 (1952), pp. 219-38; 60 (1953), pp. 41-82.

On Essene features in the Jewish-Christian Ebionite movement, see the judicious discussion of O. Cullmann, 'Die neuentdeckten Qumran Texte und das Judenchristentum der Pseudoklementinen', in *Neutestamentliche Studien für Rudolf Bultmann* (Berlin, 1951), pp. 35-51; J.A. Fitzmyer, 'The Qumran Scrolls, the Ebionites and their Literature', *Theological Studies* 16 (1955), pp. 335-72.

K.G. Kuhn, in 'Les rouleaux de cuivre...' p. 203, n. 1, has made the plausible suggestion that 2 Cor. 6.14–7.1 is cited (freely) by Paul from an Essene source.

It is extraordinary that the Essenes are not named in the New Testament. I know of no fully adequate explanation of this circumstance. Certainly it is not to be attributed to ignorance. We may find a partial explanation in the lack of antipathy of the early Church toward the Essenes. We hear of the other major parties of Judaism largely in polemical passages. On the other hand, there *are* polemical passages in the New Testament which are most easily explained as directed against the Essenes. The best example is Col. 2.16-23, where reference is made to matters of calendar, priestly laws of purity, worship of angels, etc.

1.   The later apocalyptic materials, 2 Baruch, the Similitudes of Enoch (=1 Enoch, 37-71), 2 Enoch, 2 Esdras (4 Ezra), The Assumption of Moses, the Testaments of the Twelve Patriarchs, *et al.* are not to be found at Qumrân, although in some cases sources of the above-named works or materials of a similar genre are extant. We have noted above that Testaments of Levi and Naphtali, earlier than, but related to the Testaments of the Patriarchs, have been found. The failure of the Similitudes of Enoch to put in an appearance among the multiple fragmentary copies of Enoch from Qumrân is especially noteworthy. As suggested by Milik, the silence of Qumrân in this instance is most impressive, and seems a good indication that this part at least of the Enoch cycle is post-Essene in date, and Christian in its received form. On the pseudo-Jeremianic literature, see J. Strugnell, 'Le travail d'édition...' p. 65.

relationship to the Christian apocalyptic.

Nevertheless, a new factor has entered. We have known little or nothing heretofore of the *Sitz im Leben* of the Jewish apocalyptic, the communities out of whose special faith and life the apocalyptic sprang as a characteristic expression. The background of the institutions and patterns typical of the communal life of the earliest Church in an earlier apocalyptic milieu can now be investigated seriously for the first time. The Essene literature enables us to discover the concrete Jewish setting in which an apocalyptic understanding of history was living and integral to communal existence. Like the primitive Church, the Essene community was distinguished from Pharisaic associations and other movements with Judaism precisely in its consciousness 'of being already the called and chosen Congregation of the end of days'.[1] Contrary to the tendency of New Testament theologians to assume that the 'eschatological existence' of the early Church, that is, its community life lived in anticipation of the Kingdom of God, together with the forms shaped by this life, was a uniquely Christian phenomenon, we must now affirm that in the Essene communities we discover antecedents of Christian forms and concepts.[2]

Students of the apocalyptic will immediately note that the Qumrân apocalyptic systematically fails to present materials containing allusions to the figure of the 'Son of Man' or to a Messianism strongly influenced by elements associated with the 'Heavenly Man' (the most recent discussion of these problems together with references to an extensive literature may be found in S. Mowinckel, *He That Cometh* [New York, 1956], pp. 261-450). We must assume that a developed 'transcendental' Messianism belonged either to (1) a post-Essene stage of the development of the apocalyptic or, less plausibly, to (2) another, parallel apocalyptic tradition.

1.   The phrase is taken from Bultmann (*Theology of the New Testament*; trans. K. Grobel [New York, 1951] Vol. I, p. 42). The full context of Bultmann's phrase is noteworthy: '...when regarded from the history-of-religions point of view, the earliest church presents itself as an eschatological sect within Judaism, distinguished from other sects and trends, not only by the fact that it awaits the crucified Jesus of Nazareth as Son of Man, but especially the fact that it is conscious of being already the called and chosen Congregation of the end of days.'

2.   The relation of the movement of John the Baptist to the Essenes on the one hand, and to the earliest Christian community on the other, may explain some of these continuities between the early apocalyptic traditions and the eschatological structure of early Christian thought and practice. (Cf. Cullmann, 'The Significance of the Qumran Texts...' *JBL* 74 [1955], pp. 218f.). John himself seems to have derived from priestly forebears. The little we know of his message fits very well into the context of the priestly apocalypticism of the Essenes. Moreover, it is quite likely that

In the pages to follow we shall investigate the theological language common to the Essenes and Christian sects, the common eschatological doctrines, and the related organizational and liturgical institutions belonging to the two 'apocalyptic communities'. There will be no serious attempt to deal exhaustively with the parallels between the Qumrân documents and the New Testament, even in the areas we have chosen for discussion.[1] One grows somewhat weary of the listing of

the members of his sect formed congregations, and, like the Essenes and early Christians, constituted themselves a community of the elect, baptized in repentance and in anticipation of the imminent New Age. On the other hand we cannot reconstruct either the life or teachings of the Baptist movement in any detail from the laconic, and sometimes tendentious notices in the New Testament, so that it is impossible to say, I believe, whether John and his disciples constituted an Essene splinter group or a parallel apocalyptic movement. It seems methodologically dubious to argue on the basis of John's desert life that he was at one time associated with the desert community of Qumrân. At best we can affirm that there are contacts between the preaching of John and the teaching of the Essenes of Palestine (and Qumrân).

Perhaps the strongest argument that the Baptist movement mediated between the Essene and Christian communities is to be found precisely in the ambivalence of the New Testament writers' attitude toward John. On John the Baptist's relationship to the Essenes, see further Braun, 'L'arrière-fond judaïque du quatrième évangile et la Communauté de l'Alliance', pp. 41f.; Metzinger, 'Die Handschriftenfunde am Toten Meer und das Neue Testament', *Biblica* 36 (1955), pp. 457-81; Brownlee, 'John the Baptist in the New Light of Ancient Scrolls', *Interpretation* 9 (1955), pp. 71-90. (Cf. 'A Comparison of the Covenanters of the Dead Sea Scrolls with Pre-Christian Jewish Sects', *BA* 13 [1950], pp. 49-72) Older literature may be found in Carl H. Kraeling, *John the Baptist* (New York, 1951).

1.   Among the many general studies of the Qumrân manuscripts and the New Testament, we may select the following for special reference: K.G. Kuhn, 'Die in Palästina gefundenen hebräischen Texte und das Neue Testament', *ZTK* 47 (1950), pp. 192-211; W. Grossouw, 'The Dead Sea Scrolls and the New Testament: A Preliminary Survey', *Studia Catholica* 26 (1951), pp. 289-99; 27 (1952), pp. 1-8; K.G. Kuhn, 'πειρασμός-ἁμαρτία-σάρξ im Neuen Testament und die damit zusammenhängenden Vorstellungen', *ZTK* 49 (1952), pp. 200-22; J. Coppens, 'Les documents du Désert de Juda et les origines du Christianisme', *Anal. Lovan.* II.41 (1953); F.-M. Braun, 'L'arrière-fond judaïque du quatrième évangile et la Communauté de L'Alliance', pp. 5-44 (broader than its title indicates); O. Cullmann, 'The Significance of the Qumrân Texts for Research into the Beginnings of Christianity', *JBL* 74 (1955), pp. 213-26; A. Metzinger, 'Die Handschriftenfunde am Toten Meer und das Neue Testament', pp. 457-81; Burrows, *The Dead Sea Scrolls*, Chap. XV, pp. 326-45; Frank M. Cross, '*The Dead Sea Scrolls*', *IB* XII, pp. 657-67 (cf. 'The Essenes and the New Testament', *The Christian Century*, August 24, 1955, pp. 968-71; and 'The Scrolls from the Judean Desert', *Archaeology* 9.1 [Spring,

parallels, for parallels as such may be casual or meaningful in determining relationships, depending on the integrity of each side of the parallel in its theological, dogmatic, or cultic context. Rather we propose to investigate certain parallels in theological language, cultic procedures, and ethos which appear to belong to a related apocalyptic framework, and which therefore may illuminate one of the historical lines along which the prophetic faith of 'Old Israel' passed, transmitted and transmuted by Essene Judaism, to the 'New Israel', the primitive Church.

1. *Common Theological Language: The Gospel of John*[1]

Linguistic and conceptual contacts between the scrolls and the New Testament are nowhere more in evidence than in the Gospel of John.[2] Such phrases as 'the spirit of truth and deceit' (1 Jn 4.6),[3] 'the light of

---

1956], pp. 48-53); R.E. Murphy, 'The Dead Sea Scrolls and New Testament Comparisons', *CBQ* 18 (1956), pp. 263-72; and *The Dead Sea Scrolls and the Bible* (Westminster, Maryland, 1956), pp. 55-108; W.D. Davies, 'The Dead Sea Scrolls and Christian Origins', *Religion in Life* 26 (1957), pp. 246-63.

1. This section, and parts of sections 2 and 3 of this chapter are a revised and expanded form of material published in the writer's article, 'The Dead Sea Scrolls', in Vol. XII of the *Interpreter's Bible*, copyrighted by the Abingdon Press in 1957. Copyrighted material is used here by permission.

2. Already there is an extensive literature in this field. In addition to the discussions to be found in the general articles cited in n. 1, p. 184, the following articles which deal primarily with Johannine parallels may be noted: L. Mowry, 'The Dead Sea Scrolls and the Background for the Gospel of John', *BA* 17 (1954), pp. 78-97; R.E. Brown, 'The Qumrân Scrolls and the Johannine Gospel and Epistles', *CBQ* 17 (1955), pp. 403-19; 559-74; A. Dupont-Sommer, 'La mère du Messie et la mère de l'Aspic dans un hymne de Qoumran', *RHR* 147 (1955), pp. 174-88 (parallels to Rev. 12); J.V. Chamberlain, 'Another Qumran Thanksgiving Psalm', *JNES* 14 (1955), pp. 32-41; 'Further Elucidation of a Messianic Thanksgiving Psalm from Qumrân', *ibid.*, pp. 181f.; L. Silberman, 'Language and Structure in the *Hodayot* (1QH3)', *JBL* 75 (1956), pp. 96-106; S. Mowinckel, 'Some Remarks on *Hodayot* 39.5-20', *JBL* 75 (1956), p. 276; and W.F. Albright, 'Recent Discoveries in Palestine and the Gospel of St. John', in the *Background of the New Testament and Its Eschatology*, pp. 153-71. [Most useful is Joseph Fitzmyer's paper, 'The Qumran Scrolls and the New Testament after Forty Years', *RB* 13 (1988), pp. 609-20.]

3. *rwhy 'mt w'wl* (1QS 4.23). *rwh 'mt* and *rwh 'wl* also appear standing alone often in Qumrân literature.

life' (Jn 8.12),[1] 'to do the truth' (Jn 3.21),[2] 'sons of light' (Jn 12.36),[3] 'life eternal' (Jn 3.15, 16; and *passim*),[4] familiar elements in the Johannine vocabulary, are also characteristic of the diction of the sectarian writings. More important are the repeatedly contrasted themes which sound a kind of counterpoint in both Johannine and Essene literature: light and darkness, truth and error or lying, spirit and flesh, love and hate, death and life. As in the scrolls, religious 'knowing' has a special flavor and wide usage in John; however, 'knowledge' as a revealed, especially eschatological knowledge, which belongs properly to the community of the saved, its most striking usage in the Essene literature, has its best parallels in Paul and Matthew.[5] In both John and the scrolls juridical language is common, and in both may be found a tendency to treat the inner teaching or sacraments of the community as esoteric.[6] The gift of salvation is not known by 'flesh', but through the 'spirit'. 'Unless a man be born again of water and the spirit, he cannot enter into the Kingdom of God' (Jn 3.5); 'Then God in his faithfulness (or by his truth) will purify all the works of man, and cleanse for himself

1.   *b'wr hḥyym* (1QS 3.7).
2.   *l'śwt 'mt* (1QS 1.5, etc.).
3.   *bny 'wr* (1QS 1.9; and especially 1QM *passim*).
4.   *ḥyy nṣḥ* (1QS 4.7, etc.).
5.   Typical of Johannine usage is Jn 17.3, 'And this is life eternal that they know you, the one true God and him whom you sent, Jesus Christ' (cf. 1 Jn 4.7f.). Compare 1QS 2.2-3: 'May he bless you with every good thing and keep you from all evil, and illuminate your heart with the wisdom of life, and favor you with eternal knowledge.' On the Johannine use, see R. Bultmann, 'γινώσκω, κτλ.' *TWzNT*, ed. G. Kittel, Band I, pp. 711-13.

On the usage of 'knowledge' in the scrolls and elsewhere in the New Testament, and the relationships to Gnostic usage, see especially K.G. Kuhn, 'Die Sektenschrift und die iranische Religion', *ZTK* 49 (1952), pp. 296-316; W.D. Davies, '"Knowledge" in the Dead Sea Scrolls and Mt. 11.25-30', *HTR* 46 (1953), pp. 113-29; and F. Nötscher, *Zur theologischen Terminologie der Qumran-Texte* (Bonn, 1956), pp. 15-79.

6.   On the juridical language of John, see Théo Preiss, *Life in Christ* (London, 1954) (from *La Vie en Christ* [Neuchâtel, 1951]), pp. 4-31. Preiss remarks of the Johannine literature, 'In a style of grandiose monotony, it develops a few unchanging themes...' (p. 10). No better description could be given of the theological sections of the sectarian document. There can be little doubt that the origins of the Johannine style must be sought after in Essene circles.

On the esoteric elements in John, especially in connection with the Eucharist, see J. Jeremias, *Die Abendsmahlsworte Jesu*, 2nd edn. (Göttingen, 1949), pp. 58-62.

the body of man, in order to consume every wicked spirit from the midst of his flesh, and to make him pure with (a) holy spirit from every wicked deed; and he will sprinkle on him (a) spirit of truth like water for impurity...so as to give the righteous understanding in the knowledge of the Most High...' (1QS 4.20-22).[1]

In both the Essene literature and in the Johannine writings there is the strongest emphasis on unity and community. The Essenes call themselves the Community,[2] literally the Unity. This oneness is a sign of the kingdom which is dawning and to which they belong, and is a gift of the spirit. The Johannine phrase, 'that they may be one', 'become perfectly one' (Jn 17.11, 21, 23) use typical Essene diction.[3] The quality of life in the true community is to be marked by love of brother; this is a basic theme of Essene discipline, and, of course, the repeated motive of the Johannine writings, especially 1 John. The Essene Rule also requires that one 'hate all the children of darkness', even as he must 'love all children of light'.[4] The note of hate is not characteristic of the New Testament ethic of disinterested love; however, as often has been remarked, the Johannine emphasis, unlike that of the New Testament in general, is almost exclusively on love within the 'little flock'; and a note of hostility toward the 'world' occasionally appears,[5] which, while milder than the Essene exhortation 'to hate', is nevertheless reminiscent of it.

According to Essene doctrine, the world is in the grip of two warring spirits, created by God from the beginning: the Spirit of Truth and the

---

1. Cf. Y. Yadin, 'A Note on DSD IV.20', *JBL* 74 (1955), pp. 40-43.

2. *hyhd*, 'unity' 'togetherness'. The translation 'community' is poor in English, since it permits secular connotations or the wide English usage to blur its narrow meaning. Moreover, the term in our texts has specific theological overtones; it applies to the 'eschatological' community or *Heilsgemeinschaft*, or to its activities 'in common' (*byhd*, etc.). A good number of the passages in published texts are collected by Habermann, '*dh w'dwt* (Jeruslaem, 1952), pp. 136,7. Note such phrases as *byhd 'l, byhd 'mt(w), lbryt yhd 'wlmym, bryt hyhd, lyhd qwdš, byhd 'stw, lyhd b'mtw, lyhd bryt 'wlm*, where the normal theological connotations are made explicit.

3. Note the Semitic and presumably 'Essene' form of the following: ἵνα ὦσιν τετελειωμένοι εἰς ἕν (Jn 17.23); *lhywt lyhd* (1QS 5.2); συναγάγῃ εἰς ἕν (Jn 11.52); *bh'spm lyhd* (1QS 5.7). Cf. Eph. 4.3-5.

4. 1QS 1.9-10; cf. Mt. 5.43, 44, which seems to be a reaction against such an emphasis.

5. E.g., 1 Jn 2.15; 3.13. See the discussion of Braun, pp. 19, 20; and especially Brown, pp. 561-64.

Spirit of Wickedness or Perversity.[1] The Spirit of Wickedness is none other than Belial, the 'Prince of Darkness', Satan. The Spirit of Truth is otherwise called the holy spirit (not identical with the Holy Spirit, though often hard to distinguish), the 'Prince of Lights', the 'Angel of Truth'. All men have their 'lot' in one of these spirits, and thus are children of light or darkness.[2] These two powers are locked in a titanic warfare, a struggle which mounts to a climax in the last times (compare Revelation and the War scroll). The war is waged, not only between the opposing arrays of spirits and their human hosts, but also within the heart of each 'son of light'.[3] For the people of the scrolls the end of the war is in sight. God is about to destroy forever the rule of the Spirit of Perversion, and bring an end to all darkness and wickedness. In the Johannine literature, however, although the struggle persists, and a final Armaggedon is to be fought,[4] yet the crisis of the battle is past, Jesus the Christ has 'overcome the world' (that is, the domain of the prince of Darkness).[5]

These remarks may be illustrated by the following passage from the Rule of the Community (1QS 3.17-23):

> [God] created man to rule the world and He established two spirits by which (man) would walk until the time appointed for His Visitation (that is, Last Judgment): these are the spirits of Truth and Deceit (or Wickedness). In a source of light are the origins of (the Spirit of) Truth and from a well of darkness the origins of (the Spirit of) Error. The rule of the children of righteousness is in the hand of the Prince of Light (so that) they walk in

1. On the doctrine of the Spirit at Qumrân, see E. Schweizer, 'Gegenwart des Geistes und eschatologische Hoffnung bei Zarathustra, spätjüdischen Gruppen, Gnostikern und den Zeugen des Neuen Testamentes', *The Background of the New Testament and Its Eschatology*, pp. 482-508; and W.D. Davies, 'Paul and the Dead Sea Scrolls: Flesh and Spirit', in *The Scrolls and the New Testament*, pp. 157-82.

2. Cf. Jn 8.42-47; 1 Jn 5.19 (as well as 2 Cor. 6.14–7.11), etc.; and especially 1QS 3.13–4.26.

3. 1QS 4.23-26. It is in this framework that the New Testament concepts of temptation, predestination, and justification must be understood (as well as corresponding ideas in the scrolls). See K.G. Kuhn's admirable analysis, 'πειρασμός-ἁμαρτία-σάρξ im Neuen Testament...' and Nötscher, *Zur theologischen Terminologie der Qumran-Texte* pp. 173-82. On the scrolls and 'justification' see above, Chapter 3, n. 1, p. 144.

4. *Pace* Bultmann.

5. See Father Brown's discussion, pp. 410-12. On the *Kampfsituation* in the thought of Jesus, see Kuhn, pp. 219ff., who draws attention to the following pertinent passages: Mt. 10.34; Mt. 12.28f. and parallels.

ways of light; the rule of [all] children of error is in the hand of the Angel of Darkness (so that) they walk in ways of darkness; and when any of the children of righteousness err, it is through the Angel of Darkness...and all the spirits allotted to him (attempt to) make the children of light stumble, but the God of Israel and His Angel of Truth are a help to all sons of light.

The passage may be compared with the following citations from 1 John:

Children let no one lead you astray. He who does righteousness is righteous, as he is righteous; he who commits sin is of the devil, for the devil has sinned from the beginning. To this end the Son of God was made manifest, that he might destroy the works of the devil. None that is born of God commits sin, for His seed abides in him (so that) he is not able to sin, because he is born of God. By this the children of God are made known, and the children of the devil. Everyone who does not do righteousness is not of God...(1 Jn 3.7-10).

Beloved, do not trust every spirit, but test the spirits, whether they are from God...By this you know the spirit of God: every spirit which confesses that Jesus Christ has come in flesh is from God, and every spirit which does not confess Jesus is not from God; and this is the (spirit) of the antichrist...Children, you are of God, and have conquered them, for he who is in you is greater than he who is in the world. They are of the world; for this reason what they say is of the world and the world listens (obediently) to them. We are of God; he who knows God listens to us; he who is not of God does not listen to us. By this we know the Spirit of Truth and the Spirit of Deceit. (1 Jn 4.1-6)

In both the Rule and 1 John we recognize a similar 'spirit–spirit' dualism, a powerful doctrine of predestination which allots some to God or the Spirit of Truth, others to the devil or the Spirit of Deceit. In both, the diabolical spirit struggles against the children of God (or of light). In both, the children of light have knowledge which permits them to distinguish between the spirits of truth and deceit. Because of the aid of God or the Spirit of Truth, the children of light do righteousness, but those under the dominion of the devil walk in ways of darkness. We have noted above that the work of Jesus gives a new note of victory. We may note also that the Johannine dualism is differently expressed. In the Johannine literature the Spirit is normally God's own spirit or Christ's own spirit (cf. 1 John 4.13). In the Qumrân Rule the Spirit of Truth has a 'greater distance' from God; the hypostatized Spirit *of* God has become largely identified with an angelic creature, the spirit *from* God, and their functions combined.[1]

1. Cf. the remarks of W.D. Davies on the differences between the doctrine of the

The 'Prince of Light' or 'Spirit of Truth' is appointed, according to the Essenes, as a *helper* to all children of light.[1] The figure of the *Paraclete* or Advocate of John (Jn 14.17; 15.26; 16.13, 1 Jn 5.6-8[2]) is derived from this complex of ideas. His function, described as 'to witness', to 'intercede', 'to speak', yet *'not on his own authority'* (Jn 16.13), has always been puzzling, for it does not fit the expected description of the Holy Spirit. And the origin and meaning of the term *Paraclete* as an appellation of the Spirit of Truth has been much in dispute.[3] In light of the new Essene parallels, we now understand the title and vocation of the Advocate/Spirit of Truth for the first time with some clarity.

The origin of the concept is found in the heavenly court of Yahweh in the Old Testament where in scenes of judgment Satan as prosecuting attorney stands over against the Angel of the Lord as advocate or witness.[4] In the elaborate angelology and dualism of the Essenes, partly

Spirit of God in the New Testament and the doctrine of the two spirits in the Qumrân literature in his article, 'Paul and the Dead Sea scrolls: Flesh and Spirit', *The Scrolls and the New Testament*, pp. 157-82.

1.   Cf. 1QM 13.10 *śr m'wr m'z pqdth l'wzrnw*; 1QS 3.24, 25 *w'l yśr'l wml'k 'mtw 'zr lkwl bny 'wr*; and 1QM 17.6-8.

2.   Often in the Johannine material the functions of the Spirit of Truth as (1) bearer of light, (2) leader of the armies of God, and (3) Advocate or witness are shifted to the Christ. Cf. (1) Jn 9.5; 12.46; (2) Rev. 12.7-12 parallel to 19.11-21; and (3) 1 Jn 2.1.

3.   As early as 1933, S. Mowinckel, on the basis chiefly of Essene material in the Testaments of the Twelve Patriarchs, was able to reconstruct much of the Old Testament and Jewish background of the *Paraclete* figure. See his studies, 'Die Vorstellungen der Spätjudentums von heiligen Geist als Fürsprecher und der johanneische Paraklet', *ZNW* 32 (1933), pp. 97-130; and 'Hiobs gō'ēl und Zeuge im Himmel', in K. Budde (ed.)*Vom Alten Testament* (Marti Festschrift), (Geissen, 1925), pp. 207-12; Cf. N. Johannson, *Parakletoi* (Lund, 1940), pp. 3-178; and especially Théo Preiss, *Life in Christ*, pp. 19-25.

However, Mowinckel's work has been widely ignored, especially by members of the Bultmann school in Germany; this is unfortunate since the new texts (e.g., those quoted in n. 2, above) directly support Mowinckel. The opinion of Bultmann himself has been expressed most recently in his *Theology of the New Testament* I (New York, 1955), p. 88n. For the present state (pre-Qumrân!) of the discussion, see W. Michaelis, 'Zur Herkunft des johanneische Paraklet-Titels', in *Coniectanea Neotestamentica* XI (Lund, 1947), pp. 147-62; G. Bornkamm, 'Der Paraklet in Johannesevangelium', in *Festschrift Rudolf Bultmann* (Stuttgart, 1949), pp. 12-35.

4.   See especially 1 Kgs 22.19-24; Zech. 3; and Job, especially in 16.19 and 19.25 where the 'Heavenly Witness' is to be identified with the 'Angel of the Lord',

under Iranian influence, the Old Testament origins are blurred and transmuted so that the two angels become the two opposing principles or spirits of truth and error, light and darkness. In the cosmic struggle the heavenly accuser becomes the diabolical tempter of the sons of light, the Prince of Darkness who is at war with the Prince of Light. The heavenly advocate becomes the Spirit of Truth, a holy spirit which testifies to truth in the heart of those in the 'inheritance' of truth, as well as the accuser of the children of darkness.[1] In John the Essene dualism is partly resolved, but reflections of the Essene structure of thought still survive. This is especially clear in the Johannine advocate, but also to a lesser degree in the special function of the Spirit in Acts and in Paul.

These Essene parallels to John and the Johannine Epistles will come as a surprise only to those students of John who have attempted to read John as a work under strong Greek influence. It now turns out—as a small coterie of scholars have long maintained—that John has its strongest affinities, not with the Greek world, or Philonic Judaism, but with Palestinian Judaism. Its concepts of truth, knowledge, spirit, and even the Word[2] must be seen, not as rooted in Greek or Gnostic thought, but as concepts emerging precisely out of sectarian Judaism. So that rather than being the most Hellenistic of the Gospels, John now proves to be in some ways the most Jewish.

Ultimately these conclusions will bear on critical theories in regard to the origin of John. We must look for a *Sitz im Leben* for the development of Johannine tradition where Jewish Christianity was dominant, and where Essene influences persisted. Some have suggested that John may be regarded no longer as the latest and most evolved of the Gospels, but the most primitive, and that the formative locus of its tradition was Jerusalem before its destruction. This is not to suggest that the present

as first pointed out by Mowinckel. The function of the angel, or divine messenger as witness in heavenly court scenes is found already in ancient Canaanite mythology (as I have been reminded by G.E. Mendenhall).

1. Cf. Test. of Judah 20. Preiss (*Life in Christ*, p. 20) comments on this passage, 'Similarly in Jn 16.7ff. the Spirit of Truth will convict the world of sin...It plays the part of accuser before the world...But as soon as man has received the truth in faith the roles are reversed; the Satanic Spirit of Error will seek to accuse him...while the Spirit of Truth as Paraclete will witness to him of the certainty of the love of God.'

2. Actually, no equivalent of ὁ λόγος in the Johannine sense can be documented in the scrolls. However, intimate parallels to the Prologue of John, in style, content, and vocabulary appear in the new documents. Cf. Braun, pp. 15-16; 1QS 11.11; 1QS 3.15-17.

form of the book has not had an elaborate literary history; the point is that John preserves authentic historical material which first took form in an Aramaic or Hebrew milieu where Essene currents still ran strong.

2. *Some Common Eschatological Motifs*

Both the Essenes and the primitive Church believed that the last age was imminent; indeed, they were living in the last times; they were the last generation. In some sense the new age had dawned; at least its signs were discernible in the events of their day. History had reached its crisis. The powers of darkness and light were poised for the final, decisive struggle. The Church was exhorted to 'put on the full armor of God...to stand against the wiles of the devil...to be able to withstand the evil day, and having done so to stand' (Eph. 6.10-17); the Essenes divided their little community into battle divisions and drew up a liturgy of Armageddon.

In the prophecies of the Old Testament the Essenes saw predicted the events of their own day. Where the prophets spoke of the last days and their signs (and even where they did not), the sectarian commentators discovered fulfillment in the history of their own times or in the inner life of their sect. Those with 'knowledge' should now recognize that the final war had begun. They must 'decide', understanding by faith and the spirit the fulfillment of prophecy, expectant of the consummation of history.

Of themselves the Essenes wrote, quoting Isaiah: 'When these things come to pass in Israel to the Community...they will separate themselves from the midst of the abode of perverse men to go into the desert to prepare there the way of the Lord according as it is written, '"In the desert prepare ye the Way (of the Lord), make straight in the wilderness a highway for our God"' (1QS 8.12-14).

Thus this people understood themselves to be in the situation of John the Baptist, of whom the New Testament quotes the identical passage of Isaiah. Jesus' early teachings are in much the same eschatological framework.[1] The man in the early Church lives in a 'later' moment. He believes that the Messiah has come and that his resurrection signals the beginning of the New Creation. Yet he lives in a like tension. The Kingdom delays, the 'world' remains. He must partake proleptically of

1. Cf. James M. Robinson, 'Jesus' Understanding of History', *JBR* 1955, pp. 17-24.

life in the Kingdom to come, anticipating the coming day when ambiguity will end, the world be transformed, an end be brought to all wicked flesh, and the Kingdom of God fulfilled.

The Essenes therefore search the Scriptures and interpret their prophecies eschatologically. As several scholars have pointed out, Essene exegesis has no real parallel either in Rabbinic Judaism, or in Philonic Judaism.[1] Their interpretation is neither legalistic nor allegorical. But it falls precisely into the pattern of the New Testament's use of the Old Testament. In both, exegesis is 'historical' (that is, eschatological), and pneumatic.[2]

The Essenes believed themselves to be the people of the New Covenant. They yearly celebrated the renewing of this New or 'Eternal' Covenant,[3] no doubt recalling Jeremiah's prediction of a new covenant

1.   Cf. L. Mowry, 'The Dead Sea Scrolls and the Gospel of John', pp. 93-94 G. Vermès in his article 'A propos des Commentaires biblique découverts à Qumrân', *RHPR* 35, pp. 95-102, after distinguishing the Qumrân *pĕšārîm* from both the *midrash* and Philonic exegesis, attempts to find parallels in the Targumim, but without notable success. Cf. C. Rabin, 'Notes on the Habakkuk Scroll and the Zadokite Documents', *VT* V (1955), pp. 148-62.

2.   Krister Stendahl in his volume, *The School of St. Matthew* (Uppsala, 1954), pp. 181-202, has stressed the affinity between presuppositions and style in quoting the Old Testament in Essene and New Testament composition. He notes the 'apocalyptic' character of Old Testament interpretation common to both, but also attempts more precise definition of what he calls the *pĕšer* mode of citation and interpretation, common to Qumrân commentaries and certain of the quotations of the Old Testament in the New, especially 'the formula quotations' of Matthew. Here he finds a freedom of citation based partly on a thorough knowledge of Hebrew text types and translations, partly on techniques which permit the learned expositor to manipulate an Old Testament passage to fit sectarian interests. Stendahl wrote before the character of the Old Testament text at Qumrân had become fully known, so that his work presumes a view of the Old Testament text which virtually identifies the text of the early Christian era with the single Masoretic tradition. In view of the relatively fluid state of the Old Testament in the earliest Christian period, his results must be qualified at a number of points.

The question of testimonia lists allegedly used in composition of New Testament works must also be re-examined in light of our new knowledge of the complex character of the Hebrew text in the early Christian period, and, as well, in light of the testimonia literature from Qumrân.

3.   J.T. Milik in an oral communication indicates that on the basis of new data, including a reading in an unpublished text, he can establish that the festival of the New Covenant among the sectarians fell on Pentecost (i.e., at the traditional time when the law was given at Sinai). This suggests intriguing possibilities for interpreting the

(Jer. 31.31). They understood this 'New Covenant' to be at once the 'renewed (old) covenant' and the 'eternal covenant' to be established at the end of days; that is, precisely in the New Testament sense.

The Essenes had a most developed Messianism. They expected an eschatological prophet recalling Deut. 18.15-18.[1] This figure has a counterpart in the New Testament in John the Baptist. However, it is interesting that in John's Gospel, the Baptist denies that he is Elijah, and also that he is the expected prophet, implying that Jesus is the prophet to come.[2] And in Acts 3.22 Jesus is identified in Peter's sermon precisely with the prophet of Deut. 18.15-18.[3] Moreover, the category of 'Messianic prophet' has left many traces in the earliest Church's interpretation of the work of Jesus.

A second eschatological figure is the Anointed Priest. He is the faithful priest of prophecy, the Star of Jacob, the Messiah of Aaron.[4] He is the primary figure of the New Age in the priestly apocalypticism of the Essenes. Jesus is never specifically designated the Messiah of Aaron, though there are reminiscences of this and like categories in the New Testament.[5] In the Testament of Joseph[6] the Messianic priest is called the

setting of the event of Pentecost in the New Testament.

1.   Cf. 1QS 9.11; and 4Q Testimonia.

2.   Jn 1.21, 25; 6.14; 7.40.

3.   On the Ebionite identification of Jesus with the 'true prophet', see Fitzmyer, 'The Qumrân Scrolls, the Ebionites and Their Literature', pp. 356-58.

4.   In addition to Milik's study in *DJD* I, pp. 121f., see K.G. Kuhn, 'Die beiden Messias Aarons und Israel', *NTS* 1 (1954–55), pp. 168-79; G. Friedrich, 'Beobachtungen zur messianischen Hohepriesterwartung in den Synoptikern', *ZTK* 53 (1956), pp. 265-311, especially the introductory survey; W.H. Brownlee, 'Messianic Motifs of Qumrân and the New Testament', *NTS* 3 (1956–57), pp. 12-30; the excellent study of R.E. Brown, 'The Messianism of Qumrân', *CBQ* 19 (1957), pp. 53-82; A.S. van der Woude, *Die messianischen Vorstellungen der Gemeinde von Qumrân* (Assen, 1957); and the paper of J. Liver, 'The Doctrine of the Two Messiahs in Sectarian Literature in the Time of the Second Commonwealth', *HTR* 52 (1959), pp. 149-85. Literature predating the publication of 1QSa and 1QSb, especially, and to some degree that predating the partial publication of 4Q Testimonia, 'Patriarchal Blessings', and 'Florilegium', is now antiquated. One may be singled out for its perception, M. Burrows, 'The Messiahs of Aaron and Israel', *ATR* 1952, pp. 203-6.

5.   G. Friedrich (*op. cit.*, pp. 275-305) has attempted to demonstrate that strong traces of a priestly Messianism are to be found in the Synoptics, and proposes that alongside the Christologies of the Davidic Messiah, the Suffering Servant, and the 'Son of Man', we must now make room for a high-priestly Christology. In detail,

Lamb, who takes precedence over the Lion of Judah, the royal Messiah; no doubt we must combine this figure with that of the *militant* Lamb in Revelation. Most obvious is the interpretation of Jesus as the heavenly high priest in the Epistle to the Hebrews.[1] Here Jesus is the combined priestly and royal Anointed in the type of Melchizedek, the priest-king of Salem in the days of Abraham. One suspects a conscious attempt of the early Church to adjust its Christology to the Messianic expectations of the Essenes, or rather to see in its single Messianic figure the fulfillment of all the Messianic longings of the past.[2]

The Essenes also expected the coming of the Davidic or royal Messiah. He would be lay head of the New Israel, commander of the troops in the Final War, and universal king.[3] Various proof texts of the Old Testament are quoted by the Essenes predicting the scion of David, some of which are used of Jesus in the New Testament. Of course the identification of Jesus as the Davidic Christ or Messiah of Israel dominates New Testament confessions.

The Messianic doctrine of the Essenes, including certain of its peculiar features, is closely related to that of the early Church. In both, the Messiah(s) appear in the end of days to receive an eternal kingdom; in each the royal Messiah appears bearing a sword, and defeats the earthly and cosmic powers of wickedness; in both there are priestly, royal, and prophetic elements in their Messianic expectations. There are also noteworthy distinctions. Nowhere at Qumrân, at least so far, is there a hint of 'highest' New Testament Christology: the pre-existence of the Messiah, the Second Adam, the Son of Man. In the (later edition of the) Testament of Levi, Ch. 18, in a hymn to the Messianic high priest, we find passages reminiscent of these doctrines. The Messiah here leads the return to Paradise and feeds the saints upon the tree of life. However,

---

however, his analysis is rarely convincing.

6.   Chap. 19. To be sure there is a Christian hand visible in the chapter, and any attempt to analyze the elements into older and later strands is bound to be partly subjective; nevertheless, it appears that the figures of the Lamb and Lion stand behind the present form of the text.

1.   Rev. 17.14 (cf. T. Jos. 19.8!). Cf. Charles, *The Revelation of St. John* [ICC] I, pp. cxiiif.; especially n. 2.

2.   Cf. G. Friedrich, *op. cit.*, p. 303.

3.   Cf. 4QpIsa. D: 1-5; 1QSb V.20-29; 1QM 5.1; 12.10-15 (?); 1QSa II.11-22; 4Q Patr. Blessings; 4Q Florilegium; etc.

Note in 1QSb: V.29, the prince is compared with a lion. Cf. Rev. 5.5, the 'Lion of Judah'; Test. Jos. 19.8; etc.

the material is suspect and cannot be used to establish Essene doctrine. In short, both in Essene circles and in the early Church we find a developed apocalyptic Messianism.[1] In the Qumrân literature, however, the Messiah has not yet become a heavenly savior. Nor is there any evidence in the Essene documents that the Messianic figures were confused or combined as they were in the early Church's Christology.[2] [3]

The question may be raised as to the role of the Righteous Teacher in the eschatology of the Essenes. He was an 'eschatological' figure predicted in Scripture who was to aid in bringing the New Age to birth. Is he one of the three, prophet, priest, or king?

The vocation of the Righteous Teacher during his lifetime must be described as that of forerunner of the Messianic figures. I think there can be no question of his disciples attributing Messianic rank to a Teacher who died before the full dawning of the Messianic age and remained dead during the subsequent life of the sect![4] This need not prejudice necessarily the question of a possible second coming of the Teacher in the Age-to-Come.[5] Among the least ambiguous passages relating to the Messianic figures are the following:

> All the men who entered into the New Covenant in the 'Land of Damascus',
> but have again acted faithlessly and turned aside from the well of living
> water, shall not be reckoned in the council of the people, nor inscribed in

1.   See Brown, pp. 59-63, 79.

2.   Dupont-Sommer has argued (cf. 'Le Testament de Lévi [XVII-XVIII] et la secte juive de l'alliance', pp. 47-53) that the three offices were combined and applied to the Righteous Teacher. His crucial evidence is drawn from the Testaments of the Twelve Patriarchs, evidence which appears to us to be inadmissible.

3.   W.H. Brownlee, 'Messianic Motifs of Qumrân...', pp. 17-30, has suggested that the motif of the Suffering Servant is applied to the Messiah and to the eschatological Prophet in the Qumrân literature adumbrating the identification of Jesus with the Servant of 2 Isaiah. He builds his case essentially on two crucial passages: 1QS 4.20-23 and 1QH 3.6-18. The interpretation of both is disputed. On the former, the interpretation of Y. Yadin, 'A Note on DSD IV, 20', *JBL* 74 (1955), pp. 40-43, seems clearly superior to that of Brownlee. As to the latter, I am inclined to a non-Messianic interpretation (Mowinckel, Silberman, *et al.* cf. n. 2, p. 185); but even if the Messianic interpretation is assumed, it would seem to have no necessary connection with the theme of the *suffering* Messiah.

4.   There are no references to a resurrection of the Righteous Teacher in the Qumrân literature; on pHab. 11.4-8, see Elliger, *SzHK* pp. 213-18; R. de Vaux, *RB* 58 (1951), pp. 437ff.

5.   Cf. K. Stendahl, 'The Scrolls and the New Testament, an Introduction and a Perspective'.

their book, from the day the Teacher of the Community died until the Messiah of Aaron and the one of Israel arise.[1] [*CD* 19.34 (= 8.21)-20.1]

...and they shall not deviate from the whole counsel of the Torah to walk in any stubbornness of their (own) heart but shall be judged by the first decisions (laws) by which the men of the Community commenced to be disciplined, until a Prophet comes and the Messiahs of Aaron and Israel. (1QS 9.9-11)

The former passage cleanly separates the Messianic advents from the life-time of the Teacher. The latter asserts that the rules of the Community, presumably enacted in the early days by the Teacher and his flock, are binding until the coming of an eschatological prophet and the appearance of the priestly and royal Messiahs. This appears to distinguish between the work of the Teacher in establishing the community and the work of the Prophet who appears alongside the Messiahs.[2]

While in Judaism the forerunners of the Messianic age include Elijah and the 'prophet like Moses',[3] I do not believe that the Teacher is to be thought of as a prophetic forerunner. He is, of course, a Zadokite priest. This need not disqualify him from a prophetic office. And certain of his gifts and works suggest prophetic powers. He understands all the words of the prophets by divine inspiration. He opens the books of the Law. However, the high priest properly performed an oracular function,[4] and the late high priests claimed gifts of prophecy.[5] Moreover, teaching is first of all a priestly function.[6] If our interpretation of the Testimonia is correct, the passage quoting Deut. 33.8-11 relating to the oracular and teaching duties of the priesthood is applied by the sect to the Righteous

1. ...*mywm h'sp* [] *mwrh hyh<>d 'd 'md mšyh<y>* (with Kuhn, Milik, *et al.*) *m'hrn wmyśr'l*. If the form *mšyh* is not emended, the same sense is gained by reading 'the Messiah from Aaron and (the one) from Israel'. Cf. 1QS 9.9-11. See below, pp. 187-88.

2. Cf. Brown, pp. 73-74.

3. On the concept of 'forerunner' in Jewish eschatology, see most recently, Mowinckel, *He That Cometh*, pp. 298-302. Mowinckel also takes the Righteous Teacher to be a forerunner.

4. Cf. the 'ephod of prophecy' given to Levi in T. Levi, 8.2; the title 'False Oracle' taken from prophetic contexts in sectarian exposition (see above Chapter 3, esp. p. 116, nn. 4, 5) presumes the 'prophetic' office of high priest, Cf. K. Elliger *SzHK*, p. 209.

5. Cf. Josephus, *Antiq.* XIII, 288-98; 300; etc.; Jn 11.51.

6. In *CD* 5.5 Zadok is portrayed as an inspired teacher of Torah. Cf. also the discussion of the expression *dôreš hat-tôrāh*, n. 1, p. 199.

Teacher,[1] following (1) the passage relating to the prophet like Moses, and (2) the Star and the Scepter, the priestly and royal Messiahs respectively. Moreover, the revealed title of the Essene Master is precisely 'Righteous Teacher'. While he may be referred to in other ways, the title *par excellence* chosen by the sect from ancient prophecy[2] is neither a prophetic nor Messianic designation. It is a priestly designation, chosen, we suspect, because other traditional titles were for one reason or another less appropriate. A parallel may be found in the Johannine designations of John the Baptist. Here John is portrayed as rejecting the titles of Christ, Elijah, and 'the prophet'. He is a forerunner, to be sure, but who? The solution is to name him 'the Voice crying in the Wilderness'. So a new title for the forerunner is sought out to fit John's circumstances. Similarly, to the question, 'Is the Essene master the prophet, the Messiah of Aaron or Israel?' I think we must answer: 'No, he is the Righteous Teacher of Scripture'.

We have been speaking of the Righteous Teacher's role as forerunner during his ministry. There is, however, a further question. Is the Righteous Teacher to return after death, and if so, will he appear as prophet, priest, king—or as righteous teacher?

There is one passage which can be utilized plausibly to suggest the reappearance of the Righteous Teacher in the Messianic age. This is a well-known and long-debated passage from the Damascus Document, an exposition of Num. 21.18.[3] The expositor is describing events during the epoch of the 'ruin of the land' or the epoch of 'wickedness'.

> But God remembered the covenant of the forefathers, and raised up from Aaron men of understanding, and from Israel wise men, and he made them listen (obediently), so that they dug the well, *The well which the princes dug, which the nobles of the people delved with the staff* (meḥôqēq). *The well* is the Torah, and *those who dig it* are the penitents of Israel who went out from the land of Judah and sojourned in the Land of Damascus...
>
> And the Staff (m^eḥôqēq) is the expositor of the Law (dôrēš hat-tôrāh)...and *the nobles of the people* are those that come to dig the well with precepts (m^eḥôq^{e}qôt) which the Staff laid down, that they might walk in them during the whole epoch of wickedness. Except

---

1. See above, Chapter 3, esp. p. 114, nn. 2-4.
2. Cf. Chapter 3, p. 114, n. 4.
3. Direct quotations from Numbers are in italics.

for them they cannot grasp (the Law)[1] until the Righteous Teacher[2] arises in the end of days (6.2-11).

The last phrase, 'until the Righteous Teacher arises in the end of days' is in itself ambiguous; it may apply to the contemporary life of the sect seen from the perspective of the 'whole era of wickedness' or it may refer to the Messianic era after the death of the Righteous Teacher. Context must determine which is the correct understanding. The era of the 'devastation of the land',[3] otherwise called the 'era of wrath',[4] applies to the interval between the demise of the Davidic kingdom[5] before the power of Babylon,[6] and the rise of the sect. The exposition of Num. 21.18 here as elsewhere is applied to the sect itself, not to the ancient Jewish community.[7]

The crux of the passage is the identification of the Staff, the expositor of the Law. He holds a priestly office.[8] He is a figure of the past, possibly of the remote past,[9] more likely of the time of the beginnings of the sect. In the latter case he is most easily identified with the Righteous Teacher or with an early Hasidic leader, a precursor of the Teacher at the earliest beginnings of the sect, twenty years before the initiation of the Teacher's ministry.[10] In some respects, identification with a Hasidic

---

1. See Rabin, *The Zadokite Fragments*, pp. 22, 23.

2. Usually the biblical title is distorted to *môrēh haṣ-ṣedeq*; here it is *yôrēh haṣ-ṣédeq*.

3. *CD* 5.20-21.

4. *CD* 1.5-6.

5. *CD* 3.9-10.

6. *CD* 1.5-6.

7. Cf. *CD* 8.35 (19.21); Chapter 2, p. 71, n. 2.

8. The term 'Staff' in 4Q Patr. Blessings applies to the historical, royal covenant of David. The term *dôrēš hat-tôrāh*, however, applies to the priestly office of teaching or studying the Law. In *CD* 7.18-19 it is applied to the *Star*, the priestly Messiah, the counterpart of the Scepter, the royal Messiah: 'the *Star* is the expositor of the Law who comes to Damascus' (*hb' dmśq*, i.e., who will come to the Essene community). In 4QFlor. the expositor of the Law is associated with the Davidic Messiah and hence we most easily take the expression to apply to the priestly office, in this instance again the priestly Messiah: 'He is the Scion of David who arises (*h'wmd*, i.e., who will arise; the participial construction is the same as in the preceeding quotation) with the expositor of the Law.'

9. See the writer's remarks in his *Interpreter's Bible* article, p. 664, n. 117; an identification in the remote past, with Aaron or Zadok, now appears less likely to me.

10. Cf. *CD* 1.5-11. S. Mowinckel ('The Hebrew Equivalent of Taxo in Ass. Mos.

founder seems the better solution of the two. It would explain the fact that the Staff is not specifically called the Righteous Teacher, and the expression 'until the Righteous Teacher arises in the end of days' need apply only to the ministry of the Righteous Teacher as forerunner.

If indeed we identify the Staff with the Righteous Teacher, then it follows that the Teacher is expected to return in the Messianic era. Under this hypothesis, we can then proceed to the conclusion that he will return as the priestly Messiah. His priestly lineage disqualifies him as a candidate for the Davidic Messiahship; and it is unlikely that the Righteous Teacher would properly function as an inspired interpreter of prophecy alongside the priestly Messiah.

There are obvious difficulties in this whole line of argument. The Teacher of Righteousness is nowhere explicitly identified with the coming priestly Messiah.[1] He is not specifically identified with the Staff.

---

ix', VTSup 1 [Leiden, 1953], pp. 88-96; cf. *He That Cometh*, pp. 300f.) has identified the man called Taxo in the Assumption of Moses with the Staff of the Damascus Document arguing that τάξων is the Greek equivalent of *mehôqēq*. The combination is the best suggested to date, though not wholly certain. Taxo was of the tribe of Levi, according to the Assumption, and in a time of a second dreadful visitation (that is, after the Babylonian captivity), exhorted his sons to fast three days, and then on the fourth enter a cave and die in order that God's Kingdom come. There is nothing historically impossible in identifying Taxo either with the Righteous Teacher or with a Hasidic predecessor of the Teacher.

1.   John Allegro, in his article, 'Further Messianic References in Qumrân Literature', assumes that the appearance of the epithet, 'expositor of the Law', in a context where it is clearly applied to the priestly Messiah (4Q Flor.) proves that the Teacher must be identified with the priestly Messiah. Actually the importance of the new passage is that it tends to confirm the view that the Star associated with the Scepter in *CD* 7.18-19 is the *priestly* Messiah. The expression 'expositor of the Law' is not a 'revealed' title of an eschatological figure named in Scripture. More probably it designates a priestly function appropriate to the Staff of history, to the priest of the New Age, or to the Righteous Teacher. As it happens, however, the expression is never associated directly with the title 'Righteous Teacher'.

In connection with the expression *dôrēš hat-tôrāh*, it may be noted that in 1QS 6.5 the rule is laid down that in each Essene community there must be one who functions as the expositor of the Law, *'yš dwrš btwrh*. Cf. 5.11, 8.15, Jubilees 23.26, etc.

Allegro argues in effect that the Righteous Teacher=the Staff; the Staff=the expositor of the Law; the expositor of the Law=the priestly Messiah. Therefore the Righteous Teacher=the priestly Messiah. That is, a=b; b=c; c=d; *ergo*, a=d. This logic would be excellent if Mr. Allegro were not dealing with apocalyptists, who unfortunately do not lay out their materials mathematically. One could add another step: the Staff=the Davidic covenant; *ergo*, the Righteous Teacher is the Davidic

It is noteworthy that the one passage which makes plausible this series of deductions is in the Damascus Document, and that all the literature from Qumrân has not yielded sufficient data to resolve the question. If the Essenes did expect their Teacher to return as the priestly Messiah, they have been exceedingly indirect in expressing their hope. The New Testament preoccupation with the death and Messiahship of Jesus is in significant contrast.[1] Perhaps the whole question is best left unsettled until new data are forthcoming.

3. *The Order and Liturgical Institutions of the 'Apocalyptic Communities'*

The scroll material is especially rich in materials which illuminate the origins of the organizational structure of the early Church, especially the Church in Acts.[2] Throughout the history of Christianity there have been debates concerning the nature of Church government in Apostolic times. Some have contended that the order was democratic, government without stated offices, others that it was presbyterian, following the practice of the synagogue, still others that its form of government was monarchic, governed by bishops. Actually elements of each of these types of organization appear in the New Testament. Scholars have increasingly attempted to fit them into an evolution moving from the free and congregational order to a more rigid monarchic structure.

The Essenes were a priestly and lay community, governed by hereditary priests in cultic affairs, by laymen in their common religious and 'secular' life. There is, of course no precise counterpart in Christianity to the dominance of the Aaronic office. The organization of the Essenes is most instructive, however, once this qualification is made.

The ruling assembly of the Essenes, made up of all the mature members of the covenanted community is called the *Rabbîm*, literally,

covenant (a=b; b=e; e=a). Furthermore, his first equation is not clearly established; and if our understanding of *dôrēš hat-tôrāh* as an (ideal) priestly function is correct, then Allegro can prove at best that each of these figures...expounds the Torah.

1. Cf. the writer's remarks in the *New Republic*, April 9, 1956, p. 19.

2. See especially, S.E. Johnson, 'The Dead Sea Manual of Discipline and the Jerusalem Church of Acts', *ZAW* 66 (1954), pp. 106-20; B. Reicke, 'Die Verfassung der Urgemeinde im Lichte jüdischer Dokumente', *ThZ* 10 (1954), pp. 95-112; Cross, 'The Scrolls and the New Testament', *The Christian Century*, August 24, 1955, pp. 968-71; J. Daniélou, 'La communauté de Qumrân et l'organization de l'Eglise ancienne', *RHPR* 35 (1955), pp. 104-15.

the 'Many'. It is a technical term in Hebrew which appears in literal translation in the New Testament with similar technical meaning.[1] The Jerusalem council is so designated in Acts 15.12; the assembly which chooses the Seven and places them before the Apostles is so named in Acts 6.2, 5; Silas and Judas together with Paul and Barnabas assemble the 'Many' of the Church at Antioch to hear the report of the 'Many' in Jerusalem (15.30).

Within the 'Many' was a higher judicatory consisting of twelve lay-men and three priests. These were the types of the twelve princes of the tribal assembly in the Mosaic era, together with three priests repre-senting the princes of the three clans of Levi,[2] as seems clear from the role and number of the princes in the War scroll. The circle of the Twelve in the early Church in part parallels the Essene Twelve. For example, the Essene inner circle, according to the Rule of the Community, when it is established in Israel (in the last days) will be '...an eternal planting (Isa. 60.21; 61.3), a holy temple for Israel...faithful witnesses in judgment, the Elect of (God's) favor to atone for the earth, and to mete out punishment to the wicked. It (the inner circle) is the tried (foundation) wall (misquoting Isa. 28.16), the precious corner whose foundations shall not be shaken...'[3] Rev. 21.14 (cf. Eph. 2.20; Heb. 11.10) alludes to the same passage (Isa. 28.16; cf. Ezek. 48.31), recording that the wall of the New Jerusalem 'had twelve Apostles of the Lamb'. In Lk. 22.30 Jesus addresses the Twelve: 'You are those who have continued with me in my trials; as my father appointed a kingdom for me, so do I appoint for you that you may eat and drink at my table in my kingdom, and sit on thrones *judging the twelve tribes* of Israel'. Here again is the theme of the twelve 'judges' of the *eschaton* after the pattern of the old princes of the tribal assembly of Israel.[4]

Finally, to mount another stage, the highest office of the Essene community, aside from that of the presiding priest, was that of the

1. The same term may be applied in non-sectarian Judaism with reference to members of a synagogue or *ḥᵃbûrāh*; in this case it does not, apparently, carry the technical meaning of a body with democratic powers.

2. This was first called to my attention by J.T. Milik.

3. 1QS 8.5-8.

4. Compare also the more general application of Isa. 28.16 to the Church in 1 Pet. 2.4-5. The two figures, the 'planting' and the 'building' used in the Essene text are also combined in application to the Church in 1 Cor. 3.9. Of course the description of the Church in the figure of a holy temple is a familiar motif in Pauline writings (1 Cor. 3.16; 2 Cor. 6.16).

inspector, *m^ebaqqēr*.[1] He was president of the sessions of the 'Many', fiscal agent of the community, director of labors, religious and secular, in charge of training and examining those who applied for membership in the community. He was to act as shepherd (*CD* 13.7-9). Scholars have long recognized here a parallel to the Christian shepherd, the bishop or ἐπίσκοπος, a term applied to Jesus in 1 Pet. 2.25 (together with the designation 'shepherd'), but usually to leaders in the early Church. Yet the parallel left something to be desired, since the normal Hebrew equivalent of ἐπίσκοπος is *pāqîd*. However, even this difficulty is resolved in Qumrân material. In one passage (1QS 6.12-14) the *m^ebaqqēr* is called the *pāqîd* 'at the head of the Many', that is, the 'bishop of the Many'.[2]

Thus a democratic assembly, a council of twelve, and an episcopal overseer all belong to the pattern of community organization among the Essenes. It would appear that the early Church appropriated and

---

1.   *m^ebaqqēr* probably has as its Greek equivalent ἐπιμελητής, used by Josephus of the Essene overseers.

2.   Cf. the writer's remarks, 'Qumrân Cave I', p. 124.

Recently J.T. Milik (*Découvertes, ad loc.*), has observed that the presiding priest of the community (who must be distinguished from the *m^ebaqqēr*; cf. 14.8-9) is described as follows in *CD* 14.7, *hkwhn 'šr ypqd
 'š hrbym*, 'the priest appointed overseer at the head of the Many'; and in an unpublished text, *hkwhn hmpqd 'l hrbym*, 'the priest appointed overseer over the Many'. On the basis of this data he suggests the official title of the lay official is *m^ebaqqēr*, of the priestly official, *pāqîd*.

The situation is not so simple. The *pāqîd* of 1QS 6.14 is not the presiding priest, but the *m^ebaqqēr*. This is evident not merely because of its parallelism with 6.12, but because the *pāqîd* here mentioned is functioning as *m^ebaqqēr*. The text reads, 'and everyone who volunteers from Israel to be added to the Communal Council (the Essene membership), the one who is overseer (*pāqîd*) at the head of the Many shall try him as to his intelligence and his works...he shall make him to understand all the rulings of the Community' (6.13-15). In *CD* 13.11-13 we read: 'and everyone who is added to his congregation, he [the *m^ebaqqēr*; cf. 13.6, 13] shall examine him (*ypqdhw*) as to his works and his intelligence...and he shall inscribe him in his place according to his situation in the party [lit. lot] of the truth. Let no one of all the members of the Camp assume authority to bring someone into the congregation contrary to the will of the *m^ebaqqēr* of the Camp.' The identity of function of the *pāqîd* of 1QS and the *m^ebaqqēr* of *CD* is obvious not only in the general sense of the passages, but in the frequent verbal contacts between the passages. We have here two forms of a single rule of organization.

Perhaps the term *pāqîd* could have been used of either official, at least in the early period.

modified offices and institutions belonging to older apocalyptic communities in developing its own organizational structure.

The central 'sacraments' of the Essene community appear to be its baptism(s) and its communal meal. The baptism of the Essenes, like that of John, was on repentance of sins into the eschatological community of God.[1] Contrary to early Christian usage, the Essenes seem to have practiced daily priestly lustrations as well as baptism on entrance into the New Covenant of the Community.[2] It is also possible that they repeated the initiatory rite of baptism at the yearly ceremony of covenant renewal.[3]

In the discussion of the communal meal of the Essenes in Chapter 2[4] we argued that the meal must be understood as a liturgical anticipation of the Messianic banquet. The anticipation of the banquet of the Kingdom is a strong element also in the New Testament accounts of the Lord's Supper and in the later Eucharistic practice of the Palestinian Church. In the Markan account we read, 'Truly I say to you, I shall not drink again of the fruit of the vine until that day when I drink it new in the kingdom of God' (14.25); in the Lukan version it is even stronger, especially if one follows the shorter text (22.14-19a); and it appears as well in the Pauline and later formulae; 'For as often as you eat this bread and drink the cup, you proclaim the lord's death *until he comes*' (1 Cor. 12.26); 'marana-tha, Come our Lord', and 'the holy vine of David thy servant which was made known to us through Jesus...' (*Didache* 9.2, 10.6)[5]

---

1.   1QS 5.8-23; especially 5.13-14 (the passage is discussed in detail above, Chapter 2, n. 7, p.105). Cf. 2.25–3.12, especially 3.4-7 where baptism is connected not only with repentance and covenant, but also with the gift of the spirit; 4.20-22; etc.

2.   The practice of a baptism of initiation in combination with practice of daily ritual washings persists among the Ebionites. Cf. the discussion of Fitzmyer, 'The Qumrân Scrolls, the Ebionites and their Literature', pp. 365ff.

3.   Cf. Chapter 2, p. 81, n. 2.

4.   Pp. 74-78.

5.   Many other allusions to the Messianic banquet appear which occur in Eucharistic contexts, or which seem to be shaped by liturgical usage in the early Church; e.g., Rev. 19.9, 'Blessed are those who are invited to the marriage supper of the Lamb.' In Lk. 22.30, we read '...that you may eat and drink at my table in my kingdom...'; this saying is placed in the context of a dispute over rank at the Lord's Supper. The account of the miracle at Cana has frequently been held to have Eucharistic overtones. In any case Jesus' reply to his mother when told that the wine had failed is obscure; 'O woman, what have you to do with me? My hour has not yet

The Church of Acts (Acts 2.46, etc.) ate common meals regularly, 'partaking of the food in joy'. Indeed, these banquets of joyous anticipation led to the excesses referred to in Jude 12 and 1 Corinthians 11, and to the later reforms which in turn led to the separation of the Eucharist proper from the regular common meals of the faithful.

What is the background of the institution of common meals of the entire community, eaten in anticipation of the Messianic banquet? The Passover, the other element in the background of the Lord's Supper, can give no suitable context.[1] It is a yearly feast of memorial, eaten in private in families, and is not, properly, an eschatological festival. The Essene meal gives the first suitable answer.

This is not to suggest that the Church merely took over an Essene meal. Within the Lord's Supper are notable original elements: the formulas which transform the old Passover into the feast of the New Covenant memorialize the sacrifice of the body and blood of the victim, the pledge of the covenant.[2] And there is no reason, I think, to suppose that the combination of the two elements, the memorial of the sacrifice and the anticipation of the Messianic banquet does not exist already in the most primitive traditions of the Jerusalem community.

The extreme emphasis on rank at the Essene banquet is noteworthy. It seems hardly by chance that in the Gospels of Luke (22.24-30) and John (13.12-16), teaching which repudiates the desire for rank among the disciples is placed in discourses at the Last Supper. Elsewhere we also hear Jesus condemning those who seek places of rank in his kingdom. Moreover, in the parable of the banquet in Lk. 14.15-24 (cf. Mt. 22.1-14), which in its present context is told in reply to one who says, 'Blessed is he who shall eat bread in the kingdom of God', we find

come.' Normally, 'the hour' refers elsewhere in John to his Passion and death. Why does Jesus refuse (at least at first) to provide the wine at the feast because his 'hour' has not come? Perhaps Jesus is portrayed here as alluding to the day when he properly will provide wine as host at the Messianic feast.

1. For recent attempts to equate the Lord's Supper with the Passover, see J. Jeremias, *Die Abendsmahlsworte Jesu*; and A.J.B. Higgins, *The Lord's Supper in the New Testament* (London, 1952).

A. Jaubert in a recent article (see Chapter 1, p. 46, n. 2) has argued with no little weight that the Gospel accounts are best understood if Jesus celebrated his Last Supper on the date of Passover in the Essene (and old religious) calendar, while the Crucifixion took place on the eve of the official Jewish Passover.

2. The rite of the renewal of the covenant among the Essenes is not, so far as we can tell, directly related to their communion meals, the former being an annual affair.

the remarkable expression, 'For I tell you, none of those men who were invited shall taste my banquet'; while the feast of the Essenes is for 'the Men of the Name Who are Invited to the Festival'.[1]

We have noted that the life of the sect is understood as life in antici-pation of the Kingdom of God. This eschatological community is made concrete not only in the common meal of the Messiah but also in the sharing of goods. Entry into the Essene community meant giving up all private property. In the New Testament Church, especially in Palestine, a similar practice obtains: 'Now the congregation of believers were of one heart and soul, and no one said that any of the things he possessed were his own, but they had everything in common (Acts 4.32; cf. 4.32–5.11); 'And all who believed were together and had all things in common... And day by day attending the temple together and breaking bread together (in common meals) in their homes, they partook of food with glad and generous hearts' (Acts 2.44-46).

Again, as we have seen, many (though not all) Essenes eschewed marriage.[2] They were soldiers already mustered and prepared for the Holy War of the End Time. Being engaged in the war of God, they took up the ancient ritual prescriptions of the Old Testament for Holy War, keeping the 'purity of their camps'. They refrained from sexual inter-course and marriage, which disqualified one for war, kept the stringent sanitary regulations of Holy War, and all the rest. Theirs was not a genuine asceticism, but an eschatological asceticism. They did not, it seems, reject marriage as such, but marriage in the present circumstances.

Compare this structure of thought with the following passage in Paul's letter to the Corinthians: 'I mean, brethren, the appointed time has grown very short; from now on, let those who have wives live as though they had none, and those who mourn as though they were not mourning, and those who rejoice as though they were not rejoicing, and those who buy as though they had no goods, and those who deal with the world as though they had no dealings with it. For the form of this world is passing away' (1 Cor. 7.29-31).

---

1.   J.T. Milik and D. Barthélemy (*DJD I*, p. 117) have called attention to this parable of the banquet in connection with the list of rules which prohibited men who were maimed, unclean, blind, etc., from entering into the inner councils and cultus of the Essene community. Jesus, in absolute contrast, asserts that 'the poor and maimed and blind and lame' will be brought in to the banquet (Lk. 14.21)! It is difficult to suppose that the parable is not told in conscious reaction to sectarian doctrine.

2.   Chapter 2, pp. 81-84.

Chapter 6

NOTES ON A GENERATION OF QUMRÂN STUDIES[1]

I have chosen the title 'Notes on a Generation of Qumrân Studies' to make clear that this essay will be a desultory, not a systematic approach to recent scroll research and publication. This is not the place to give a comprehensive overview of forty years of research. If one wishes to read an insightful and judicious review of Qumrân studies he can do no better than to read Devorah Dimant's essay on 'Qumrân Sectarian Literature' in the volume *Jewish Writings of the Second Temple Period* edited by Michael Stone.[2] I wish rather to comment on progress of recent date in areas of my own interest and competence, to register pleasure over some confirmations of the results of early synthetic efforts to comprehend the rich data of the discoveries, and finally, to express some doubts about, and even displeasure at, some recent trends in Qumrân studies.

1. Let me begin with the palaeography of the Qumrân scrolls. In 1961 when I published my monograph on 'The Development of the Jewish Scripts', we depended heavily on typological dating, that is relative dating by typological sequence, for the Archaic scripts and for the Hasmonaean scripts.[3] Only in the Herodian period was there a sufficient number of inscriptions which could be dated absolutely to provide firm dating pegs in the typological sequence. Even here there was no super-abundance of dated scripts in the formal character. In the intervening

---

1.   This chapter is a revised and expanded version of a lecture prepared for the Madrid meetings, published in *The Madrid Qumran Congress: Proceedings of International Congress on the Dead Sea Scrolls, Madrid 18-21 March, 1991* (Leiden and Madrid: Brill and Editorial Complutense, 1992): Volume I: 1-14.

2.   *Compendia Rerum Iudicarum ad Novum Testamentum.* Section Two (Assen and Philadelphia: Van Gorcum and Fortress Press, 1985), pp. 483-550.

3.   G. Ernest Wright (ed.), *The Bible and the Ancient Near East* (Garden City, New York: Doubleday, 1961), pp. 133-202.

three decades much new palaeographical material from this period has been found, including the great mass of inscriptions from Masada recently published by Joseph Naveh, inscriptions with an absolute *terminus ad quem* of 73 AD.[1] For dating the earlier scripts we depended on fourth and third-century papyri and ostraca in Aramaic from Egypt, they in turn being dated primarily by typological sequence and on indirect data from Palmyrene and Nabataean inscriptional data. Thirty years have brought marvelous new controls. Most important perhaps are the dated papyri executed in Samaria, found in the Wâdî-ed-Dâliyeh.[2] The latest is dated March 19, 335 BC.[3] Hirbet-el-Kôm has produced ostraca in Greek and Aramaic, including a bilingual text dated in the sixth year of a Ptolemy who can only be Ptolemy II, Philadelphus, 277 BC. And a recently published papyrus from a Jericho cave is contemporary, written in a beautiful formal hand.[4] Its script is breathtakingly close to the script of 4QSam[b] and, as well 4QEx[f] and 4QJer[a]. My 1961 dates for the three third-century manuscripts may in fact be minimal, as I noted soon after the discovery of the Samaria papyri.[5] That is, the old Samuel is probably no later than 250 BCE, and the old Jeremiah scroll late third century. The archaic Exodus, more difficult to date because of its cursive tendencies, should probably date in the range 275–225 BC. Other finds, including the Raphia Ostracon and the Jerusalem Sherd, the latter probably from the time of Ptolemy Philadelphus, the former from the end of

---

1.   Y. Yadin and J. Naveh in *Masada I: The Aramaic and Hebrew Ostraca and Jar Inscriptions* (Jerusalem: Israel Exploration Society and The Hebrew University of Jerusalem, 1989), pp. 1-68 and Plates 1-60.

2.   See the writer's discussion in Paul W. Lapp and Nancy L. Lapp (eds.), *Discoveries in the Wâdî ed-Dâliyeh* AASOR XLI (Cambridge, 1974), pp. 17-29, and Pls. 59-63.

3.   See F.M. Cross, 'Samaria Papyrus I: A Slave Conveyance of 335 B.C.E. Found in the Wâdî ed-Dâliyeh', *EI* 18, pp. 7-17* and Pl. II [The Avigad Volume]; and 'A Report on the Samaria Papyri', in the *Jerusalem Congress Volume, 1986. Supplements to Vetus Testamentum* 40, pp. 17-26.

4.   For the Hirbet el-Kôm text, see Lawrence T. Geraty, 'The Khirbet el-Kom Bilingual Ostracon', *BASOR* 120 (1975), pp. 55-61; the Jericho Papyrus was published by Hanan Eshel and Hagai Misgav, 'A Fourth Century B.C.E. Document from Ketef Yeriho', *IEJ* 38 (1988), pp. 158-76 and Pls. 25-26. It will be noted that the dates of Eshel are, in my opinion, too high. In very recent days a large number of ostraca from the end of the Persian era and the beginning of the Hellenistic era have come to light, apparently from the vicinity of Mareshah. When published they will provide a series of precise dates including some from the years of Alexander himself.

5.   See above in the paper cited in note 4.

the fourth century, give additional data for the palaeography of the Archaic era of the Jewish character.[1] I should say that I know of only three third-century manuscripts from Qumrân, despite claims to the contrary, and all of these are in the Jewish character, not the Palaeo-Hebrew character. Archaic manuscripts of the first half of the second century need to be shifted up little if any, and I believe that the dates of manuscripts in the Jewish character which I have dated to the Hasmonaean and Herodian periods need no adjustment.

New materials for the analysis of the Palaeo-Hebrew character have been used in the dissertation of Mark McLean.[2] In general he lowers the date of manuscripts written in this script on the basis of comparative data, notably coins with absolute dates. For example, the date given to 4QEx[m] by Monsignor Skehan, 200–175, and by Richard Hanson, 225–175, McLean correctly lowers to c. 50 BC. The date of 11Q Lev, dated by Hanson to c. 100 BC in the *editio princeps*, McLean dates to 1–50 CE and again I believe his arguments to be sound.[3] The rich new finds in the Samaritan remains on Mount Gerizim, excavated by Yiṣḥaq Magen, when fully published, will provide a firm absolute *terminus ad quem* for a number of inscriptions in both the Palaeo-Hebrew and the Jewish scripts.[4] The date in question is 128 BC, the destruction of the sacral area and city on Gerizim by John Hyrcanus I. Several of the inscriptions, both in Palaeo-Hebrew and in the Jewish character were exhibited in the Rockefeller Museum in the summer of 1990. From my observations in the Museum (but without photographs for careful, precise study) I am

1. The Raphia sherd was published by J. Naveh, "Published and Unpublished Aramaic Ostraca', *'Atiqot* 17 (1985), pp. 118-19, and Pl. XX, 9. The Jerusalem Sherd was published by F.M. Cross, 'An Aramaic Ostracon of the Third Century B.C.E. from Excavations in Jerusalem', *Eretz-Israel* 15 (1981), pp. 67*-69* and Pl. IV, 2 [The Aharoni Volume].

2. Mark David McLean, 'The Development and Use of Palaeo-Hebrew in the Hellenistic and Roman Periods' (unpublished Harvard University dissertation, 1982).

3. See Richard Simon Hanson in D.N. Freedman and K.A. Mathews, *The Paleo-Hebrew Leviticus Scroll: (11QpaleoLev)* (Winona Lake, Indiana: ASOR, 1985), pp. 15-23.

4. See provisionally Y. Magen, 'A Fortified Town of the Hellenistic Period on Mount Gerizim', *Qadmoniot* 19 (1983), pp. 91-101; and 'Mount Gerizim—A Temple City', *Qadmoniot* 23 (1990), pp. 70-96. See also Reinhard Plummer, 'Samaritan Remains and Archaeology', in Alan D. Crown (ed.), *The Samaritans* (Tübingen: Mohr, 1989), pp. 167-77.

under the impression that my chronology of both the Palaeo-Hebrew and Jewish scripts is correct.

In 1991 Magen Broshi, curator of the Shrine of the Book, announced at the Madrid Congress the results of a series of carbon$_{14}$ dates made on papyri of the fourth century BC (papyri bearing date formulae), on a sequence of Qumrân scrolls, on materials from the Bar Kokheba caves, and on Khirbet Mird material.[1] The dates achieved by this technique for the Qumrân documents conform remarkably well to the results gained by palaeographical analysis. And the agreement between carbon$_{14}$ dates and the documents with date formula confirm the accuracy of the carbon$_{14}$ techniques in dating objects of this era.

2. From palaeography let us move the short distance to another technical subject, that of the orthography of the scrolls. At Qumrân in both biblical books and in sectarian works we find several types of orthography, an archaic orthography less *plene* than that of the Rabbinic Recension of the Pentateuch, and which does not use *waw* as a *mater lectionis* for long-ō derived from older long-ā, the so-called Canaanite shift.[2] This is the orthography of the earliest of the biblical scrolls, 4QSam^b. A frequent orthography is a style slightly fuller in its use of *waw* and *yod* as vowel markers than the Rabbinic Recension, a style found also in inscriptions and coin legends of the second century BC. This orthography appears as early as the old Exodus scroll of the third century, and continues as late as the Herodian period (e.g., 4QDt^n). Orthography in the Rabbinic mode is also found early and late. Perhaps the most interesting and instructive orthography found in the Qumrân Manuscripts is what I have called the baroque style. It is a full orthography in its use of *matres lectionis*, but is marked as well by a series of alternate, long pronominal elements. In most cases the long form of the pronoun or pronominal suffix is distinguished by the preservation of a

---

1.   See now G. Bonani, M. Broshi, I. Carmi, S. Ivy, J. Strugnell, and W. Wölfli, 'Radiocarbon Dating of the Dead Sea Scrolls', *'Atiqot* XX (1991), pp. 27-32. A wrong result was produced in one instance among fourteen documents tested: the Testament of Qahat [4Q534]. The script of this manuscript is coeval with that of the Samuel manuscript labeled 4QSam^c, dated palaeographically to ca. 100–75 BC, by carbon$_{14}$ to 192–63 BC. But the carbon$_{14}$ for the Testament of Qahat is 388–353 BC, an impossible dating, some two centuries too early.

2.   See D.N. Freedman, 'The Massoretic Text and the Qumran Scrolls: A Study in Orthography', in F.M. Cross and S. Talmon (eds.), *Qumrân and the History of the Biblical Text* (Cambridge and London: Harvard University Press, 1975), pp. 196-211.

final long-ā vowel: in the second person masculine singular, for example, –*kh* with nouns, –*th* with verbs. Old case endings on adverbs, and volitive endings in –ā on verbs are also restored, and indeed leveled through in contexts where they do not belong. These a-vowels are survivals of old Canaanite. In vernacular speech final-a vowels were lost about 1200 BC. The suffix of the second masculine singular, for example, was pronounced –*ak* in vernacular Hebrew in pre-Exilic times, and as observed in *Early Hebrew Orthography*, this is the dominant pronunciation of the suffix in the second column of the Hexapla, in Jerome's transcriptions in Latin, in manuscripts with Palestinian punctuation, and, as well, in Samaritan sources.[1] Sporadically we also find the suffix transcribed as –*kh*, –*kā*. I have used the second person pronoun to illustrate, but a similar pattern is found in the contrasts, *hū'*, *hū'āh*, *hī'*, *hī'āh*, etc. The baroque orthography was devised as an attempt to preserve archaic, elevated or poetic speech, lost in vernacular or prosaic Hebrew. The devisers of the baroque orthography overstepped themselves, and leveled through long forms in –ā in biblical prose, where such forms are probably artificial. In any case the memory of such forms is based, no doubt, on manuscripts which used a final *mater lectionis hē* to mark the literary long form. In pre-Exilic Hebrew we have only two inscriptions which are literary or poetic. One, the Beit Lei inscription, is well-known; the second, a spectacular ostracon from Ḥirbet 'Uzza, is only recently published.[2] In these two inscriptions the second-person singular pronouns are spelled –*kh* (e.g., *qbrkh*) and in verbal forms in the Khirbet 'Uzza Sherd, the verbal suffix is written –*th* (e.g., *wht'r'rth*), as in the baroque style. Evidently such spelling survived in later manuscripts, the basis of the restoration of such forms in baroque orthography. In the case of Rabbinic orthography, these forms were freely revised to vernacular or non-literary forms in –*k*, that is –*ak*. The verbal suffix, –*tā(h)* was revised to –*t*. Oddly some forms were preserved in the Rabbinic Recension, for example *ntth* [*nātattāh*], written with *hē* in more than

1.   F.M. Cross and D.N. Freedman, *Early Hebrew Orthography* (New Haven: American Oriental Society, 1952), pp. 65-60.

2.   See especially the papers of F.M. Cross, 'The Cave Inscriptions from Khirbet Beit Lei', in *Near Eastern Archaeology in the Twentieth Century: Essays in Honor of Nelson Glueck* (Garden City, New York: Doubleday, 1970), pp. 299-306; Patrick D. Miller Jr, 'Psalms and Inscriptions', *Congress Volume, Vienna 1980. Supplements to Vetus Testamentum*, pp. 311-32, esp. 320ff.; and especially Itzhaq Beit-Arieh, 'A Literary Ostracon from Ḥorvat 'Uza', with an Appendix by Frank Moore Cross, 'A Suggested Reading of the Ḥorvat 'Uza Ostracon', *Tel Aviv* 20 (1993), pp. 55-65.

half of its occurrences. In short we have an interesting and characteristic phenomenon in which one style of orthography levels through short, non-literary or prosaic forms of pronouns; the other levels through elevated or poetic long forms of the pronouns. Which orthography is to be preferred? Which is 'free'? The Massoretes, *sensu stricto*, did not like some of the vernacular forms in the Rabbinic Recension. They changed vernacular forms properly *–ak* and *–t*, into the archaic forms *–kā* and *–tā* by placing a *qameṣ* anomalously in the bosom of *kap* and under *taw*. Most Hebraists, strangely, never ask why all final vowels in Massoretic Hebrew are marked by a *mater lectionis* except *–kā* and *–tā*. Why?— because the Massoretes are freely archaizing on the basis either of oral tradition, or more likely on the basis of old manuscripts which preserve these forms. My point is this: both the baroque orthography and the orthography of the Rabbinic Recension are revisionist and mixed orthographies. Neither approximates pre-Exilic orthography. Neither approximates the orthography of the fourth and early third centuries BC. Both exhibit a long process of revision. The Rabbinic orthography is as artificial as the baroque. Its only advantage is familiarity. To call it a conservative orthography is to mislead. Better to call it the vernacular or the popular orthography of c. 200 BC. The baroque orthography first appears at Qumrân in the third quarter of the second century BC. The scribes responsible, perhaps Sadducean in affiliation, understood what they were doing as a learned exercise in preserving archaic Hebrew pronunciation.

Emanuel Tov in a recent paper has argued that what I have called baroque orthography is actually a style invented by and limited to the Qumrân community in the desert.[1] He calls it 'Qumrân orthography and language'. It is true that the earliest extant exemplar of this orthography is the old Isaiah scroll which dates to c. 150-125 BC, very close to the time of the withdrawal of the Essene community into the desert. But the system of orthography surely was not invented with the great Isaiah scroll. The slightly different styles of baroque orthography in the first half and the second half of the scroll suggest that it was copied from two scrolls in baroque script of earlier date which presses us very close to the date of the separation of the sect into the desert. I think that the baroque orthography is a learned attempt at archaism, much like the Massoretic pointing correcting the Rabbinic consonantal text, and was known in

1.   See E. Tov, 'The Orthography and Language of the Hebrew Scrolls Found at Qumran and the Origins of These Scrolls', *Textus* 19 (1986), pp. 31-57.

Palestine in the Hasmonaean and Herodian eras quite widely. At the same time I think it is true that the scribes in the Qumrân scriptorium were enchanted with this archaizing style, and that Tov is correct in recognizing that many if not all baroque texts were copied at Qumrân.

Where I disagree categorically with Tov is in his claim that the baroque orthography is 'free', Rabbinic orthography 'conservative'. The Proto-Rabbinic style is the result of revision, the leveling through of short forms where they were original and where they were not. In the case of the baroque style there is the leveling through of long forms whether they were original or not. To term one tradition conservative is to misuse language. Tov's 'conservative' really means familiar, his 'free' means unfamiliar. Still the baroque style is almost certainly a Palestinian fashion rejected by the Pharisees in favor of a different type of text, just as they rejected the Palaeo-Hebrew script in favor of the vernacular Jewish script in selecting their Pentateuchal model. In one instance they selected the popular script, not the national script of Palestine, in the other instance they selected an orthographic style popular towards 200 BC, neither an old orthography nor the baroque. Actually, they probably chose texts which had this style of script and orthography rather than revising systematically. This would explain the unevenness of the orthography of the Rabbinic Recension, especially in late books. As I have long argued, I believe that the most plausible explanation of these surprising choices is to be found in the choice of Babylonian manuscripts of the Pentateuch as the model for the Recension promulgated by Hillel and his house in the early first century AD.

3. Let me turn to some comments on the history of the biblical text and the contribution of the Qumrân scrolls to our understanding of this history. In a series of articles Emanuel Tov has attacked my attempts to organize the multiplicity of textual data from Qumrân using a theory of local texts, a commonplace phenomenon in the textual history of groups of ancient documents.[1] To borrow the language of a colleague in

---

1.   The writer's papers include 'The History of the Biblical Text in the Light of Discoveries in the Judaean Desert', 'The Contribution of the Qumrân Discoveries to the Study of the Biblical Text', and 'The Evolution of a Theory of Local Texts', all found collected in F.M. Cross and S. Talmon (eds.), *Qumrân and the History of the Biblical Text* (Cambridge and London: Harvard University Press, 1975), pp. 177-95, 278-92, and 306-20; and 'Problems of Method in the Textual History of the Hebrew Bible', in Wendy Doniger O'Flaherty (ed.), *The Critical Study of Sacred Texts* (Berkeley: Graduate Theological Union, 1979), pp. 31-54. For Tov's critique, see his *Text Critical Use of the Septuagint in Biblical Research* (Jerusalem: Simor, 1981),

evolutionary biology, there are 'splitters' and there are 'clumpers'.[1] Splitters see a new species in every individual. Clumpers wish to include variation of minor sort within a single species. There is, of course, debate concerning what is minor. Is Neandertal man *homo sapiens*? There are those who say yes and those who say no, and I believe the current prevailing opinion is that we must speak of *homo sapiens neandertalensis* and of *homo sapiens sapiens*—neatly leaving the question finessed by the invention of subspecies. Tov is a splitter (or diversifier). I am a clumper (or unifier). Tov admits that the scrolls with long series of so-called Proto-Samaritan readings belong in a 'group' with the Samaritan tradition—despite the unique readings of the Samaritan. He admits that the manuscript 4QJer[b] is closely linked with the Old Greek of Jeremiah. And he sees the Proto-Rabbinic manuscripts as a group. That is, he recognizes manuscripts related to the Samaritan, the Septuagint, and the proto-Massoretic or Proto-Rabbinic text as extant at Qumrân. Having done so he then denounces the theory of text types or textual families. He carefully avoids the language of filiation, families, types. Having admitted the existence of at least the traditional three families, he then asserts that there is a sea of 'independent' manuscripts, and apparently finds no 'group', other than the traditional three. It must be insisted against Tov, however, that certain patterns of data require genetic

and especially, 'A Modern Textual Outlook Based on the Qumran Scrolls', *HUCA* 53 (1982), pp. 11-27; and his references to earlier papers. Professor Tov kindly has given me an advance copy of his new paper provisionally entitled 'Groups of Biblical Texts Found at Qumran' [the paper is published now in the volume *Time to Prepare the Way in the Wilderness: Papers on Qumran Scrolls*, edited by D. Dimant and L.H. Schiffman (Leiden: E.J. Brill, 1995), pp. 85-102]. In this paper he modifies his positions somewhat, particularly in regard to the affinities of texts related to the *Vorlage* of the Old Greek. But his assignment of 'non-aligned' or 'independent' texts I still find unsatisfactory. Cf. Eugene Ulrich, 'The Biblical Scrolls for Qumran Cave 4: An Overview and a Progress Report on Their Publication', *RB* 54 (1989), pp. 207-28; and especially 'Horizons of Old Testament Textual Research at the Thirtieth Anniversary of Qumran Cave 4', *CBQ* 46 (1984), pp. 613-36.

1.   Freeman Dyson has expressed more elegantly a similar contrast between two schools in the history of science: 'Unifiers are people whose driving passion is to find general principles which will explain everything. They are happy if they can leave the universe looking a little simpler than they found it. Diversifiers are people whose passion is to explore details. They are in love with the heterogeneity of nature and they agree with the saying "Le bon Dieu aime les détails". They are happy if they can leave the universe a little more complicated than they found it'. See his *Infinite in All Directions* (New York: Harper & Row, 1988), pp. 44-45.

explanation or description. Manuscripts have bad genes and good genes. Bad genes are secondary or corrupt readings which have been introduced into a manuscript by a scribe and copied and recopied by scribes in his vicinity or who otherwise had access to his manuscript or one of its descendants. A cluster or long list of bad genes—secondary readings and errors—held in common by two manuscripts require filiation as an explanation. Coincidence can be appealed to in simple, typical errors of limited number. But not in cases where there is an extended list of secondary or corrupt readings held in common by two manuscripts, for example, by the *Vorlage* of the Old Greek and the manuscript 4QSam[a]. These texts must be related and the only question is how closely or how recently. Filiation based on a series of bad genes or corrupt readings suggests that we designate the filiated texts with an appropriate genetic designation: a textual family, or a text type. I prefer family. To call such filiated texts a 'group' as does Tov is to underplay the fact of filiation, and its local ambience. What is an independent manuscript for Tov? He does not really tell us. He mentions that such manuscripts were marked by unique readings. But of course in this period before external controls were placed on scribal transmission there are no manuscripts—I know of none—*without* unique readings. All scribes make errors. Unique, but original readings are excessively rare. One may speak of an 'independent' manuscript only when it exhibits corrupt or secondary readings in large number, few or none of which are held in common with a known textual family. The only manuscript with a sizable number of unique but original readings is the old Samuel manuscript, 4QSam[b], reflecting, I believe, a very early stage of the Palestinian text. Its other traits reinforce this view. Of its agreements with the Old Greek against the Massoretic text, of which there are thirty instances, all but five are superior readings in my judgment. The five secondary readings are explicating pluses. The manuscript has five readings in common with the Massoretic Text against the Old Greek, all of them transparently original readings. There are also four variants in which the manuscript agrees with the Massoretic Text and the Lucianic Greek against the Egyptian Greek family where the Egyptian family is corrupt and the Lucianic family is in fact the Old Greek. Finally, there are five proto-Lucianic readings, where 4Q Samuel stands with the Lucianic Greek against both the Massoretic Text and the Egyptian Greek. Can we describe this text as standing in the tradition of the Massoretic Text? Obviously not. It shares with the Massoretic text no bad genes. Agreement only in a few variant readings we deem superior gives no basis for establishing a relationship. What of the agreement with the Old Greek in thirty variants? These agreements are impressive but of the thirty readings only five, seven counting the proto-Lucianic readings, are corrupt readings held in common. Are these seven bad genes sufficient to warrant filiation with the *Vorlage* of the Old Greek? We should like more fragments in order to make a confident decision. It could be called an independent text. It possesses three unique readings, all of which I consider to be superior readings. More likely it is a remote ancestor of the manuscripts of Samuel which were taken to Egypt from Palestine. Its failure to agree with any of the Massoretic Text's secondary readings in these twenty-five instances is of major significance for judging the text of Samuel chosen by the Rabbis in the promulgation of their recension. It was not an Old Palestinian text. So both good genes and bad genes have significance in writing the history of the text. However, primary data for establishing filiation is the sharing of a significant group of bad genes. Tov admits that the later Samuel, 4QSam^a, has a long, long list of secondary variants held in common with the Old Greek. Thus in my view, the two texts are necessarily related, filiated. How else explain agreement in an extended series of mistakes, some of them as long as twenty-five words? The two texts are related. The only question is how closely. There are a number of secondary readings in common with the Lucianic Greek, the Old Latin, Josephus, and the Massoretic Text. These phenomena require explanation too. I do not think that we have here a mixture or conflation of traditions—there is surprisingly little of this in the Qumrân biblical texts. I think rather that we are dealing here with a text related to the *Vorlage* of the so-called Proto-Lucianic Greek text.

Tov warmly embraces the notion that there is a group—we should say family—of Proto-Rabbinic manuscripts to be detected at Qumrân, and not surprisingly, in the texts from the southern desert which actually date after the promulgation of the Rabbinic Text. The latter group is really irrelevant to our discussion here since they are Rabbinic texts, not Proto-Rabbinic. The Proto-Rabbinic texts according to Tov are marked by their *approach* to the text. This approach, he says, 'disallowed after a certain period the insertion of changes in the transmitted text'. Tov is thinking of the baroque orthography. We have discussed above that it is a conservative impulse, not a free impulse, the attempt to preserve archaic forms, improving on the vernacular orthography that hides the earlier stages of the language. It is true that this baroque orthography is introduced probably in early Maccabaean times. But the orthography of the Rabbinic Recension is decades not centuries earlier. Further in my view there are Proto-Rabbinic texts in both orthographies. Isaiah at Qumrân, both 1QIsa^a and 1QIsa^b, are Proto-Rabbinic in my judgment. They are very closely affiliated, sharing errors, conflations, and parallel readings. The fact that one is written in baroque orthography, the other in common orthography is a purely superficial matter. The texts of Isaiah, Jeremiah (save 4QJer^b), and Ezekiel at Qumrân are all Proto-Rabbinic, are all full, poor texts, and of the Palestinian family. As I have often argued, the Rabbis did not select the same local textual family in all instances.[1] In the Pentateuch they chose a superb, short text, indeed a conservative text. In the major prophets they chose quite another text, a full, conflate text. Each biblical book must be examined for itself.[2]

Finally a word or two about recensions or editions. The Rabbis rejected the short, superb text of Jeremiah we find at Qumrân in a single exemplar and in the Greek Bible. We do not know why. In the Pentateuch they rejected the late Palestinian recension of Proto-Samaritan type in favor of a short text. We do not know why. It is not possible to speak of a 'conservative tendency' in view of this apparently random result. I have published some speculations to explain what happened which I will not reiterate here. We should note that in the case of the Pentateuch at Qumrân we have very early texts of Palestinian type without the pattern of parallel readings, and other bizarre traits of the Proto-Samaritan family. Most of them are not, in my opinion, Proto-Rabbinic texts. To be sure in some Pentateuchal books—Leviticus is a prime example—there is little variation among Qumrân manuscripts, in the Old Greek, and in the Massoretic Text. In such relatively stable texts we have far less to go on in establishing filiations than in texts like Samuel or Jeremiah where the textual traditions are at wide variance.

While on the subject of editions of biblical books, I cannot resist a remark or two. Jastram's edition of 4QNum^b reinforces the view that it may be better to speak of the Proto-Samaritan text of the Pentateuch as a recension rather than merely as a textual family. That is, there is the evidence of conscious and extensive expansion and revision of the text,

---

1. See most recently my comments in 'The Text Behind the Text of the Hebrew Bible', *Bible Review* 1 (1985), pp. 12-25; and my forthcoming chapter, 'The Fixation of the Text and Canon of the Hebrew Bible', in *The Cambridge History of Judaism*.

2. See now Emanuel Tov's detailed reply to my criticism in *The Madrid Qumran Congress*, Volume I, pp. 15-21.

not merely the usual accumulation of inadvertent errors, minor explicating pluses, modernizing, and intrusion of isolated parallel readings, the
usual stuff of scribal transmission. Something much more systematic
appears to have been undertaken.[1] This is obviously the case with
Jeremiah. It should be observed, however, that much of the text
common to both editions of Jeremiah, the Massoretic and the Greek, can
be analyzed in terms of ordinary textual development. So the studies of
both Tov and Janzen are useful.[2] We should also term the contrasting
texts of Job in Hebrew and in the Old Greek two editions, and jettison
explanations which assert that the Greek translator has abbreviated his
text. Each time such claims have been made—in Jeremiah and in the
Tabernacle sections of Exodus to name two egregious examples—new
textual evidence has proved them false. Orlinsky's arguments that Job
was translated into Greek from a Palaeo-Hebrew *Vorlage* are probably
valid, and not without interest. Emanuel Tov has argued that the
Hebrew and Greek texts of Proverbs exhibit recensional differences.[3]
Daniel exists in more than one edition. We must also assert, in accord
with an older scholarly consensus, recently under attack, that the
Chronicler's Work existed in two editions, a long edition of which the
Rabbinic Text is an exemplar, and a short edition, omitting the
Nehemiah memoirs, of which First Esdras is a translation, and Josephus
a witness. On the other hand, I have not been convinced by those who
argue that the 11QPs is an expanded edition of the Psalter.[4]

The recovery of editions and literary levels in biblical works begins a

1.   'The Text of Numbers', *The Madrid Qumran Congress* I, pp. 177-98.

2.   J Gerald Janzen, *Studies in the Text of Jeremiah*, HSM 6 (Cambridge:
Harvard University Press, 1973), and E. Tov, 'L'Incidence de la critique textuelle sur
la critique littéraire dans le livre de Jérémie', *RB* 79 (1972), pp. 189-99.

3.   'Recensional Differences Between the Masoretic Text and the Septuagint of
Proverbs', in H.W. Attridge, John J. Collins, and T.H. Tobin (eds.), *Of Scribes and
Scrolls* [Strugnell Volume] (Lanham, Maryland: University Press of America, 1990),
pp. 43-56; and more generally, Tov, *The Text Critical Use of the Septuagint* (cited in
note 15), pp. 293-306. For other evidence of recensional activity, see Eugene Ulrich,
'Pluriformity in the Biblical Text, Text Groups, and Questions of Canon', *The
Madrid Qumran Congress* I, pp. 23-41.

4.   For example, James A. Sanders, 'The Qumran Psalms Scroll (11QPsa)
Reviewed', in M. Black and W.A. Smalley (eds.), *On Language, Culture, and
Religion* [Eugene A. Nida Volume] (The Hague: Mouton, 1974), pp. 79-99, with a
complete bibliography (up to the date of his publication) of discussion of the Cave 11
Psalms.

process of no small importance in biblical studies: the uniting of text-criticism and literary criticism in scholarly approaches to biblical literature. During the past century there has been a divorce between higher and lower criticism, a scandal of excessive specialization, with dreary results. The marriage, or rather the remarriage of the two disciplines, particularly in the books and papers of Julio Trebolle Barrera, is therefore an event of unusual promise.[1]

4. Let me turn finally to some brief comments on the history of the community at Qumrân, and to the history of the sectarian movement we call the Essenes. In my Haskell Lectures I argued that the best derivation of the Greek term 'Essene' was from Aramaic *hasên, hasayyâ*, 'holy ones'.[2] This received indirect support from Philo who in two passages connects the name with ὁσιότης, 'holiness'.[3] The only serious objection to this etymology has been that the root *hsn* appeared only in East Aramaic. This objection is now removed by a passage in the Testament of Levi (4QTLev ar[b] [new notation]; PAM 43.242) which reads, 'And the name of his holy one not blotted out from all names...' (מתמחא שם חסיה מן כול שמחא ולא).[4]

The discoveries on Mount Gerizim have clarified the history of Hasmonaean coinage. Coins of Yoḥanan in the city on the mountain destroyed in 128 BC certify that Hasmonaean coinage began with John Hyrcanus I, and not with Alexander Jannaeus as claimed by Yaakov Meshorer and accepted by most numismatists. Meshorer himself quickly

---

1. Julio C. Trebolle Barrera, *Salomon y Jeroboan: Historia de la recensión y redactión de 1 Reyes, 2-12; 14* (Valencia: Institución San Jerónimo, 1980); *Jehú y Joás: Texto y composición literaria de 2 Reyes 9–11* (Valencia: Institución San Jerónimo, 1984); 'Testamento y Muerte de David', *RB* 87 (1980), pp. 87-103; 'El estudio de 4Q Sam[a]: Implicaciones exegéticas e históricas', *Estudios Biblicos* 39 (1981), pp. 5-18; 'From the "Old Latin" Through the "Old Greek" to the "Old Hebrew" (2 Kings 10:23-25)', *Textus* 11 (1984), pp. 1-20; 'Textual Variants in 4QJud[a] and the Textual and Editorial History of the Book of Judges', *RevQ* 54 (1989), pp. 229-45.

2. See above, Chapter 2, note 1.

3. *Quod omnis probus liber sit*, XII, 75 [cf. XIII, 91]; *Hypothetica, apud* Eusebius, *Praep. evang.* VIII, 11; cf. Josephus, *War* II, 119.

4. This unpublished quotation is here cited thanks to the kindness of Professor Michael Stone (who reported it to me) and to Professor Jonas Greenfield who are editing the text for publication. Cf. recently M. Petit, 'Les Esséens de Philon d'Alexandrie et les Esséniens', in D. Dimant and U. Rappaport (eds.), *The Dead Sea Scrolls: Forty Years of Research* (Leiden and Jerusalem: Brill, Magnes, and Yad Ben-Zvi, 1992), pp. 139-55.

abandoned his earlier theories in light of the new data.[1] This confirms anew De Vaux's chronology of the Qumrân community center, placing its origin in the time of Jonathan or Simon. The latter was De Vaux's choice and indeed my view as well, on the basis of archaeological and palaeographical evidence in the first instance, and then on an analysis of the literary evidence. I remain convinced that one must begin with hard evidence—that is, the evidence of the typological sciences. Then one moves to the few overt references in the sectarian literature, notably those in the *Pešer* Nahum, and as well, examines Pliny and the classical source used by Josephus and Philo to describe the Essene sect, and only then, finally, turns to the obscure and esoteric allusions in the sectarian literature.[2] This order of procedure is to my mind the only methodologically sound approach to writing the history of the Qumrân sect. If one begins looking for Wicked Priests he will find in this era, as in all eras no doubt, an overabundance of candidates.

There has been a great deal of discussion lately about the date of the Temple Scroll, and the Halakhic Epistle (a title I prefer to *Miqṣat Ma'aśê Hat-tôrāh* or MMT).[3] In the case of the Temple Scroll, the argument that the lore on kingship contains polemic against the institution of monarchy introduced by the Hasmonaeans, developed by Hengel, Charlesworth, and Mendels, I find convincing.[4] The absence of the theological jargon found, for example in the *Serek Hay-yaḥad*, is not troubling. The document is primarily concerned with halakhic matters,

---

1.   A personal communication from Professor Meshorer.

2.   This line of argument is stressed in my essay, 'The Early History of the Apocalyptic Community of Qumrân', in *CMHE*, pp. 326-46. For Josephus and Philo's source, see Morton Smith, 'The Description of the Essenes in Josephus and the Philosophumena', *HUCA* 29 (1958), pp. 273-313.

3.   See provisionally the paper of E. Qimron and J. Strugnell, 'An Unpublished Halakhic Letter', in *Biblical Archaeology Today* (Jerusalem: Israel Exploration Society, 1985), pp. 400-407. My discussion is based on the penultimate version of the *editio princeps* of the text now in press by the same two authors, made available to me by Professors Strugnell and Qimron. [Published now in *DJD X, Qumran Cave 4 V.*]

4.   M. Hengel, J.H. Charlesworth, D. Mendels, 'The Polemical Character of "On Kingship" in the Temple Scroll: An Attempt at Dating 11QTemple', *JJS* 37 (1986), pp. 28-38. See already, Y. Yadin, *The Temple Scroll* (Jerusalem: The Israel Exploration Society, The Institute of Archaeology of the Hebrew University of Jerusalem, and The Shrine of the Book, 1983) I, pp. 387-88; and more recently L.H. Schiffman, 'The Law of the Temple Scroll and Its Provenance', *Folia Orientalia* 25 (1988), pp. 85-98.

an entirely different genre from that of cosmic speculation and apocalyptic eschatology. Its calendar and its legal lore are sectarian, and, as we shall see, with Sadducean elements. Further, its treatment of Jerusalem as the wilderness camp with similar rules of purity is shared by other sectarian documents: the Damascus Document, the Halakhic Epistle, and Enoch's Animal Apocalypse which, with Dimant, I believe to be Essene.[1] Similarly I view the Halakhic Epistle as sectarian, Essene. It speaks of the separation of its authors' group from Jewry. The term used is *prš* interestingly enough. It speaks in the first person plural, not singular. I see no reason to think it is written by the Teacher of Righteousness. I find myself here in agreement with Schiffman.[2] Further it is addressed to a leader and group admired for wisdom and understanding by the authors. This is most easily understood as a collateral line of Zadokite priests who have not joined the Essene community and its priests of the Zadokite house. After all, such priests, a rich and aristocratic group, are well documented. John Hyrcanus I turned to such a group, repudiating Pharisaic regulations, and in the days of Herod such a collateral line was restored to the high priesthood. Schiffman speaks of the epistle as addressed to 'compromising Sadducees', a designation I find appropriate. I am inclined to think that the new halakhic lore of the Temple Scroll and the Halakhic Epistle confirms the views of those who held that Zadokite priests, ousted from their traditional positions of power, led pious supporters into the desert to dream apocalyptic dreams and to await the final restoration of the legitimate house of Zadok to power.[3]

1. D. Dimant, 'Qumran Sectarian Literature' (cited in n. 1), p. 544 and n. 287. It has not been noticed that in the Animal Apocalypse the Ethiopic word *bēt*, 'house', is a mistranslation through the Greek of Aramaic *mašrītâ* which can mean both 'dwelling' and 'camp' (and is used to translate Hebrew *mahǎnê*).

The *pěšārîm* are an exception, dating late in the sect's history, but based on oral lore of exegesis from early and late. See F.M. Cross, 'Introduction', in *Scrolls from Qumrân Cave I: The Great Isaiah Scroll; The Order of the Community; The Pesher to Habakkuk*. From Photographs by John C. Trever (Jerusalem: The Albright Institute of Archaeological Research and The Shrine of the Book, 1972), pp. 1-5.

2. Schiffman, 'The Significance of the Scrolls', *Bible Review* 6 (1990), pp. 19-27 and 52. Cf. James C. VanderKam, 'The People of the Dead Sea Scrolls: Essenes or Sadducees?', *Bible Review* 7 (1991), pp. 42-47.

3. F.M. Cross, *The Ancient Library of Qumrân*, Revised Edition (Garden City, New York: Anchor Books, 1961), p. 129. On the so-called Groningen Hypothesis, see most recently Florentino Garcia Martinez, 'Qumran Origins and Early History: A

The fact that Essene halakhic lore holds much in common with Sadducean (Zadokite) legal teachings reflected in later Rabbinic debate should not mislead—as it has some scholars versed in Rabbinic texts—into the view that the sectaries are Sadducees and *not* Essenes. Joseph Baumgarten recently has given a balanced review of the divergences as well as the agreements between the aristocratic Sadducees of Jerusalem, and the self-styled poor of the desert.[1]

There have been a number of attempts to develop a typology of the theological and sociological development of the Qumrân or Essene sect, and to use such a theoretical sequence of stages as the basis for the literary dissection of sectarian works. I must confess that I am skeptical about the methods being used to develop these theories and doubtful about their results. Such developments, of course, must be squeezed into a very short period of time. Devorah Dimant suggests a maximum range of one or two generations for the major sectarian writings.[2] Recent scholars wish to see in the orders of the camps and the cities of Judah an early stage of the sect, in the celibate order of the *Yaḥad* a later development. But the document used by Josephus and Philo speaks of these Essene communities in the cities of Judâh, and the most parsimonious explanation is to suppose that the Community in the desert and the less ascetic communities throughout Judah were contemporaneous. I should suggest that in the wider Essene movement, celibacy was vocational, marriage fully acceptable, precisely as in the communes of primitive Christianity. J. Murphy-O'Connor's elaborate analyses, laying bare

Groningen Hypothesis', *Folia Orientalia* 25 (1988), pp. 113-36; and the literature cited.

1.   Joseph Baumgarten, 'The Disqualifications of Priests in 4Q Fragments of the "Damascus Document", a Specimen of the Recovery of pre-Rabbinic Halakha', *The Madrid Qumran Congress*, Vol. II, pp. 503-13, and his references to the literature, notably to his own earlier papers; and 'The Purification Rituals in *DJD 7*', in D. Dimant and U. Rappaport (eds.), *The Dead Sea Scrolls: Forty Years of Research* (Leiden and Jerusalem: Brill, Magnes, and Yad Ben-Zvi, 1992), pp. 199-209. Cf. Lawrence Shiffman, 'The New Halakhic Letter (4Q MMT) and the Origins of the Dead Sea Text', *BA* 53 (1990), pp. 64-73; 'The Significance of the Scrolls', *BR* 6 (1990), pp. 19-27, 52; 'The Sadducean Origins of the Dead Sea Scroll Sect', in *Understanding the Dead Sea Scrolls*, ed. Hershel Shanks, Daniel R. Schwartz, 'Law and Truth: On Qumran-Sadducean and Rabbinic Views of Law', in D. Dimant and U. Rappaport (eds.), *The Dead Sea Scrolls: Forty Years of Research*, pp. 229-40.

2.   D. Dimant, 'Qumran Sectarian Literature' (cited in n. 1), p. 532.

various strata, I have not found convincing.[1] Sidnie White's text-critical analysis of the Damascus Document proves to be a devastating repudiation of Murphy-O'Connor's two-recension theory.[2] A number of scholars still separate the 'admonitions' (a misnomer) from the 'laws' on form-critical grounds. But Klaus Baltzer long ago in his volume *The Covenant Formulary* showed that precisely on form-critical grounds the two sections of the Damascus Document belong together, and that the Damascus Document as a whole belongs to a genre which is pre-biblical, biblical, Jewish, and New Testament.[3] And, of course, they are together at Qumrân.

One of the arguments has been that different Messianic doctrines are found in the two sections of the Damascus Document.[4] This is not so. There is a consistent doctrine of two messiahs, one of Aaron, one of Israel, throughout the Qumrân literature. Indeed the doctrine of two Messiahs has its roots in the Restoration establishment of a diarchy. Joshua the high priest and the 'scion', namely Zerubbabel, are the two 'anointed ones', *běnê hay-yiṣhar*, who 'shall take office standing by the side of the Lord of the whole earth'. The elaboration of a doctrine of two ages took place in later apocalypticism, in which a typology of the events and offices of old Israel were projected into the new age. David, the ideal king of the old days is taken as the archetype of the ideal king of the New Age. Zadok, priest of David and of Solomon, scion of Aaron is the archetype of the new Zadok, the messiah of Aaron. The two figures, priestly and royal, persist in later Jewish doctrine of eschatological offices down to Christian times. At Qumrân, in the Damascus Document, in the Rule, in the War Scroll, in the Testimonia, and, as well,

1. J. Murphy-O'Connor, 'La Genèse littéraire de Règle de la Communauté', *RB* 76 (1969), pp. 528-49; 'An Essene Missionary Document? CD II,14–VI,1', *RB* 77 (1970), pp. 201-29; 'A Literary Analysis of Damascus Document VI,2–VIII,3', *RB* 78 (1971), pp. 210-32; 'The Critique of the Princes of Judah (CD VIII, 3-19)', *RB* 79 (1972), pp. 200-216; 'A Literary Analysis of Damascus Document XIX,33–XX,34', *RB* (1972), pp. 544-64; 'The Original Text of CD 7:9–8:2=19:5-14', *HTR* 64 (1971), pp. 379-86; 'The Essenes and Their History', *RB* 81 (1974), pp. 215-44; 'The *Damascus Document* Revisited', *RB* 92 (1985), pp. 223-46.

2. Sidnie Ann White, 'A Comparison of 'A' and 'B' Manuscripts of the Damascus Document', *RQ* 48 (1987), pp. 537-53.

3. Klaus Baltzer, *The Covenant Formulary*, trans. David E. Green (Philadelphia: Fortress Press, 1971), esp. pp. 112-22.

4. See the classic if flawed study of the late Jean Starcky, 'Les Quatre étapes du messianisme à Qumran', *RB* 70 (1963), pp. 481-505.

in the Testaments of the Twelve Patriarchs, there is the doctrine of the two messiahs, with the Balaam Oracle concerning the Star and the Scepter, the two eschatological figures, a favorite proof text. Confusion has been introduced by a reading in CD XIV, 19: [*mšy*]*ḥ 'hrwn wyśr'l*. It is to be read 'the messiah of Aaron and the one of Israel'. This constitutes no problem in Hebrew grammar as recognized long ago by Ginzburg. This expression cannot mean anything but the (priestly) messiah of Aaron and the (secular) messiah of Israel. The expression Aaron and Israel regularly refers to the priestly and the secular division of the community. A single priestly messiah would be called simply 'the messiah of Aaron'. Further confusion has been created by the following phrase *ykpr 'wnm* [   ]. The verb is singular. But it must be taken as a passive, *yĕkuppar*. Compare the passive constructions with this verb, the *nitpa'el* in Deut. 21.8 and in 1 Sam. 6.3 (4QSam^a and OG), or the more familiar *pu'al* as in Isa. 22.14 and 27.9. Were *'wnm* the object of the verb *ykpr* here, and *mšyḥ* the subject, the word *'wnm* would have been preceded by the particle *'et*. So the case is clear. The putative single messiah is a phantom of bad philology.

It is true that the royal messiah is usually meant when otherwise unspecified. Even in 1QSa II: 11-13, the rule for the celebration of the eschatological banquet, the Messiah of Israel is juxtaposed to 'the Priest', the *latter* taking precedence. Further there are texts which mention only the royal messiah; but to argue that these texts represent circles where the traditional doctrine of the diarchy had been replaced by a merging of the two figures into one—as happened in Christianity, and to some degree in later Judaism after the fall of the temple when the rule of the high priest was permanently broken—is a precarious argument from silence. It has long been argued—against Josephus' plain testimony—that the Essenes of Qumran had no doctrine of resurrection. But a recently published text makes reference to a proof text promising resurrection. 'As it is written, he shall heal the slain, and the dead he shall resurrect (literally, "make alive")'.[1]

The reverse case may be illustrated by reference to the Daniel literature. Here scholarly consensus has held that while the Book of Daniel testifies explicitly to a doctrine of the resurrection of the righteous, the author (or editor) possessed no doctrine of the Messiah(s). In fact a

---

1. For a preliminary edition of this text, 4Q521, see Robert Eisenman and Michael Wise, *The Dead Sea Scrolls Uncovered* (Rockport, Maine: Element, 1992), pp. 19-23; and Pl. 1.

famous document from Cave 4 Qumran 4Q246 belonging to the wider
Daniel literature, pseudo-Daniel[d] (so called because it is not a part of the
canon) there is a dramatic reference to the expected messiah using familiar soubriquets to identify him. A portion text reads as follows:

I

1 [ע]לוהי שרת נפל קדם כרסיא

2 [ואמר לה חיי מ]לכא [ל]עלמא אתה רגיז ושנוך

3 [זיוך ואפשר מלכ]א חזוך וכלא אתה עד עולם

4 [חזית די ישפלון ר]ברבין עקה תתא על ארעא

5 [להוה קרב בעממיא] ונחשירון רב במדינתא

6 [ולקצח יומיא יאבד] מלך אתור [ומ]צרין

7 [ויקום בר אנש ומלך] רב להוה על ארעא

8 [כלה וכל אנש לת י]עבדון וכלא ישמשון

9 [לה קדיש אלהא ר]בא יתקרא ובשמה יתכנה

II

1 ברה די אל יתאמר ובר עלין יקרונה כזיקיא

2 די חזיתא כן מלכוחהן שנ[ין] ימלכון על

3 ארעא וכלא ידשון עם לעם ודוש ומדינה למד[ינ]ה

4   עד יקום עם אל וכלא יניח מן חרב

5 מלכוחה מלכות עלם וכל ארחתה בקשוט ידין

6 ארעא בקשוט וכלא יעבד לשלם חרב מן ארעא יסף

7 וכל מדינתא לה יסגדין אל רבא באילה

8 הוא יעבד לה קרב עממין ינתן בידה וכלהן

9 ירמה קדמוהי שלטנה שלטן עלם וכל תהומי

I

(1) [   ]on him settled;
He fell before the throne,
(2) [and said to him, 'Live O k]ing forever!'[1]
You are disturbed and your (3) [appearance] changed;[2]
[And I shall interpret O kin]g your dream
And all that comes to pass unto perpetuity;
(4) [You saw in your vision that the] might[y [shall fall];
Affliction shall come on earth.

1.   My reconstruction is based on Dan. 2.4, 3.89, and 5.10.
2.   The reading *wšnwk zywk* is precisely the impersonal usage with the suffix as
subject found in Dan. 5.6 with the same terms: *zywhy šnwhy*.

(5) [There shall be war with the nations,]
And great carnage among the countries.
(6) [And at the end of days][1] the king of Assyria and of Egypt [shall
perish].
(7) And there shall arise a son of man]
And he shall be a great [king][2] over the earth (8)—all of it.
[And all of mankind] shall serve [him],
And all shall minister (9)[to him].
[Holy One[3] of the g]reat [God] he shall be called,
And by his name he shall be surnamed.

II

(1) Son of God he shall be called,
And Son of the Most high he shall be surnamed.

. . . .
(5) His kingdom shall be an eternal kingdom,
And all his ways truth.
He shall judge (6) the earth with truth,
And all will make peace (with him).
The sword shall cease from the earth,
(7) And all the countries shall worship him.
The great God shall be his patron.
People he will give in his hand
And all of them (9) he shall cast before him.
His rule shall be an eternal rule...

'Great', 'Holy One'. 'Son of the Most High', 'Son of God'—these
parallels to the messianic titles in Lk. 1.32-35 (where the messianic interpretation is patent) are so striking as to suggest, if not to require, that the
author of the hymn quoted in Luke is dependent on a Danielic text. It
should be noted that in the Aramaic epithets, the names of god—*'El*

---

1.   On this expression, see Dan. 4.31.
2.   [*mlk*] *rb* is a quotation from Ps. 48.3, 'Mount Zion in the extremities of the
north, the city of the great king (*mlk rb*)'. See also *mlk rb* in Dan. 2.10. Evidently it is
taken here as the son of David.
3.   The reconstruction *qdyš 'lh'* is based on Lk. 1.32-35. Here we find the same
series of Messianic titles piled up (though not in the same order): 'Son of the Most
High' (v. 32), 'Holy One' (v. 35b), and 'Son of God' (v. 35b). Compare also *mlk
rb*. 'Great King' in line 7 with Lk. 1.32: ουτος εσται μεγας και υιος υψιστου
κληθησεται, 'He shall be (called) great and called the Son of the Most High'.

and *'Elyon*—are nevertheless given their Hebrew forms. This makes it most implausible that they be applied to any but an Israelite king.[1]

I have held this messianic interpretation of the 'Son of God' text since J.T. Milik read a paper on the text at Harvard University in 1972. Indeed I sent to him the reconstruction given above shortly after his American visit, arguing strongly against his interpretation of the epithets as belonging to a Seleucid king (Alexander Balas).[2]

One final text may be cited: an Apocryphon of Levi (4Q540 and 4Q541).[3] If Puech's interpretations and reconstructions are roughly sound, we have to do here with a salvific figure who is evidently the Messiah Priest. At the same time the royal messiah goes without mention—which by no means can be construed to mean that the author of the Levi Testament possessed no doctrine of the royal messiah, son of David.

There are many other issues which I should like to discuss, but they must await another occasion. For example, in the past I have stressed the shift from Zadokite to Hasmonaean lineage as the basis for the crisis which led to sectarian withdrawal. But it is increasingly clear that issues of calendar and purity contributed heavily as well to the crystallization of the Essene sect. Our early views have been too simple, and as the years of study and publication pass, so our understanding of the richness of sectarian history must be changed and refreshed.

---

1.   If these were pagan titles we should expect *'lh'* and *'ly'*.

2.   See John Collins, 'A Pre-Christian "Son of God" Among the Dead Sea Scrolls', *BR* 9 (1993), pp. 34-38 and 57, esp. n. 4. The *editio princeps* of 4Q246 (=4Q psDan[d]) is by Émile Puech to whom Milik assigned the text, 'Fragment d'une apocalypse en araméen (4Q246 = pseudo-Dan[d]) et le "royaume de Dieu"', *RB* 99 (1992), pp. 98-131. See also the reconstruction of Joseph Fitzmyer in his latest studies of the text, '4Q246: "The Son of God" Document from Qumran', *Biblica* 74 (1993), pp. 153-74; and 'The Aramaic "Son of God" Text from Qumran Cave 4', in M. Wise *et al.* (eds.), *Methods of Investigation of the Dead Sea Scrolls and the Khirbet Qumran Site: Present Realities and Future Prospects*, Annals of the New York Academy of Sciences 722 (New York: New York Academy of Sciences, 1994), pp. 163-78; cf. R. Eisenman and M. Wise, *The Dead Sea Scrolls Uncovered*, pp. 68-71.

3.   The *editio princeps* is by E. Puech, 'Fragments d'un apocryph de Lévi et le personnage eschatologique: 4Q TestLévi[c-d](?) et 4QAJa', *The Madrid Qumran Congress* II, pp. 449-501.

Postscript

The Essene Faith and the Christian Gospel

In drawing on the Qumrân library in the discussion of Christian origins, we have dealt primarily with parallels, with data which reveal continuities between the Essenes and the early Church. We have noted common language, common doctrines, common institutions. We have made no attempt to draw up systematically the differences between Christianity and Essenism.

Some few comments on the relation of Essenism to Christianity may be in order, however, in light of the current popular discussion of the scrolls. We have discovered the greatest similarities between these in their common apocalyptic point of view. Both were apocalyptic communities which in their common life attempted to bridge the gap between the Old Age and the New Age. There are, however, distinctions to be made between Essene apocalypticism and New Testament eschatology.

The Essene and the Christian live in the Old Age, yet by anticipation in the new. Thus in some sense we can speak of the 'overlapping' of the ages in their existence as members of the New Covenant. For the member of the early Church, however, the time is 'later'. He stands on a new ground. The Messiah has come. He has been raised. The resurrection is not merely an anticipatory event. It shows that the New Age has come. Professor Stendahl has expressed the distinction by saying that 'the degree of anticipation' is greater in the New Testament, its eschatology 'higher'.[1]

This 'later moment' of the Christian's existence, this 'greater degree of anticipation' of the early Church has radical effects upon Christian doctrine. The legal framework of Judaism, including Essene Judaism is

1. 'The Scrolls and the New Testament, an Introduction and a Perspective' in *The Scrolls and the New Testament*, pp. 1-17. This is perhaps the best short discussion of this topic; I am indebted at many points in the following remarks to my colleague's paper.

broken. The New Age is one in which the law is engraved in the heart. The gift of the Holy Spirit—anticipated in Essene doctrine—is poured out on the early Church, so that life is Spirit-dominated, and a new freedom replaces or rather fulfills the law.

The peculiarly priestly flavor of Essene apocalypticism is largely missing in early Christianity. 'The hour is coming when neither on this mountain nor in Jerusalem will you worship the father...the hour is coming and now is when the true worshipers will worship the Father in spirit and truth' (Jn 4.21-23). The destruction of the Temple caused no strain upon early Christianity. The work of the old sacrificial system was completed in Jesus' sacrifice. The community of Qumrân dreamed of a new Temple and a new Jerusalem. Its details in remarkable refinement are laid out in the Temple Scroll

To be sure, the rejection of the priestly laws of purity, separations from sinners, the hierarchical distinctions in rank, and the dominance of the priesthood rests, however, on factors other than the 'lateness of the hour' in which the early Christian existed. Christian eschatology is more directly rooted in Old Testament prophetism, the Essene in Old Testament priestly traditions. The sure signs of the New Age, according to Jesus, were the healing of the sick, the blind seeing, the dead rising, the dumb speaking. God gathered the poor, the maimed, the abandoned, the sinner into his banquet. The Essene excluded from the eschatological banquet all the unclean, those distorted in body and spirit. Such were unworthy of the New Age. Jesus' "poor" were the humble outcasts of Palestine. The Essene "poor" were in some sense an "artificial" poor, the elite of the desert who shared their goods.

But to return to our central theme. The Christian lived in that 'later moment' in the history of redemption when the Gentiles were to be brought into the Kingdom of God.[1] Hence Christianity turned out to the world. The Essenes, of course, looked forward to the day when Israel would atone for the sins of the world[2] and the nations would flow to Jerusalem. But they lived in an 'earlier' moment, before the full manifestation of God's Kingdom, when salvation was to be preached only to the Jews. Priestly separatism and what is inaccurately called Jewish 'particularism' belong to one phase in the history of redemption. Freedom and what is wrongly called Christian 'universalism' to a later

1. Cf. Stendahl, *op. cit.*; J. Jeremias, *Jesu Mission für die Völker*, Chap. III; Munck, *Paulus und die Heilsgeschichte* (Copenhagen, 1954), pp. 242-76.
2. 1QS 8.10.

phase of the history of redemption...after the Messiah has come.

All this is to say that the 'event' of Jesus as the Christ, his exaltation, his resurrection, the gift of his Spirit, distinguishes the two eschatological communities. It is possible that the Righteous Teacher of the Essenes was *expected* to return as a Messiah. But for the Church, Jesus had been resurrected as Messiah.[1] The event was past. The New Age was fully begun. The Messiah *had* come, had been resurrected and enthroned, though he would come again in glory.

We should emphasize that the New Testament faith was not a new faith, but the fulfillment of an old faith. The Church is precisely Israel in its own self-understanding.[2] Jesus did not propose to present a new system of universal truths. He came to fulfill the past work of God, to confirm the faith of the fathers, to open the meaning of the Law and Prophets. The New Testament does not set aside or supplant the Old Testament. It affirms it and, from its point of view, completes it. Lines of continuity between Moses and Jesus, Isaiah and Jesus, the Righteous Teacher and Jesus, John the Baptist and Jesus should occasion no surprise. On the contrary, a biblical faith insists on such continuities. The biblical faith is not a system of ideas, but a history of God's acts of redemption.

It is not the idea of redemption through suffering but the 'event' of the crucifixion understood as the atoning work of God that distinguishes Christianity. It is not the doctrine of resurrection but faith in the resurrection of Jesus as an eschatological event which forms the basis of the Christian decision of faith. It is not faith that a Messiah will come that gives Christianity its special character, but the assurance that Jesus rules as the Messiah who has come and will come. It is not the hope of a New Creation that lends uniqueness to Christianity, but the faith that Jesus is the New Adam, the first of the New Creation. Finally, it is not a 'love ethic' that distinguishes Christianity from Judaism—far from it. The Christian faith is distinguished from the ancient faith which brought it to birth in its knowledge of a new act of God's love, the revelation of His love in Jesus' particular life and death and resurrection.

1.   Compare Stendahl's remarks in this connection, *op. cit.*, pp. 14f.
2.   Cf. the writer, the *New Republic*, April 9, 1956, p. 18.

INDEXES

INDEX OF REFERENCES

OLD TESTAMENT

INDEX OF AUTHORS